JUSt ANOTHER MEAt-EATiNG DIRTBAG

JUST ANOTHER MEAT-EATING DIRTBAG

A MEMOIR BY
MICHAEL ANTHONY

WITH ART BY
CHAI SIMONE

STREET NOISE BOOKS • BROOKLYN, NEW YORK

Edited by Ada Price
Book Design by Liz Frances and Dev Kamath
Cover Design by Zoe Norvell

ISBN 978-1951-491-19-2

Printed in Mexico

9 8 7 6 5 4 3 2 1

First Edition

To anyone who has been in love and done something stupid because of it.

CHAPTER 1

LOVE IS THE ABSOLUTE WORST.

BECAUSE WHEN YOU LOVE SOMEONE, LIKE, REALLY LOVE SOMEONE, THEN YOU'RE LIABLE TO DO ANYTHING TO KEEP THEM IN YOUR LIFE—*ANYTHING*.

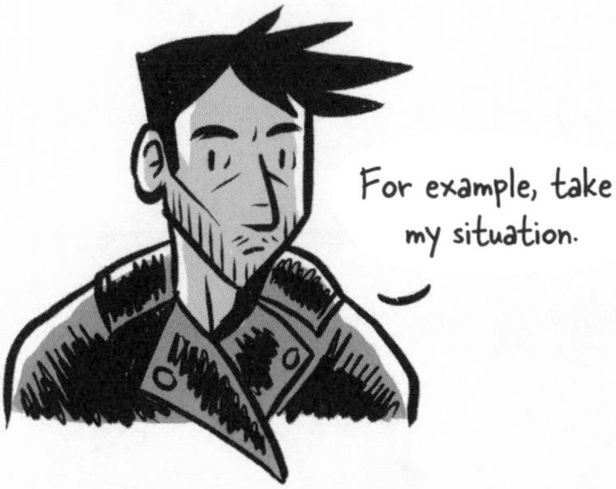
For example, take my situation.

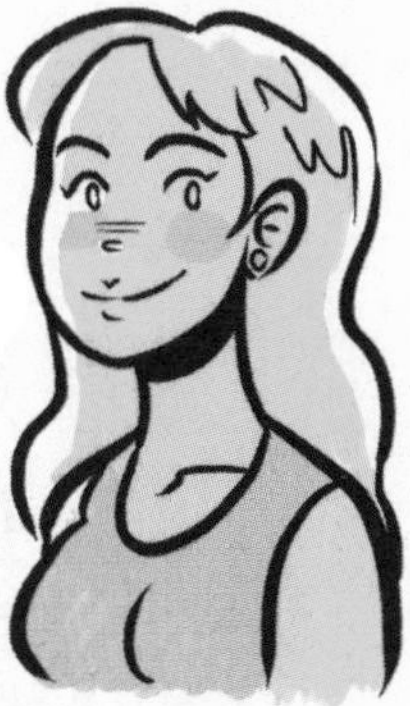

THAT WAS ME . . . AND THAT WAS MY GIRLFRIEND, COCONUT.

A FEW YEARS AGO, COCONUT AND I FELL IN LOVE. LIKE, STUPIDLY IN LOVE, THE SO-CUTE-IT-MAKES-YOU-WANT-TO-VOMIT KIND. THE KIND THAT HAD US KISSING IN PUBLIC, COMING UP WITH CUTE PET NAMES (HENCE COCONUT), AND EVEN HAD US FALLING ASLEEP HOLDING HANDS.

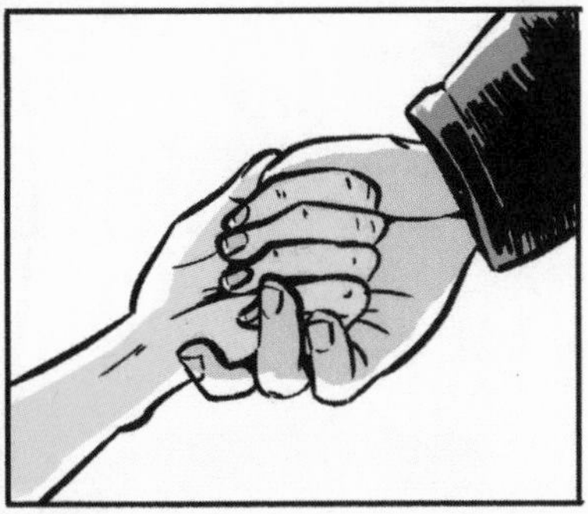

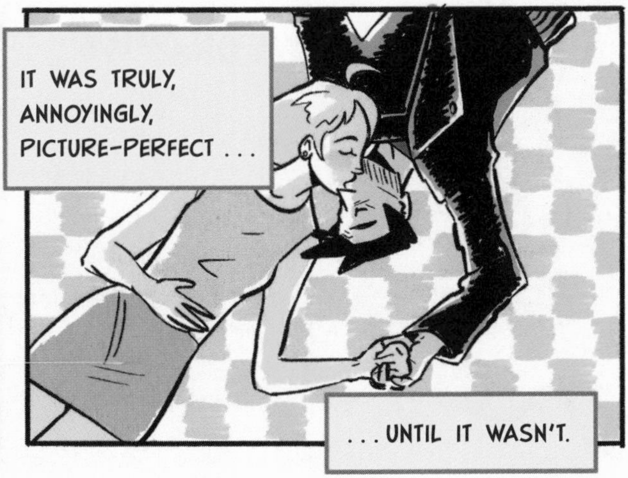
IT WAS TRULY, ANNOYINGLY, PICTURE-PERFECT . . .
. . . UNTIL IT WASN'T.

BUT BEFORE WE DIVE INTO WHAT WENT WRONG, AND THE STUPID DIRTBAG THINGS I DID TO KEEP COCONUT AROUND, YOU SHOULD FIRST KNOW A FEW THINGS ABOUT US.

FIRST OFF, THERE WAS COCONUT (THE ANGEL)

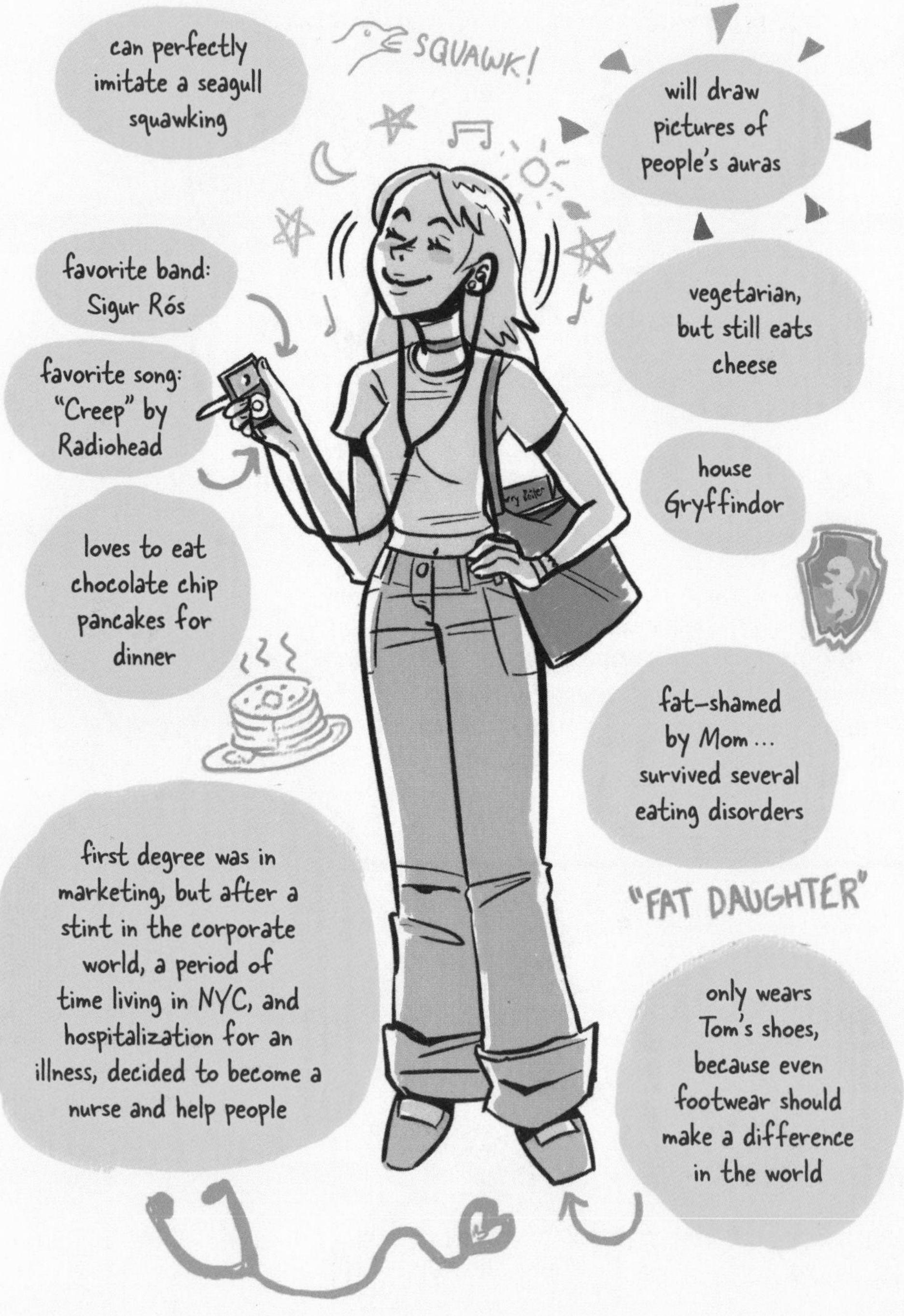
can perfectly imitate a seagull squawking
SQUAWK!
will draw pictures of people's auras
favorite band: Sigur Rós
vegetarian, but still eats cheese
favorite song: "Creep" by Radiohead
house Gryffindor
loves to eat chocolate chip pancakes for dinner
fat-shamed by Mom... survived several eating disorders
"FAT DAUGHTER"
first degree was in marketing, but after a stint in the corporate world, a period of time living in NYC, and hospitalization for an illness, decided to become a nurse and help people
only wears Tom's shoes, because even footwear should make a difference in the world

AND THEN, OF COURSE, THERE WAS ME, MICHAEL (THE DIRTBAG)

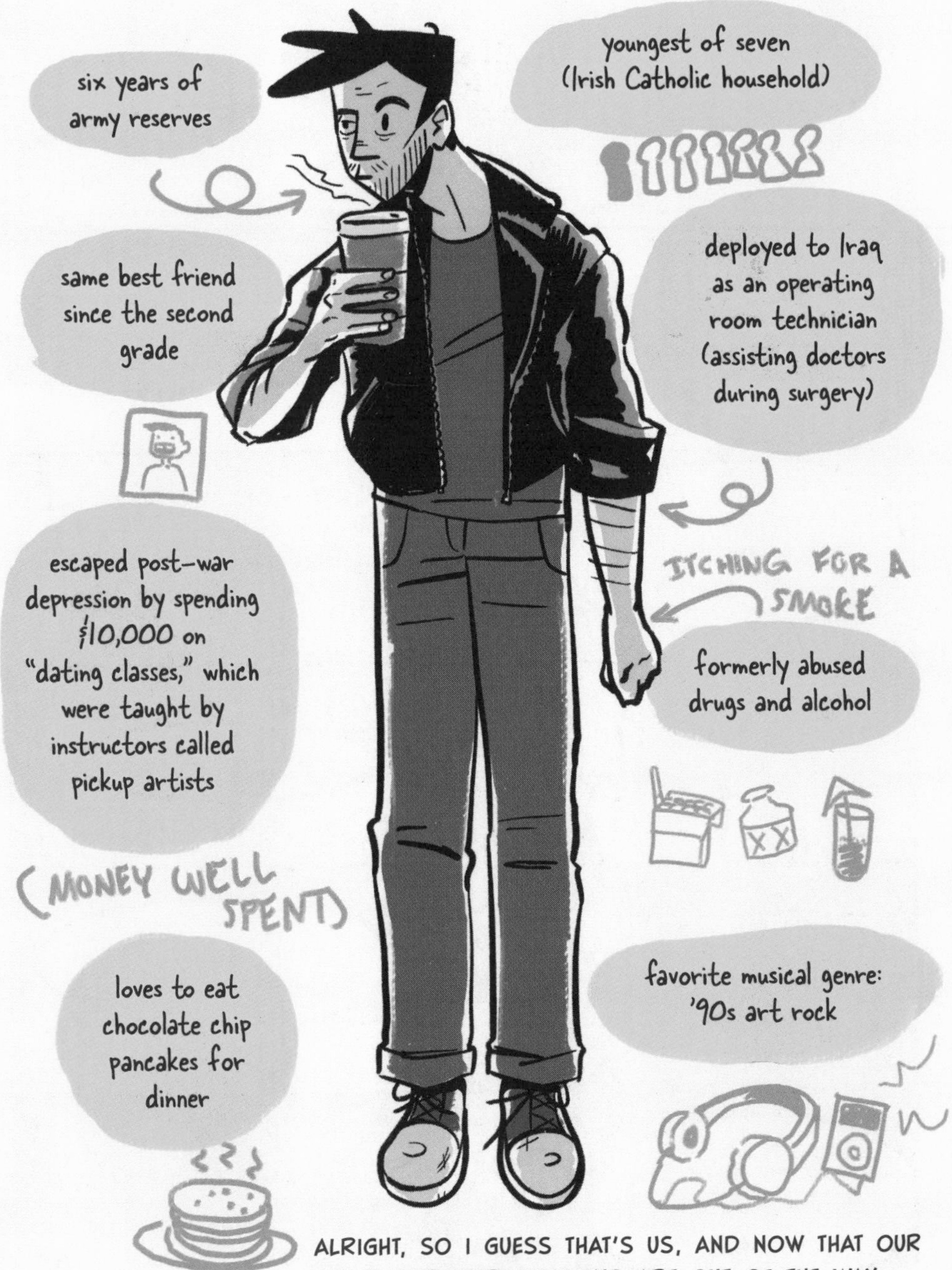
six years of army reserves
youngest of seven (Irish Catholic household)
same best friend since the second grade
deployed to Iraq as an operating room technician (assisting doctors during surgery)
escaped post-war depression by spending $10,000 on "dating classes," which were taught by instructors called pickup artists
ITCHING FOR A SMOKE
formerly abused drugs and alcohol
(MONEY WELL SPENT)
loves to eat chocolate chip pancakes for dinner
favorite musical genre: '90s art rock

ALRIGHT, SO I GUESS THAT'S US, AND NOW THAT OUR CHARACTER INTRODUCTIONS ARE OUT OF THE WAY, LET'S DIVE INTO HOW EVERYTHING WENT TO HELL . . .

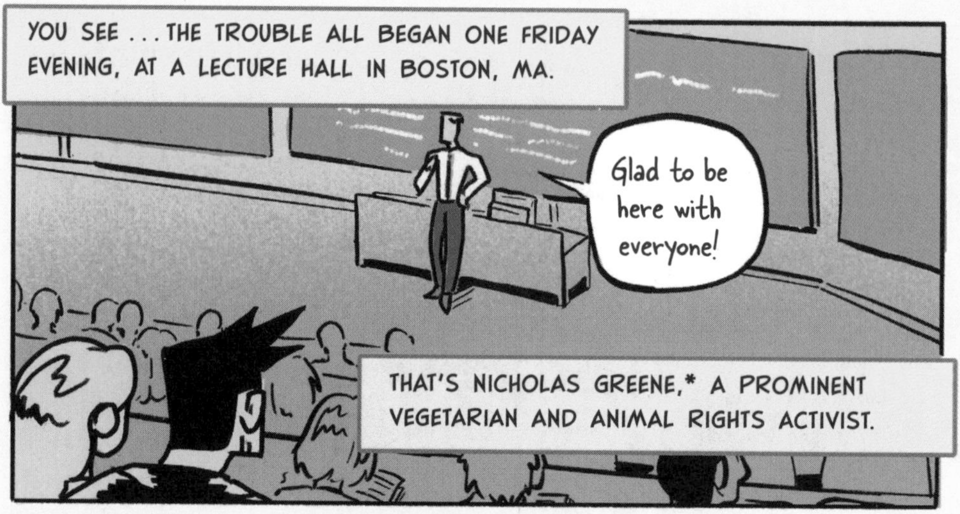
YOU SEE . . . THE TROUBLE ALL BEGAN ONE FRIDAY EVENING, AT A LECTURE HALL IN BOSTON, MA.
Glad to be here with everyone!
THAT'S NICHOLAS GREENE,* A PROMINENT VEGETARIAN AND ANIMAL RIGHTS ACTIVIST.

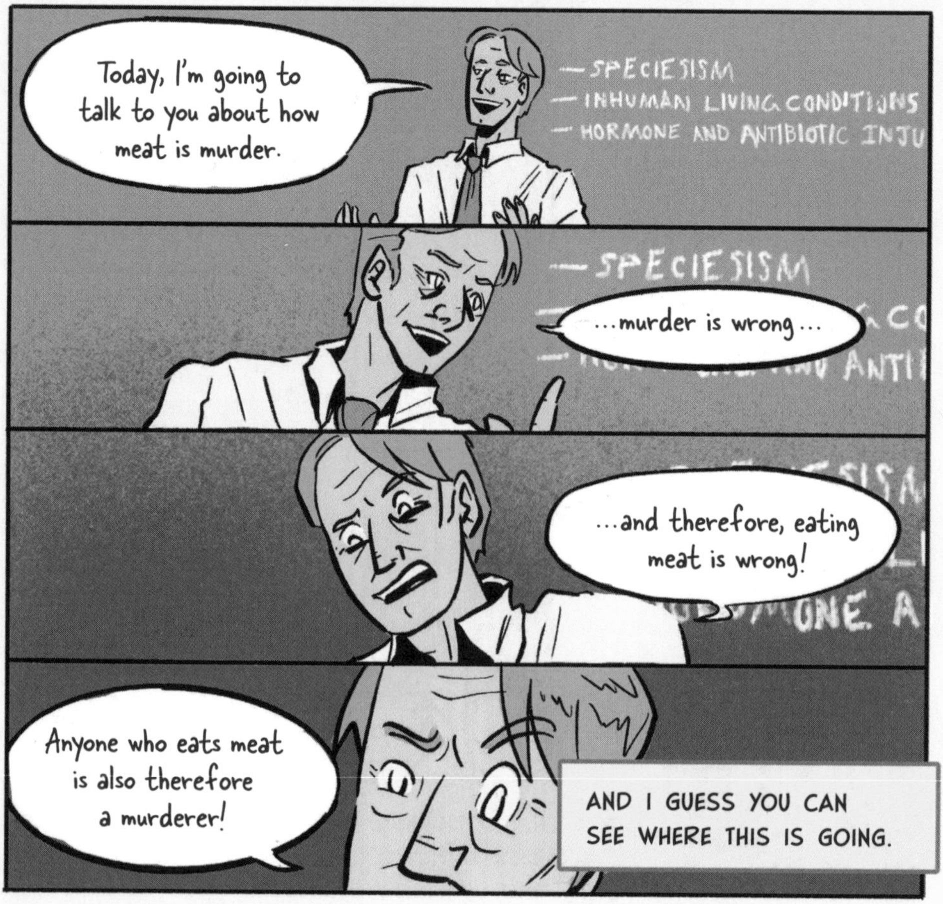
Today, I'm going to talk to you about how meat is murder.
—SPECIESISM
—INHUMAN LIVING CONDITIONS
—HORMONE AND ANTIBIOTIC INJU
. . . murder is wrong . . .
. . . and therefore, eating meat is wrong!
Anyone who eats meat is also therefore a murderer!
AND I GUESS YOU CAN SEE WHERE THIS IS GOING.

*NOT HIS REAL NAME, JUST FYI.

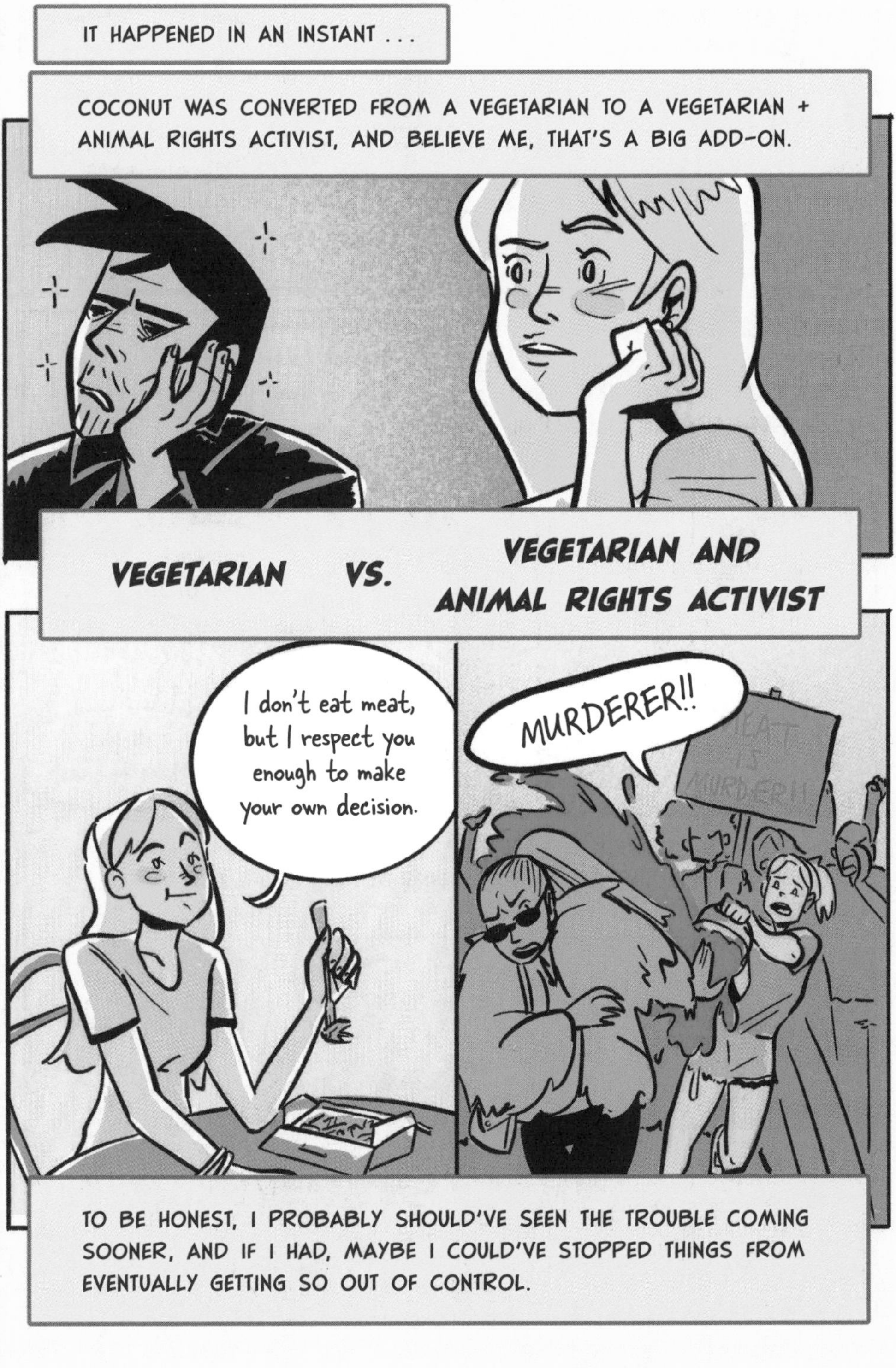
IT HAPPENED IN AN INSTANT . . .
COCONUT WAS CONVERTED FROM A VEGETARIAN TO A VEGETARIAN + ANIMAL RIGHTS ACTIVIST, AND BELIEVE ME, THAT'S A BIG ADD-ON.
VEGETARIAN VS. VEGETARIAN AND ANIMAL RIGHTS ACTIVIST
I don't eat meat, but I respect you enough to make your own decision.
MURDERER!!
MEAT IS MURDER!!
TO BE HONEST, I PROBABLY SHOULD'VE SEEN THE TROUBLE COMING SOONER, AND IF I HAD, MAYBE I COULD'VE STOPPED THINGS FROM EVENTUALLY GETTING SO OUT OF CONTROL.

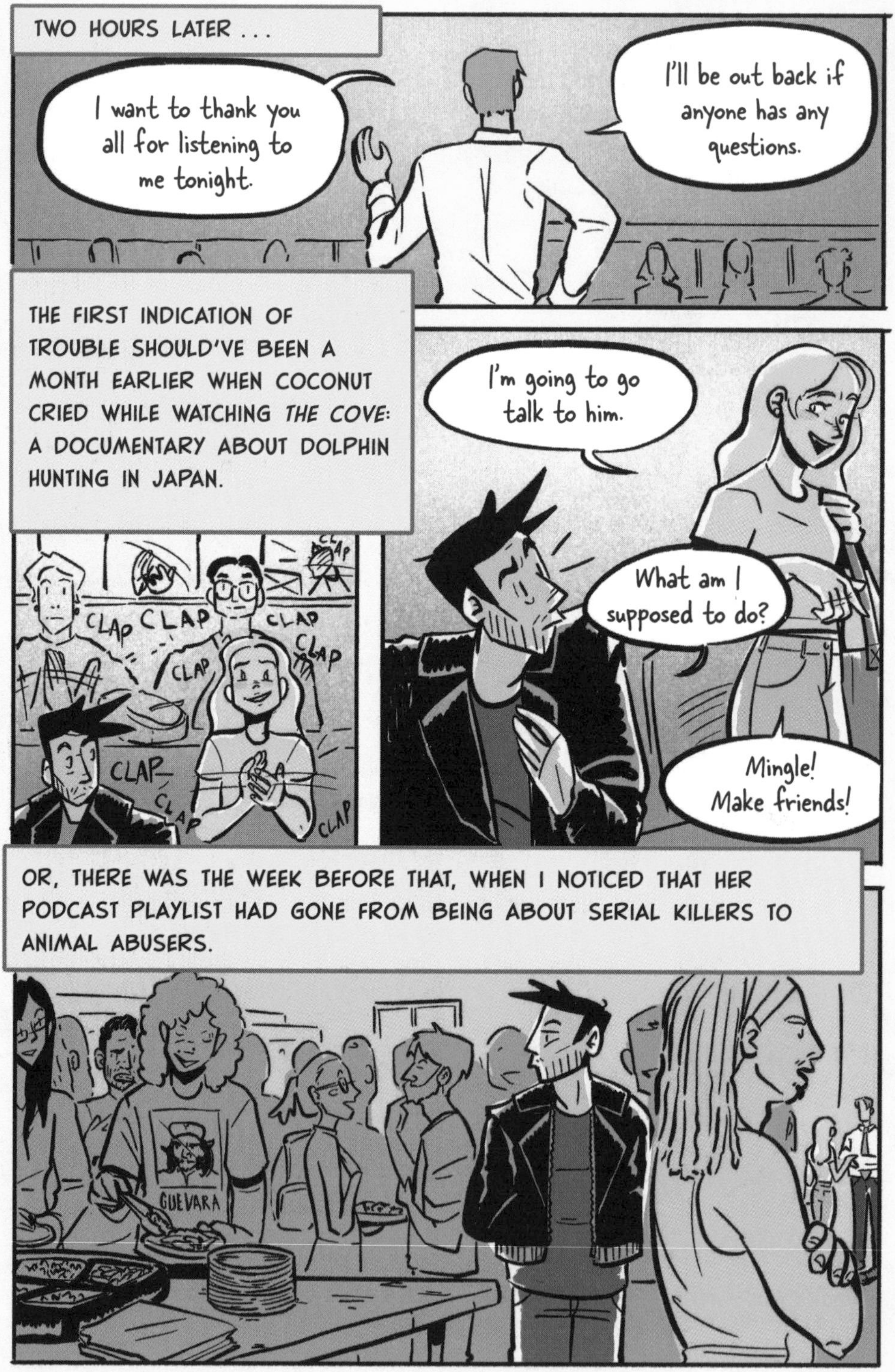
TWO HOURS LATER . . .
I want to thank you all for listening to me tonight.
I'll be out back if anyone has any questions.
THE FIRST INDICATION OF TROUBLE SHOULD'VE BEEN A MONTH EARLIER WHEN COCONUT CRIED WHILE WATCHING *THE COVE*: A DOCUMENTARY ABOUT DOLPHIN HUNTING IN JAPAN.
CLAP CLAP CLAP CLAP CLAP CLAP CLAP CLAP CLAP CLAP
I'm going to go talk to him.
What am I supposed to do?
Mingle! Make friends!
OR, THERE WAS THE WEEK BEFORE THAT, WHEN I NOTICED THAT HER PODCAST PLAYLIST HAD GONE FROM BEING ABOUT SERIAL KILLERS TO ANIMAL ABUSERS.
GUEVARA

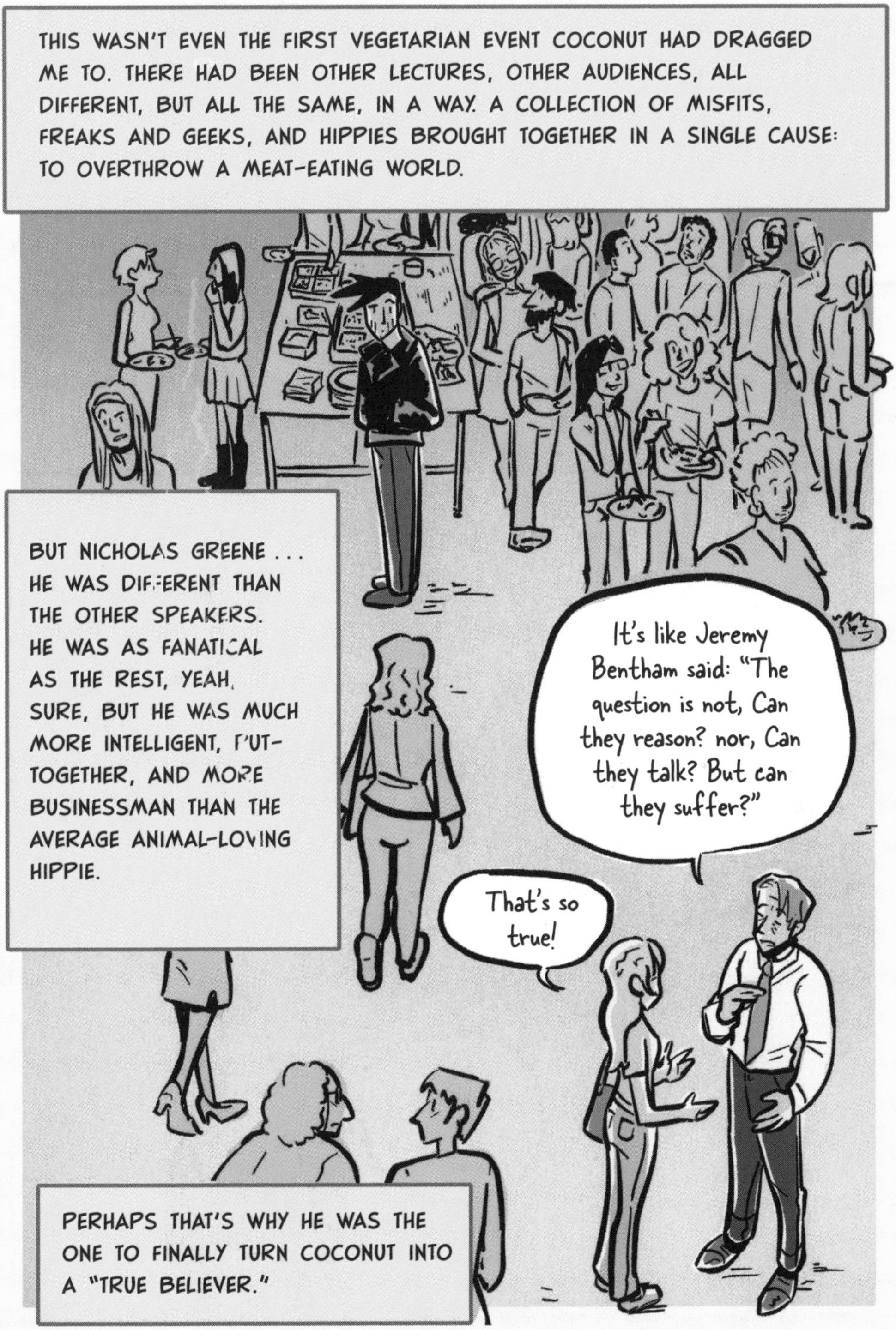
THIS WASN'T EVEN THE FIRST VEGETARIAN EVENT COCONUT HAD DRAGGED ME TO. THERE HAD BEEN OTHER LECTURES, OTHER AUDIENCES, ALL DIFFERENT, BUT ALL THE SAME, IN A WAY. A COLLECTION OF MISFITS, FREAKS AND GEEKS, AND HIPPIES BROUGHT TOGETHER IN A SINGLE CAUSE: TO OVERTHROW A MEAT-EATING WORLD.
BUT NICHOLAS GREENE . . . HE WAS DIFFERENT THAN THE OTHER SPEAKERS. HE WAS AS FANATICAL AS THE REST, YEAH, SURE, BUT HE WAS MUCH MORE INTELLIGENT, PUT-TOGETHER, AND MORE BUSINESSMAN THAN THE AVERAGE ANIMAL-LOVING HIPPIE.
It's like Jeremy Bentham said: "The question is not, Can they reason? nor, Can they talk? But can they suffer?"
That's so true!
PERHAPS THAT'S WHY HE WAS THE ONE TO FINALLY TURN COCONUT INTO A "TRUE BELIEVER."

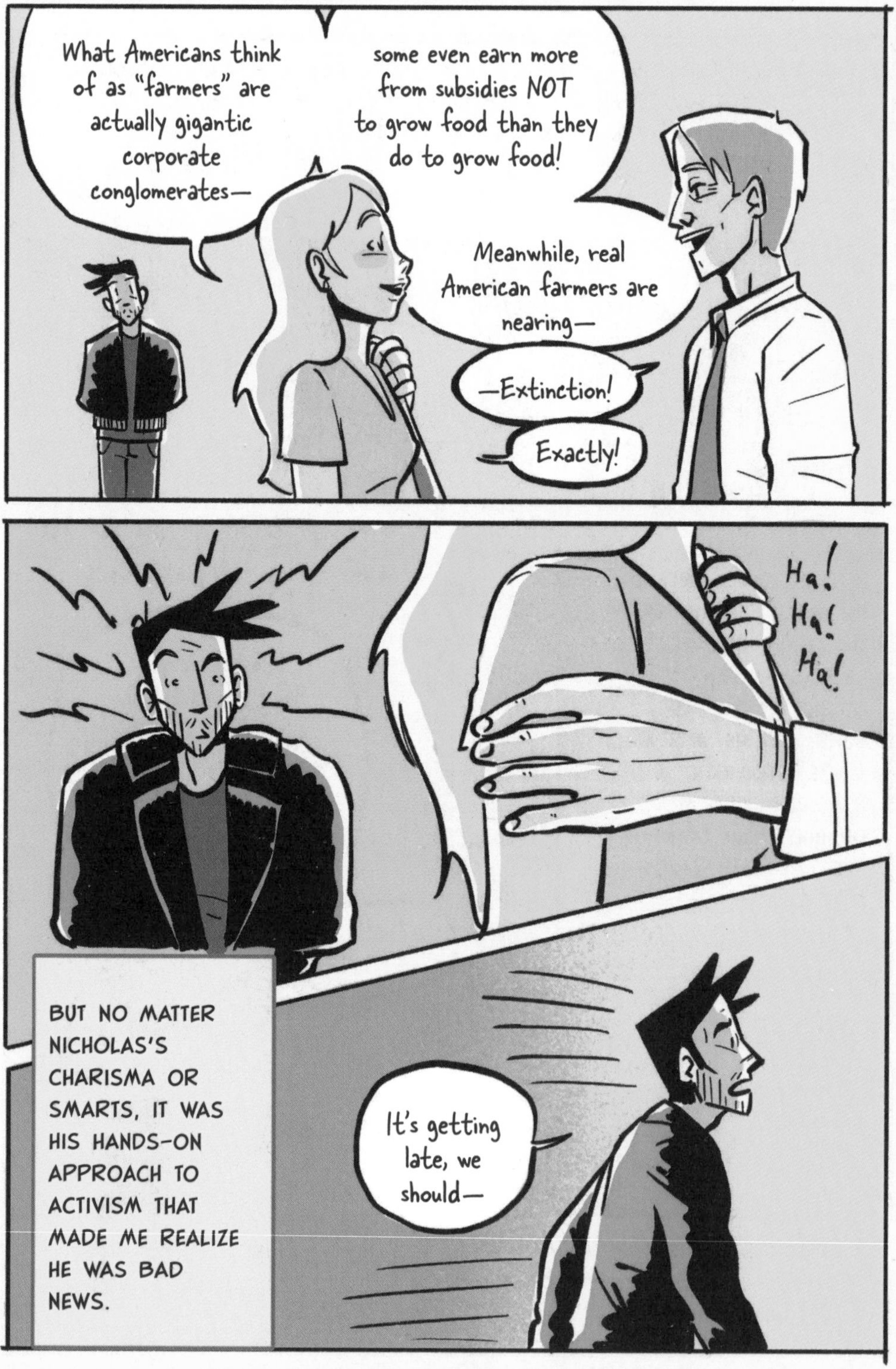
What Americans think of as "farmers" are actually gigantic corporate conglomerates—
some even earn more from subsidies NOT to grow food than they do to grow food!
Meanwhile, real American farmers are nearing—
—Extinction!
Exactly!
Ha! Ha! Ha!
BUT NO MATTER NICHOLAS'S CHARISMA OR SMARTS, IT WAS HIS HANDS-ON APPROACH TO ACTIVISM THAT MADE ME REALIZE HE WAS BAD NEWS.
It's getting late, we should—

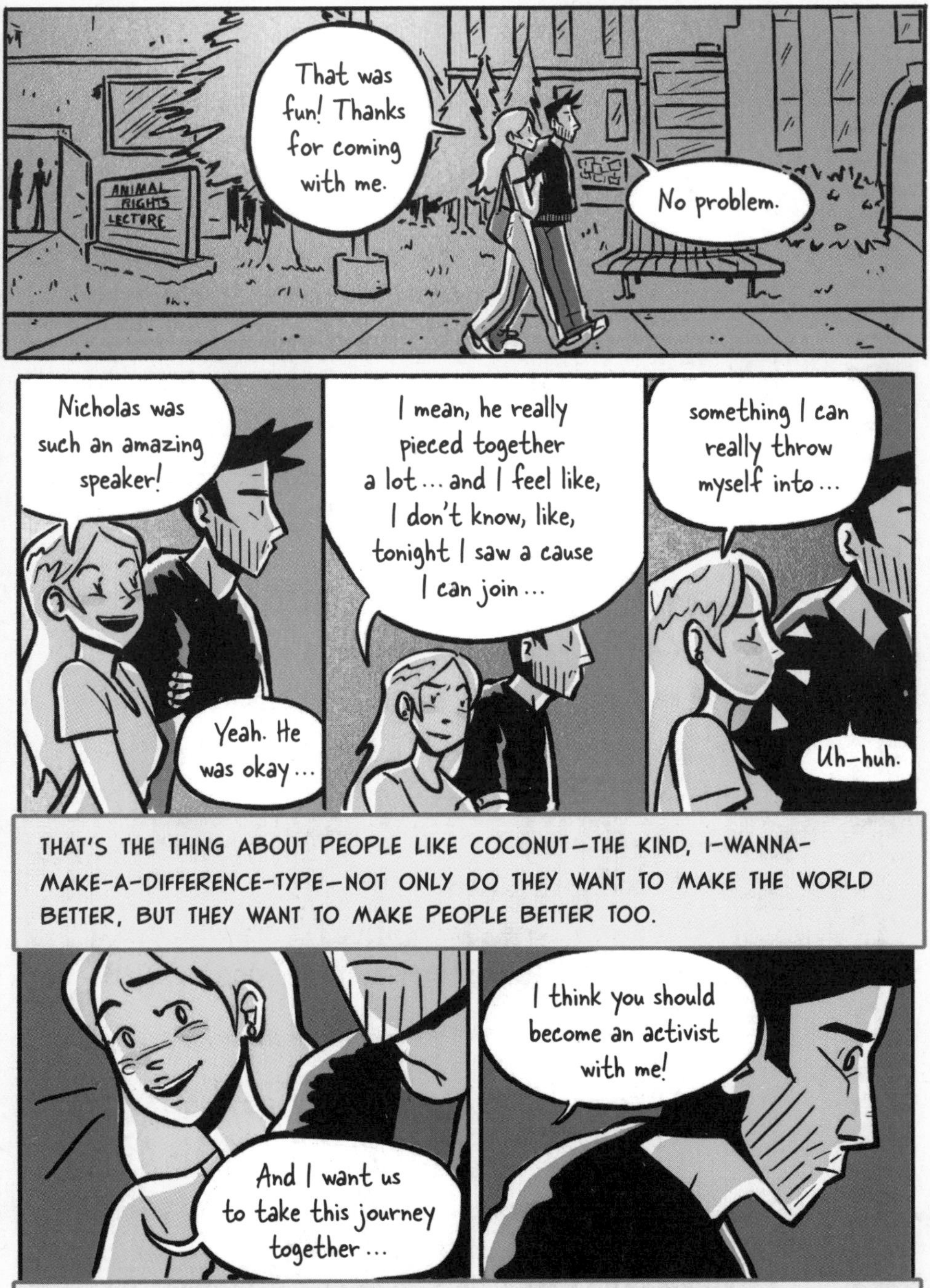

ANIMAL RIGHTS LECTURE
That was fun! Thanks for coming with me.
No problem.
Nicholas was such an amazing speaker!
Yeah. He was okay...
I mean, he really pieced together a lot... and I feel like, I don't know, like, tonight I saw a cause I can join...
something I can really throw myself into...
Uh-huh.
THAT'S THE THING ABOUT PEOPLE LIKE COCONUT—THE KIND, I-WANNA-MAKE-A-DIFFERENCE-TYPE—NOT ONLY DO THEY WANT TO MAKE THE WORLD BETTER, BUT THEY WANT TO MAKE PEOPLE BETTER TOO.
And I want us to take this journey together...
I think you should become an activist with me!
AND THE PROBLEM IS PEOPLE, PEOPLE LIKE ME—THE NOSTALGIC, ALONE-IN-YOUR-HEAD NARRATOR TYPE—WE HATE CHANGE, EVEN IF IT IS SUPPOSEDLY FOR OUR OWN GOOD.

Lecture Notes

Speciesism - When one species discriminates against another because of perceived intellectual + emotional superiority.

EX. It's illegal to rape a human, and it's illegal to eat another human; HOWEVER, it's LEGAL to force-inseminate an animal, and then eat the resulting offspring.

INHUMANE LIVING CONDITONS

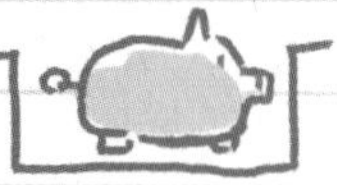

Pigs: Kept in cages so small that there's no room to even turn around.

Chickens: Fattened up so much that they can't fly, much less walk.

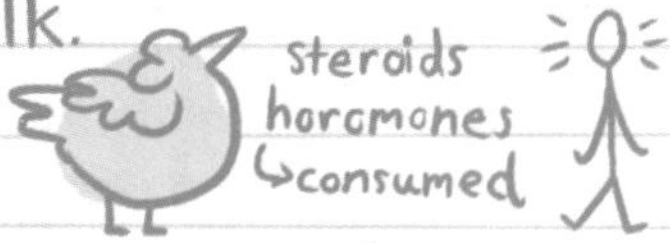
steroids
hormones
↳consumed

Cows: Kept pregnant year round and when their calves are born, they're ripped away. Then they're force inseminated again, cycle continues.

DISEASES / CONDITIONS THAT CAN ALLEGEDLY BE CURED / BETTERED / PREVENTED BY A PLANT-BASED DIET: weight loss, some cancers, osteoarthritis, diabetes

Recommended reading: *Animal Liberation*, by Peter Singer

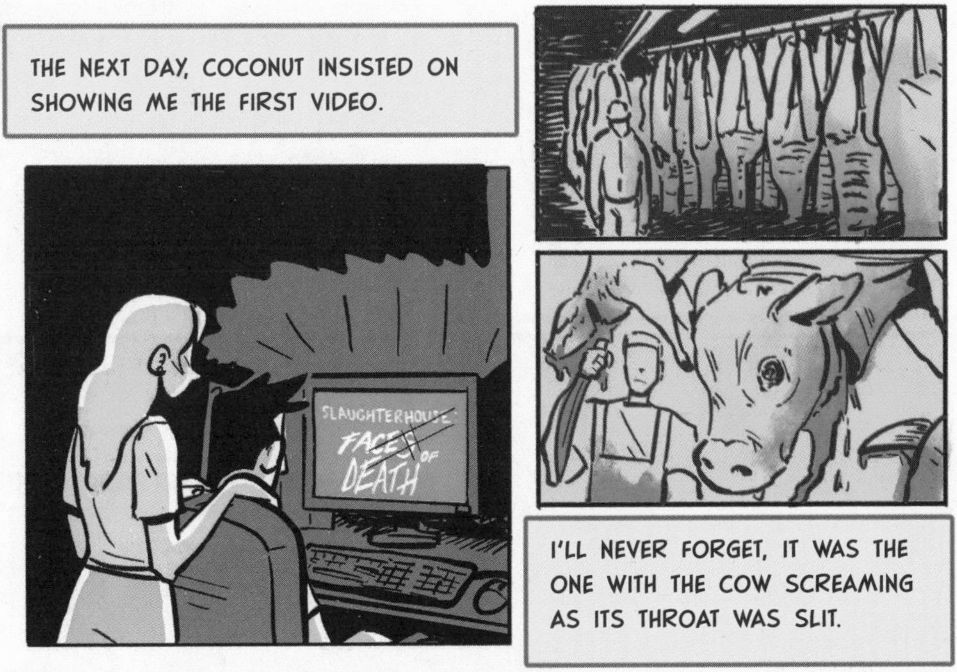
THE NEXT DAY, COCONUT INSISTED ON SHOWING ME THE FIRST VIDEO.
SLAUGHTERHOUSE:
FACES OF DEATH
I'LL NEVER FORGET, IT WAS THE ONE WITH THE COW SCREAMING AS ITS THROAT WAS SLIT.

CHAPTER 2

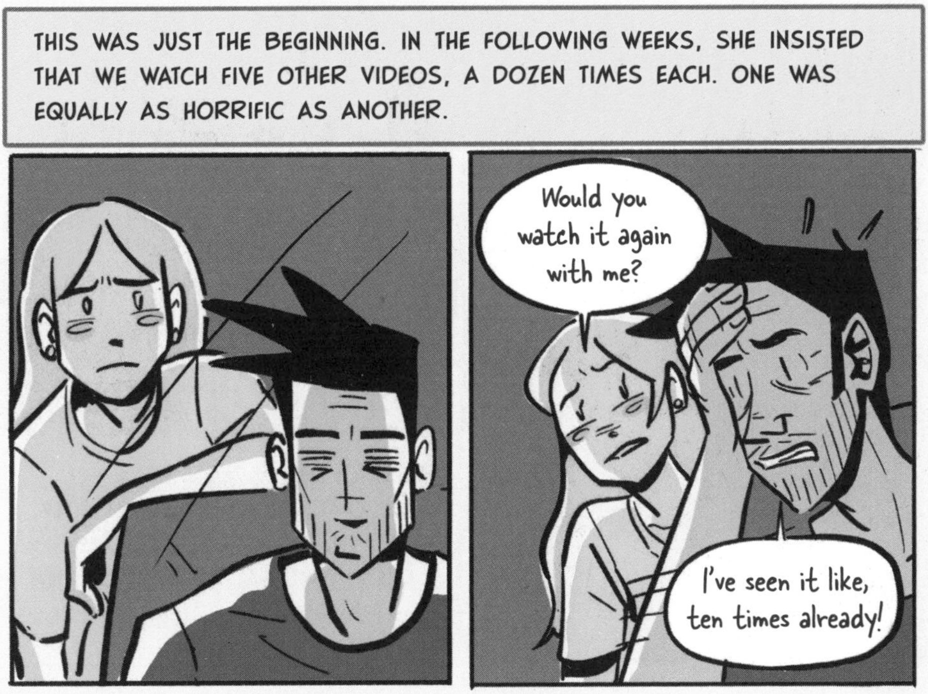
THIS WAS JUST THE BEGINNING. IN THE FOLLOWING WEEKS, SHE INSISTED THAT WE WATCH FIVE OTHER VIDEOS, A DOZEN TIMES EACH. ONE WAS EQUALLY AS HORRIFIC AS ANOTHER.
Would you watch it again with me?
I've seen it like, ten times already!

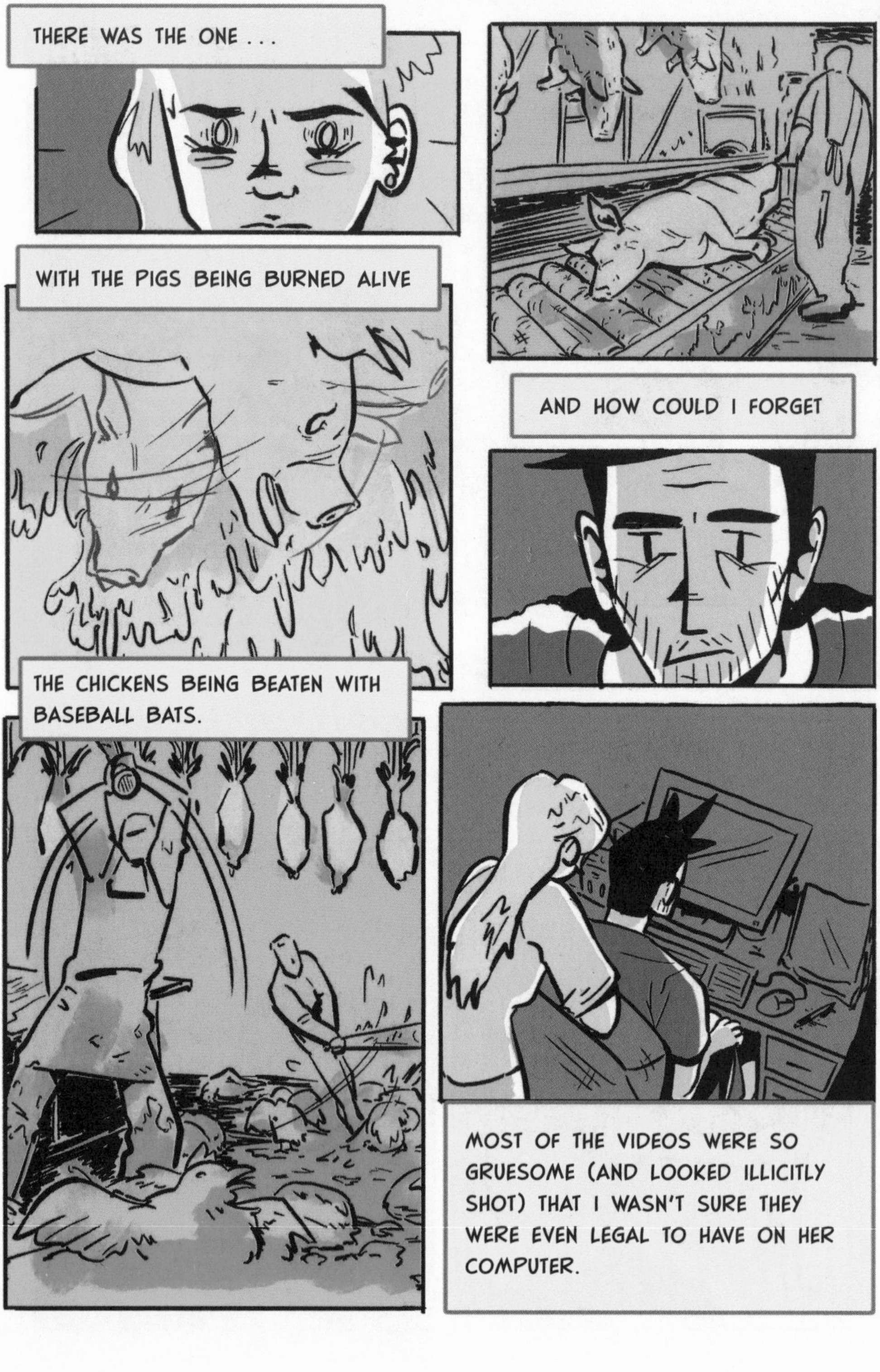
THERE WAS THE ONE . . .
WITH THE PIGS BEING BURNED ALIVE
THE CHICKENS BEING BEATEN WITH BASEBALL BATS.
AND HOW COULD I FORGET
MOST OF THE VIDEOS WERE SO GRUESOME (AND LOOKED ILLICITLY SHOT) THAT I WASN'T SURE THEY WERE EVEN LEGAL TO HAVE ON HER COMPUTER.

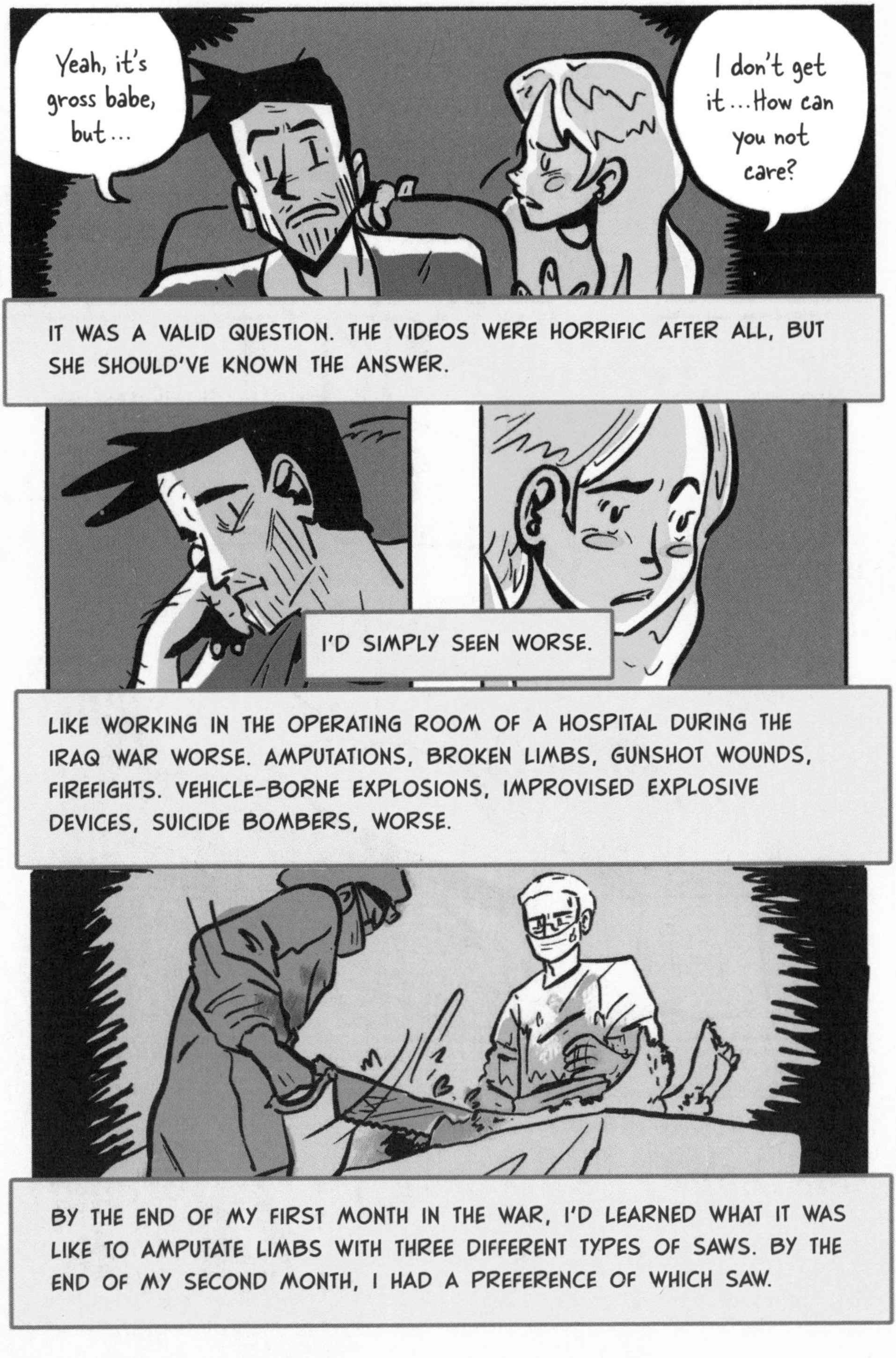
Yeah, it's gross babe, but...
I don't get it...How can you not care?
IT WAS A VALID QUESTION. THE VIDEOS WERE HORRIFIC AFTER ALL, BUT SHE SHOULD'VE KNOWN THE ANSWER.
I'D SIMPLY SEEN WORSE.
LIKE WORKING IN THE OPERATING ROOM OF A HOSPITAL DURING THE IRAQ WAR WORSE. AMPUTATIONS, BROKEN LIMBS, GUNSHOT WOUNDS, FIREFIGHTS. VEHICLE-BORNE EXPLOSIONS, IMPROVISED EXPLOSIVE DEVICES, SUICIDE BOMBERS, WORSE.
BY THE END OF MY FIRST MONTH IN THE WAR, I'D LEARNED WHAT IT WAS LIKE TO AMPUTATE LIMBS WITH THREE DIFFERENT TYPES OF SAWS. BY THE END OF MY SECOND MONTH, I HAD A PREFERENCE OF WHICH SAW.

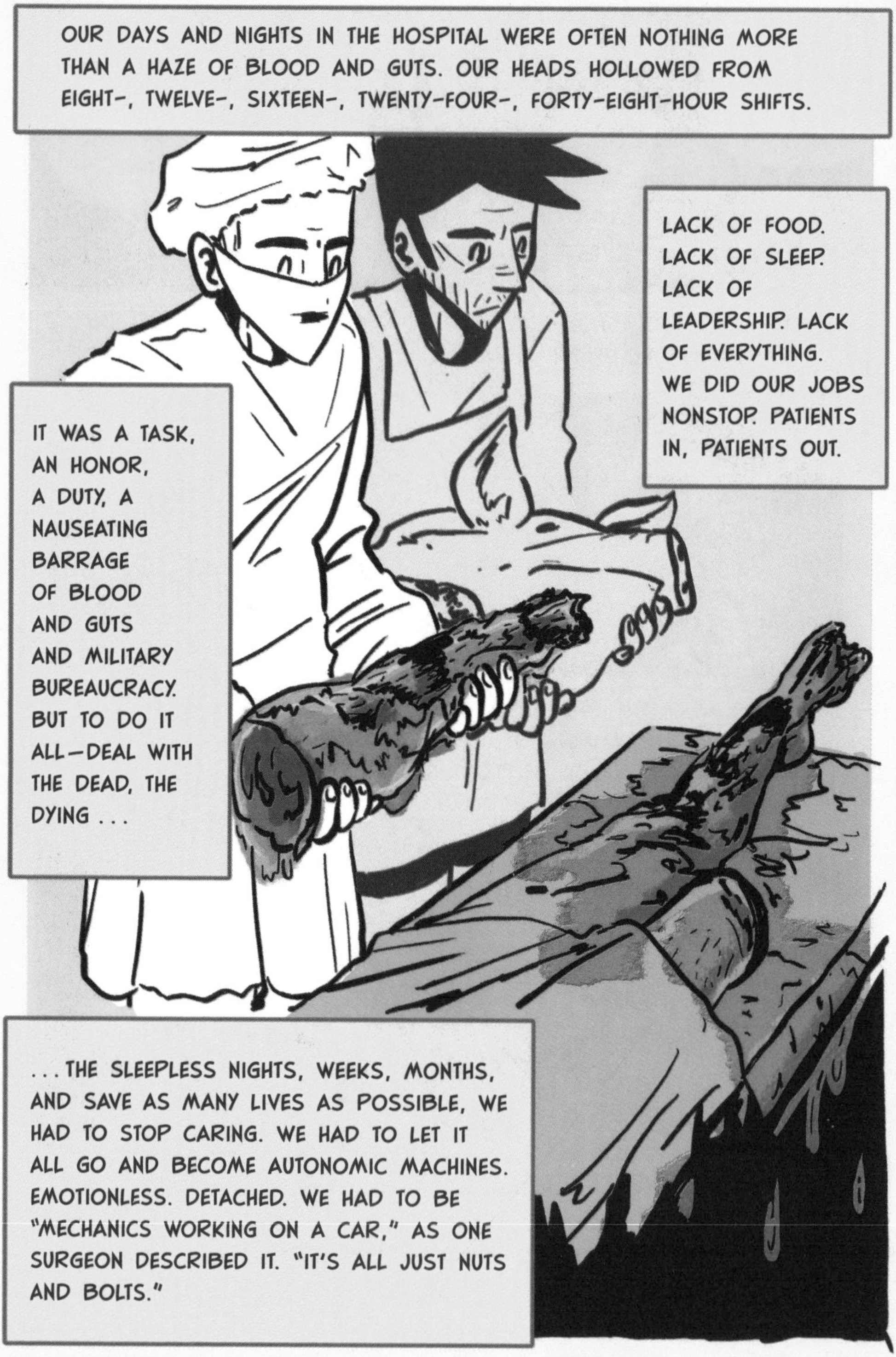
OUR DAYS AND NIGHTS IN THE HOSPITAL WERE OFTEN NOTHING MORE THAN A HAZE OF BLOOD AND GUTS. OUR HEADS HOLLOWED FROM EIGHT-, TWELVE-, SIXTEEN-, TWENTY-FOUR-, FORTY-EIGHT-HOUR SHIFTS.
LACK OF FOOD. LACK OF SLEEP. LACK OF LEADERSHIP. LACK OF EVERYTHING. WE DID OUR JOBS NONSTOP. PATIENTS IN, PATIENTS OUT.
IT WAS A TASK, AN HONOR, A DUTY, A NAUSEATING BARRAGE OF BLOOD AND GUTS AND MILITARY BUREAUCRACY. BUT TO DO IT ALL—DEAL WITH THE DEAD, THE DYING . . .
. . . THE SLEEPLESS NIGHTS, WEEKS, MONTHS, AND SAVE AS MANY LIVES AS POSSIBLE, WE HAD TO STOP CARING. WE HAD TO LET IT ALL GO AND BECOME AUTONOMIC MACHINES. EMOTIONLESS. DETACHED. WE HAD TO BE "MECHANICS WORKING ON A CAR," AS ONE SURGEON DESCRIBED IT. "IT'S ALL JUST NUTS AND BOLTS."

U.S. SERVICE MEMBERS. MULTINATIONAL FORCES. TERRORISTS. INSURGENTS. CIVILIANS. ADULTS. CHILDREN. EVEN SERVICE DOGS. THEY ALL CAME THROUGH OUR HOSPITAL DOORS.

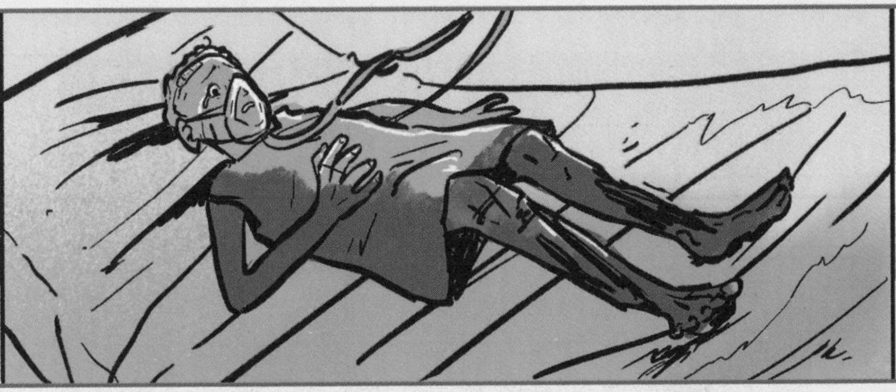

CHILDREN WERE ALWAYS THE TOUGHEST TO WORK ON; EVEN THE ONES LABELED "COMBATANTS," BECAUSE NO MATTER WHAT THEY'D DONE, THEY WERE STILL JUST KIDS. MANY WERE SO MALNOURISHED THAT YOU'D SWEAR A CHILD ON THE OPERATING TABLE WAS ONLY SEVEN OR EIGHT, BUT THEY'D END UP BEING FOURTEEN OR FIFTEEN.

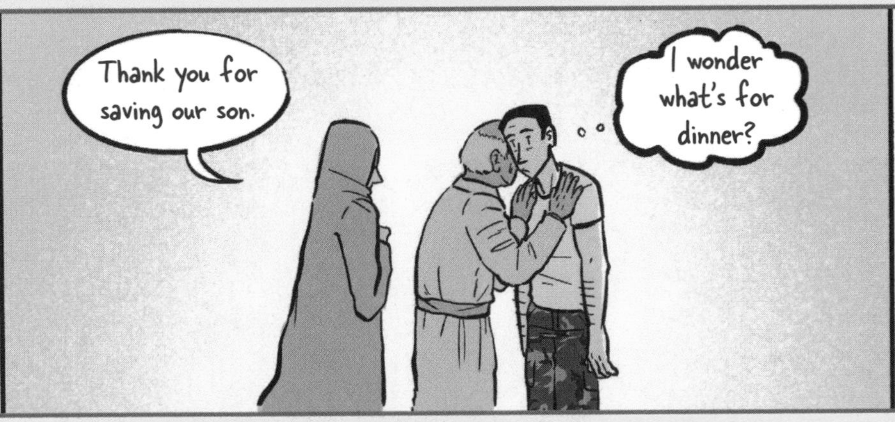
Thank you for saving our son.
I wonder what's for dinner?

KIDS, EVEN MALNOURISHED ONES, HAVE 300 GROWING AND FUSING BONES COMPARED TO 206 FOR ADULTS. THIS MEANS X-RAYS CAN'T DISTINGUISH BETWEEN BONE SHRAPNEL FROM A BOMBER AND THE NORMAL BONES OF A PATIENT.

AND THEN THERE WERE THE TIMES OUR SUPPLY LINES WERE ATTACKED AND OUR HOSPITAL RAN LOW ON SUPPLIES, AND EVEN BLOOD—BAD NEWS IN A WARZONE. ON DAYS LIKE THAT, I WOULD DONATE IN THE MORNING AND AFTERWARD ASSIST IN MY USUAL ROUND OF SURGERIES.

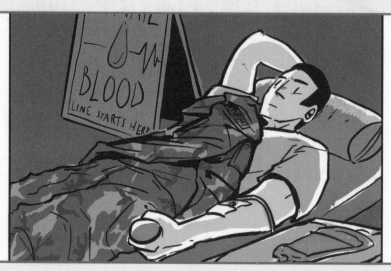

ONE OF THE MORNINGS I DONATED, WHEN SUPPLIES WERE ESPECIALLY LOW, I ASSISTED AFTERWARD ON A SURGERY WITH A PATIENT OF THE SAME BLOOD TYPE. A SUICIDE BOMB VICTIM, HE WAS LITTERED WITH SHRAPNEL AND HIS VITALS KEPT DROPPING DUE TO BLOOD LOSS. WHICH MEANT THAT HE KEPT NEEDING TRANSFUSIONS, AND AS THE NEED CONTINUED . . .

WE REACHED THE DAY'S DONATIONS, WHICH MEANT THAT EVENTUALLY MY OWN BLOOD WAS SHOOTING OUT AT ME FROM THE PATIENT.

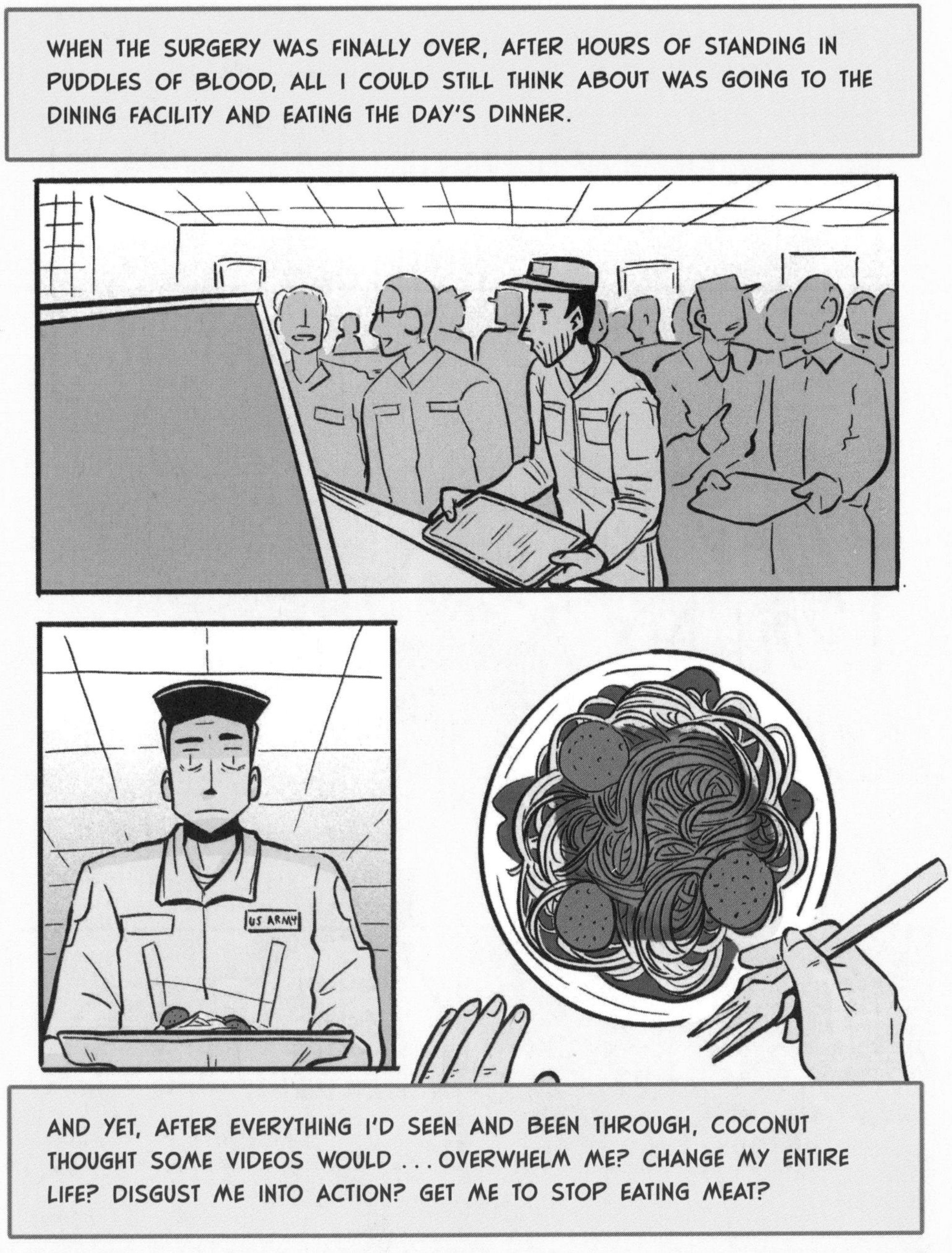
WHEN THE SURGERY WAS FINALLY OVER, AFTER HOURS OF STANDING IN PUDDLES OF BLOOD, ALL I COULD STILL THINK ABOUT WAS GOING TO THE DINING FACILITY AND EATING THE DAY'S DINNER.
US ARMY
AND YET, AFTER EVERYTHING I'D SEEN AND BEEN THROUGH, COCONUT THOUGHT SOME VIDEOS WOULD . . . OVERWHELM ME? CHANGE MY ENTIRE LIFE? DISGUST ME INTO ACTION? GET ME TO STOP EATING MEAT?

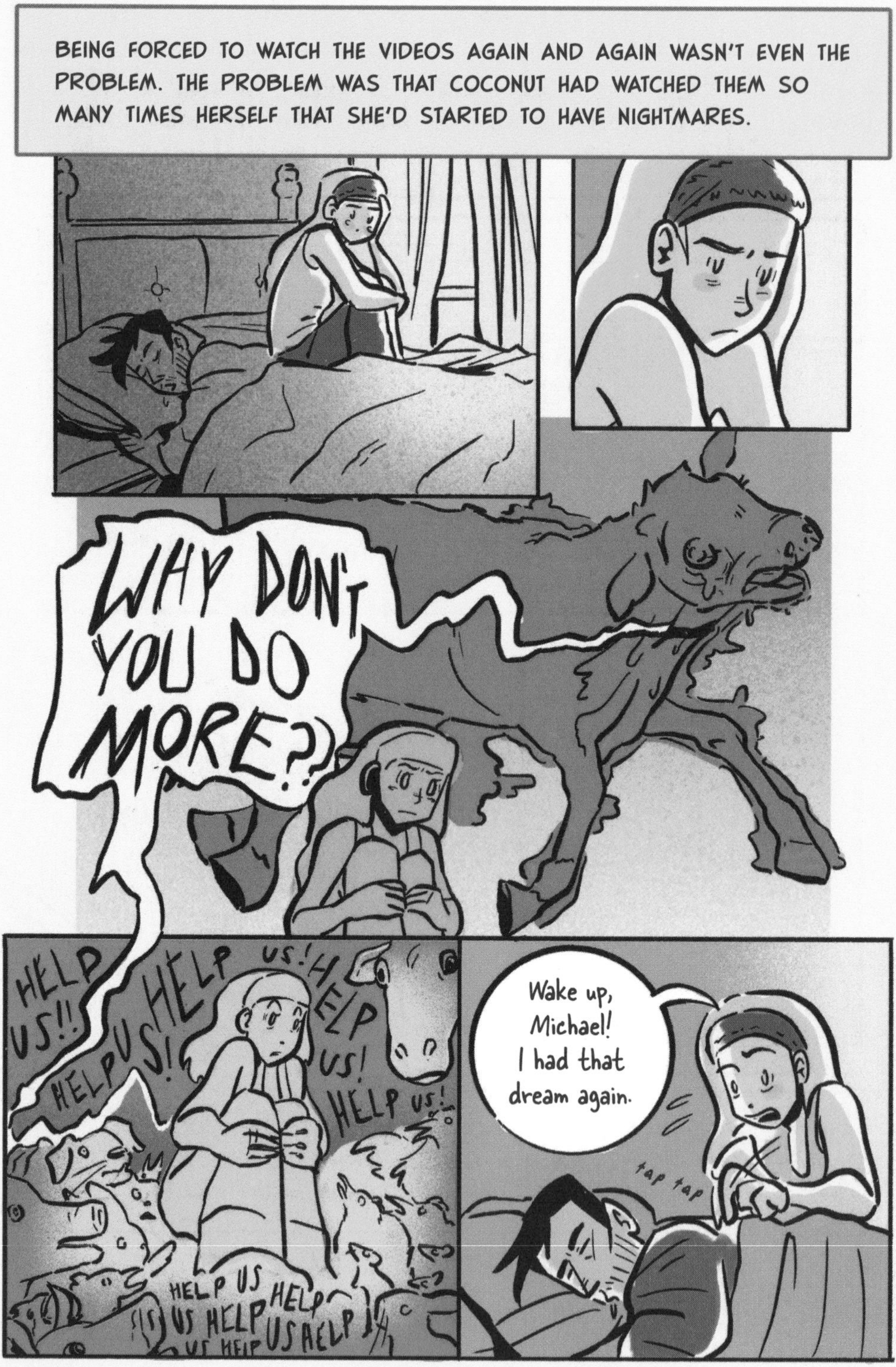
BEING FORCED TO WATCH THE VIDEOS AGAIN AND AGAIN WASN'T EVEN THE PROBLEM. THE PROBLEM WAS THAT COCONUT HAD WATCHED THEM SO MANY TIMES HERSELF THAT SHE'D STARTED TO HAVE NIGHTMARES.
WHY DON'T YOU DO MORE?
HELP US!!
HELP US!
HELP US!
HELP US!
HELP US!
HELP US HELP US HELP US HELP US HELP
Wake up, Michael! I had that dream again.
tap tap

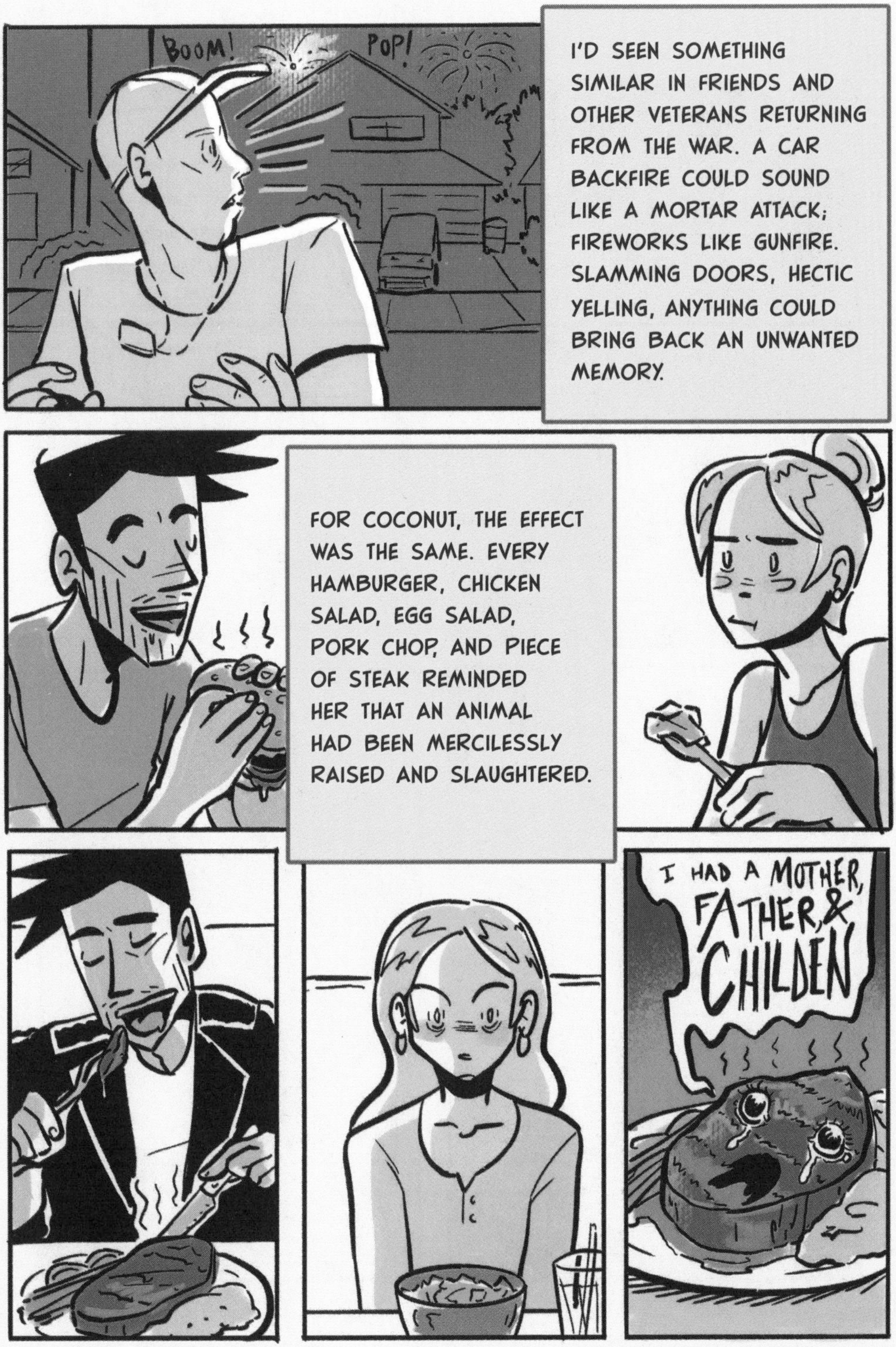
BOOM!
POP!
I'D SEEN SOMETHING SIMILAR IN FRIENDS AND OTHER VETERANS RETURNING FROM THE WAR. A CAR BACKFIRE COULD SOUND LIKE A MORTAR ATTACK; FIREWORKS LIKE GUNFIRE. SLAMMING DOORS, HECTIC YELLING, ANYTHING COULD BRING BACK AN UNWANTED MEMORY.
FOR COCONUT, THE EFFECT WAS THE SAME. EVERY HAMBURGER, CHICKEN SALAD, EGG SALAD, PORK CHOP, AND PIECE OF STEAK REMINDED HER THAT AN ANIMAL HAD BEEN MERCILESSLY RAISED AND SLAUGHTERED.
I HAD A MOTHER, FATHER, & CHILDEN

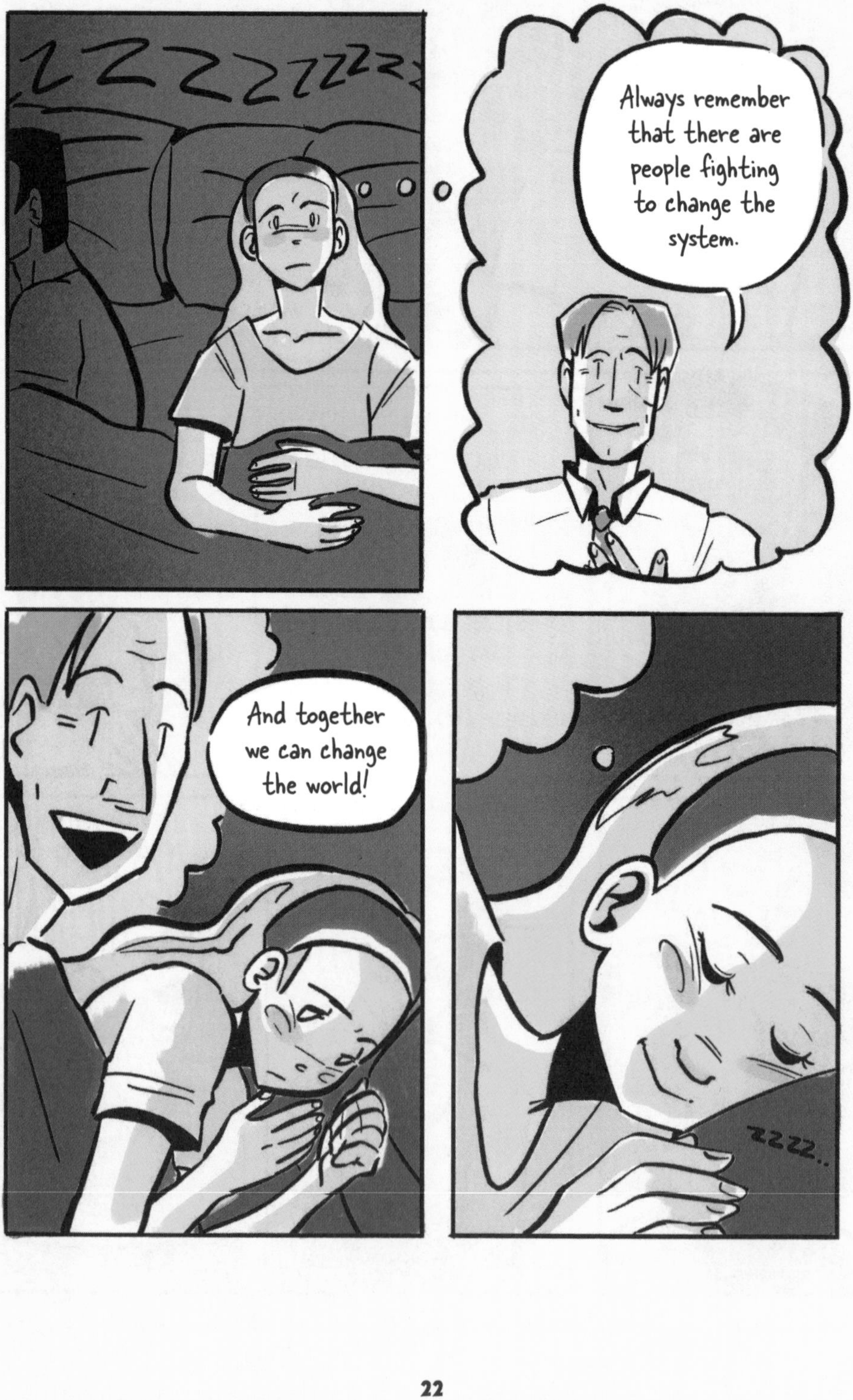
ZZZZZZZZZ
Always remember that there are people fighting to change the system.
And together we can change the world!
ZZZZ..

THE SLAUGHTERHOUSE PROCESS

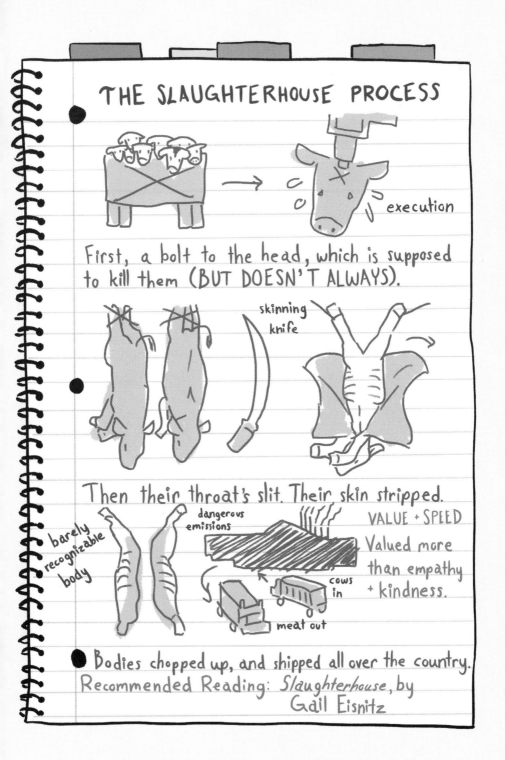

execution

First, a bolt to the head, which is supposed to kill them (BUT DOESN'T ALWAYS).

skinning knife

Then their throat's slit. Their skin stripped.

barely recognizable body

dangerous emissions

VALUE + SPEED
Valued more than empathy + kindness.

cows in

meat out

Bodies chopped up, and shipped all over the country.
Recommended Reading: *Slaughterhouse*, by
Gail Eisnitz

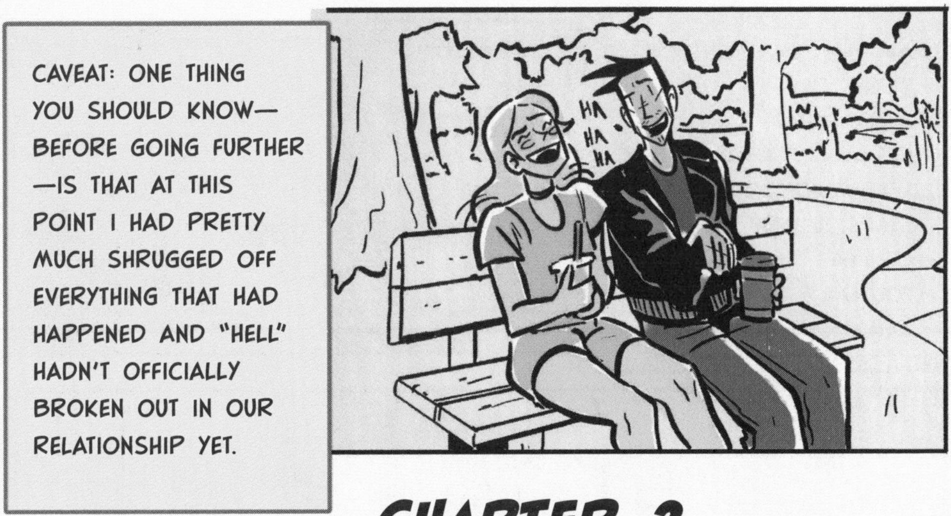
CAVEAT: ONE THING YOU SHOULD KNOW—BEFORE GOING FURTHER—IS THAT AT THIS POINT I HAD PRETTY MUCH SHRUGGED OFF EVERYTHING THAT HAD HAPPENED AND "HELL" HADN'T OFFICIALLY BROKEN OUT IN OUR RELATIONSHIP YET.
HA HA HA

CHAPTER 3

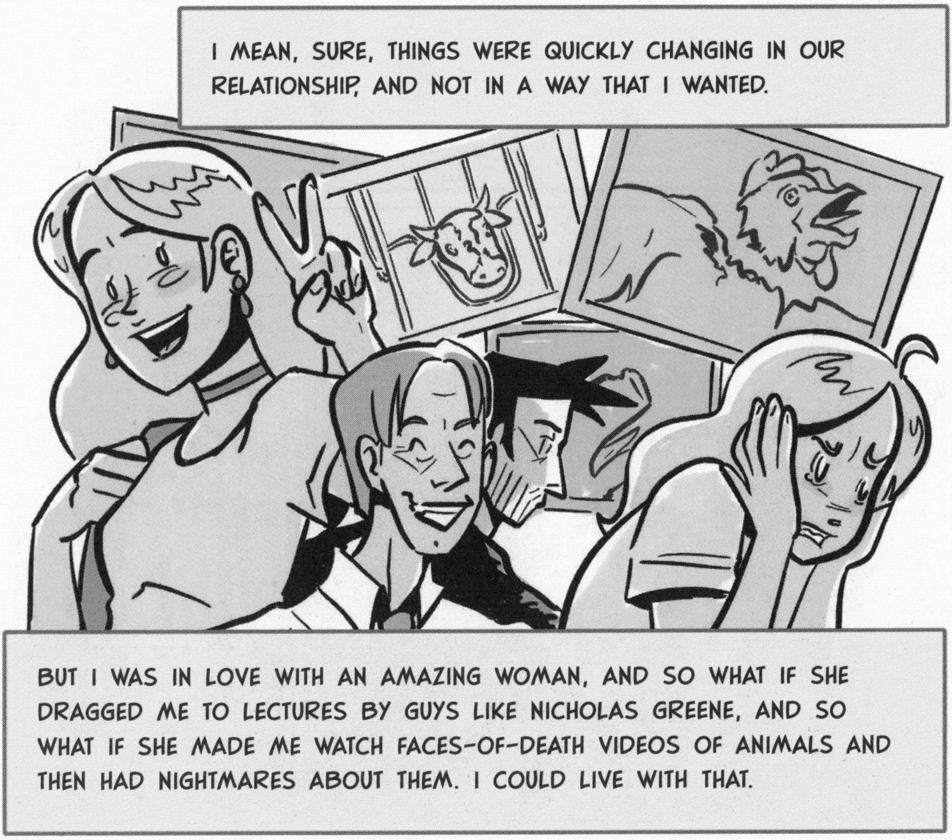
I MEAN, SURE, THINGS WERE QUICKLY CHANGING IN OUR RELATIONSHIP, AND NOT IN A WAY THAT I WANTED.
BUT I WAS IN LOVE WITH AN AMAZING WOMAN, AND SO WHAT IF SHE DRAGGED ME TO LECTURES BY GUYS LIKE NICHOLAS GREENE, AND SO WHAT IF SHE MADE ME WATCH FACES-OF-DEATH VIDEOS OF ANIMALS AND THEN HAD NIGHTMARES ABOUT THEM. I COULD LIVE WITH THAT.

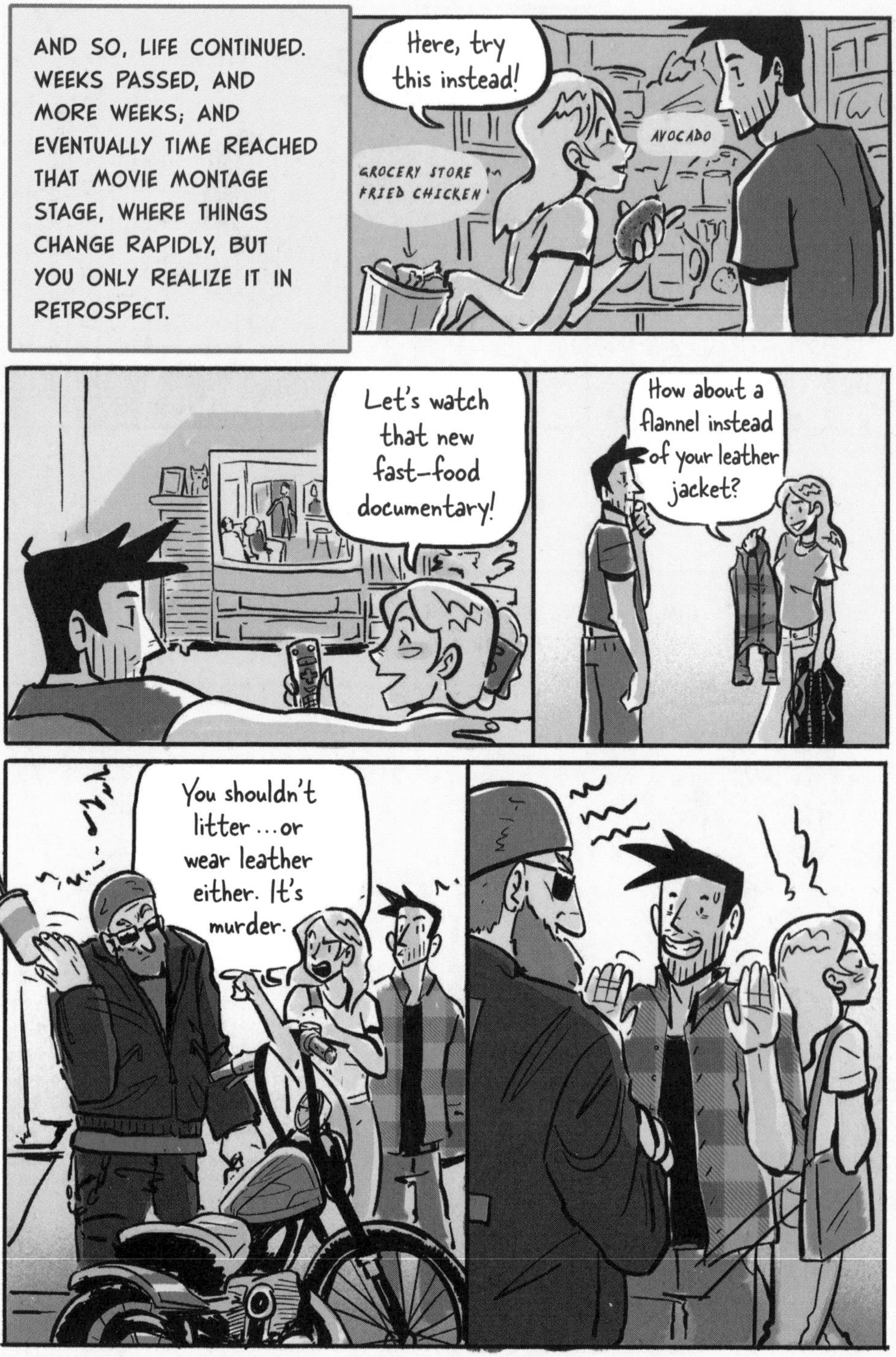
AND SO, LIFE CONTINUED. WEEKS PASSED, AND MORE WEEKS; AND EVENTUALLY TIME REACHED THAT MOVIE MONTAGE STAGE, WHERE THINGS CHANGE RAPIDLY, BUT YOU ONLY REALIZE IT IN RETROSPECT.
Here, try this instead!
AVOCADO
GROCERY STORE FRIED CHICKEN
Let's watch that new fast-food documentary!
How about a flannel instead of your leather jacket?
You shouldn't litter ...or wear leather either. It's murder.

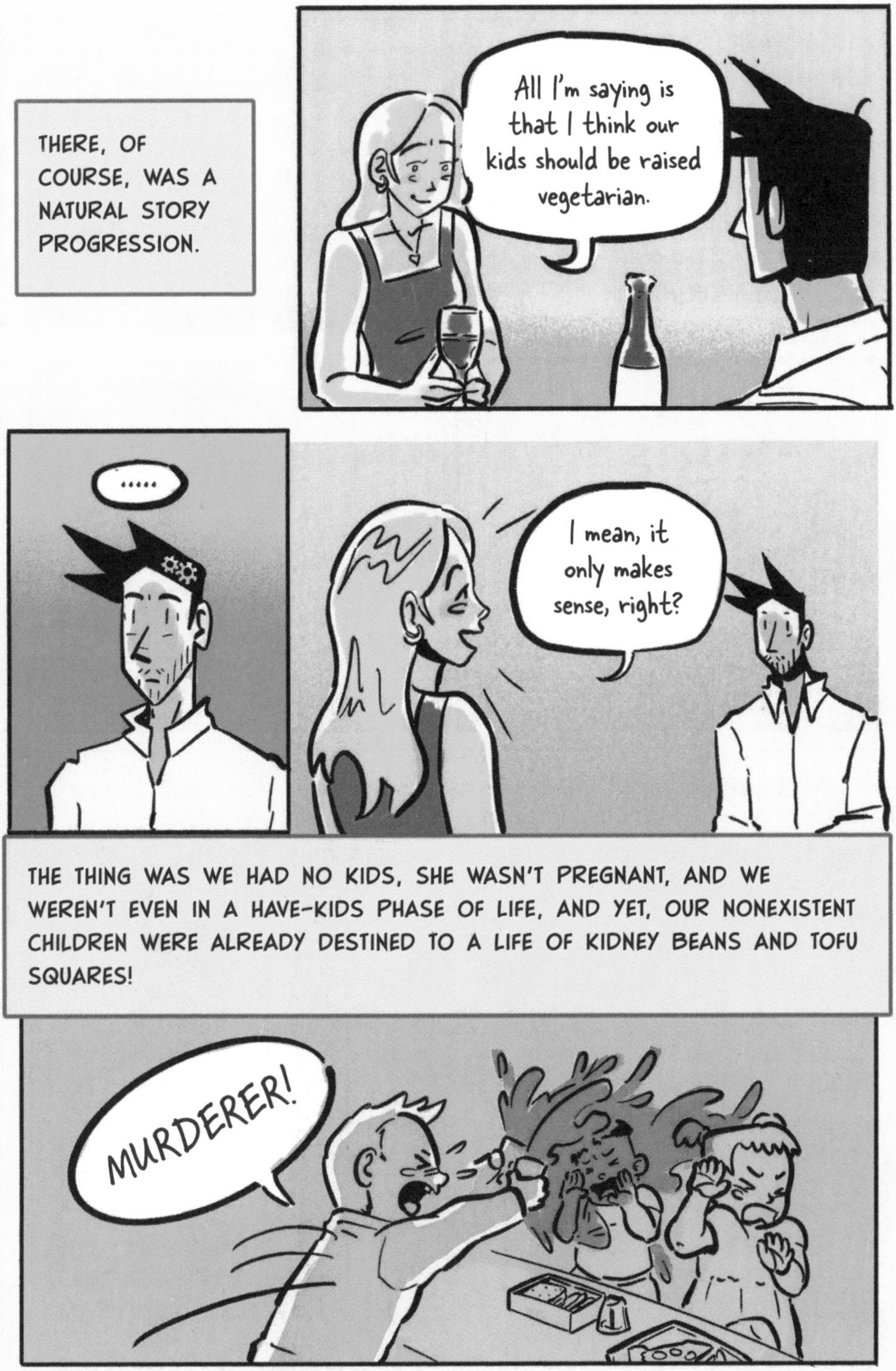
THERE, OF COURSE, WAS A NATURAL STORY PROGRESSION.
All I'm saying is that I think our kids should be raised vegetarian.
.....
I mean, it only makes sense, right?
THE THING WAS WE HAD NO KIDS, SHE WASN'T PREGNANT, AND WE WEREN'T EVEN IN A HAVE-KIDS PHASE OF LIFE, AND YET, OUR NONEXISTENT CHILDREN WERE ALREADY DESTINED TO A LIFE OF KIDNEY BEANS AND TOFU SQUARES!
MURDERER!

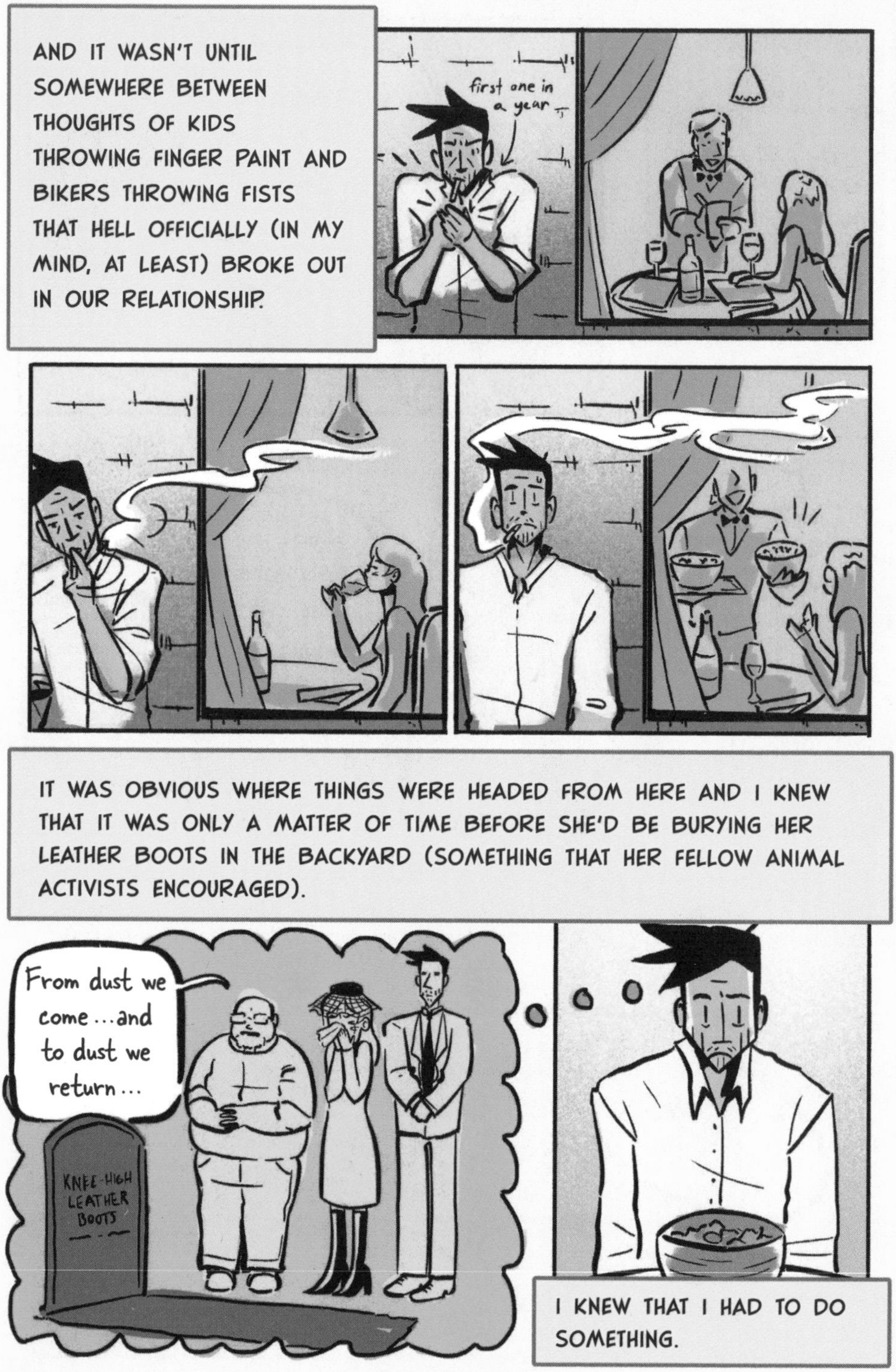
AND IT WASN'T UNTIL SOMEWHERE BETWEEN THOUGHTS OF KIDS THROWING FINGER PAINT AND BIKERS THROWING FISTS THAT HELL OFFICIALLY (IN MY MIND, AT LEAST) BROKE OUT IN OUR RELATIONSHIP.
first one in a year
IT WAS OBVIOUS WHERE THINGS WERE HEADED FROM HERE AND I KNEW THAT IT WAS ONLY A MATTER OF TIME BEFORE SHE'D BE BURYING HER LEATHER BOOTS IN THE BACKYARD (SOMETHING THAT HER FELLOW ANIMAL ACTIVISTS ENCOURAGED).
From dust we come ...and to dust we return ...
KNEE-HIGH LEATHER BOOTS
I KNEW THAT I HAD TO DO SOMETHING.

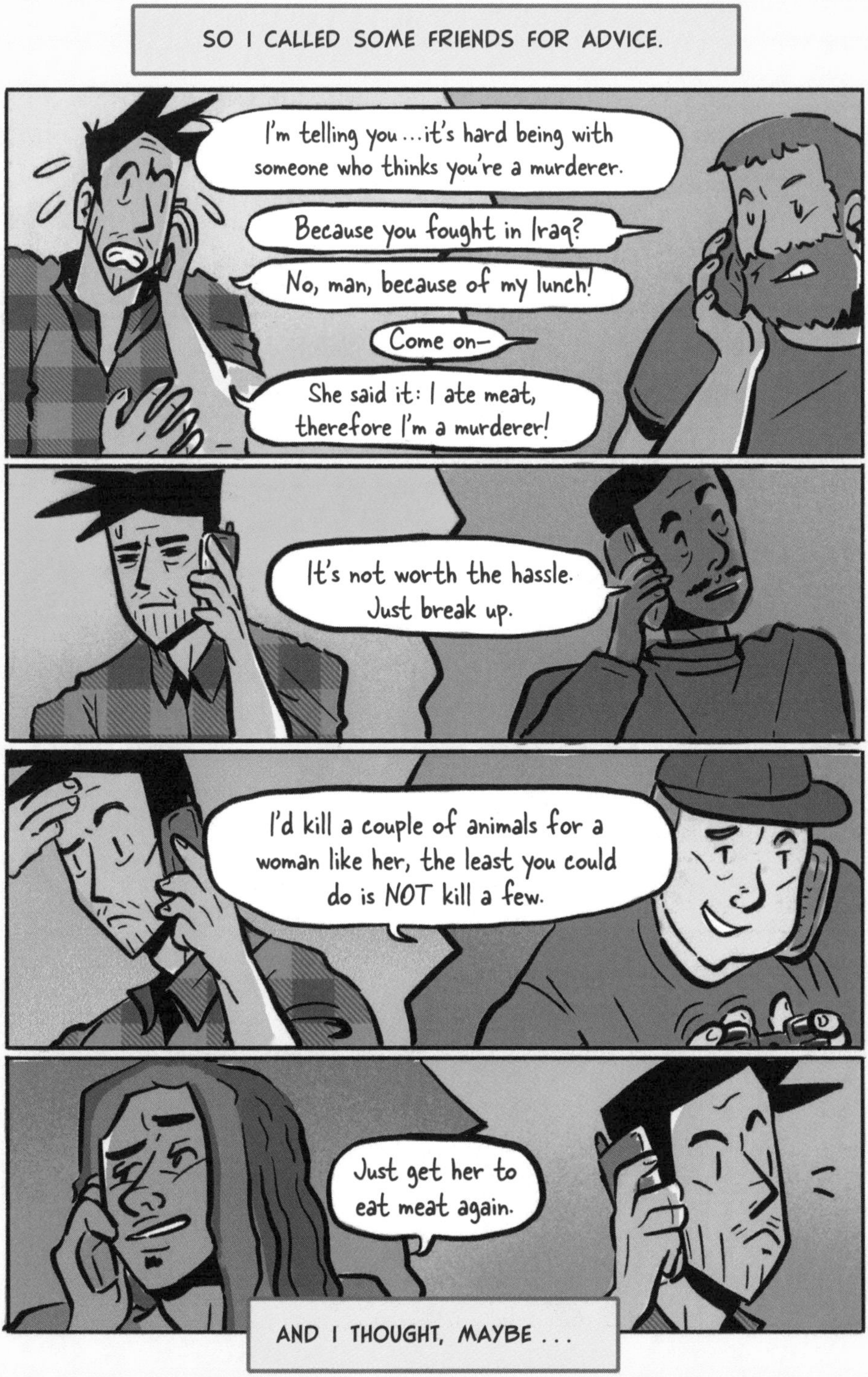
SO I CALLED SOME FRIENDS FOR ADVICE.
I'm telling you...it's hard being with someone who thinks you're a murderer.
Because you fought in Iraq?
No, man, because of my lunch!
Come on–
She said it: I ate meat, therefore I'm a murderer!
It's not worth the hassle. Just break up.
I'd kill a couple of animals for a woman like her, the least you could do is NOT kill a few.
Just get her to eat meat again.
AND I THOUGHT, MAYBE . . .

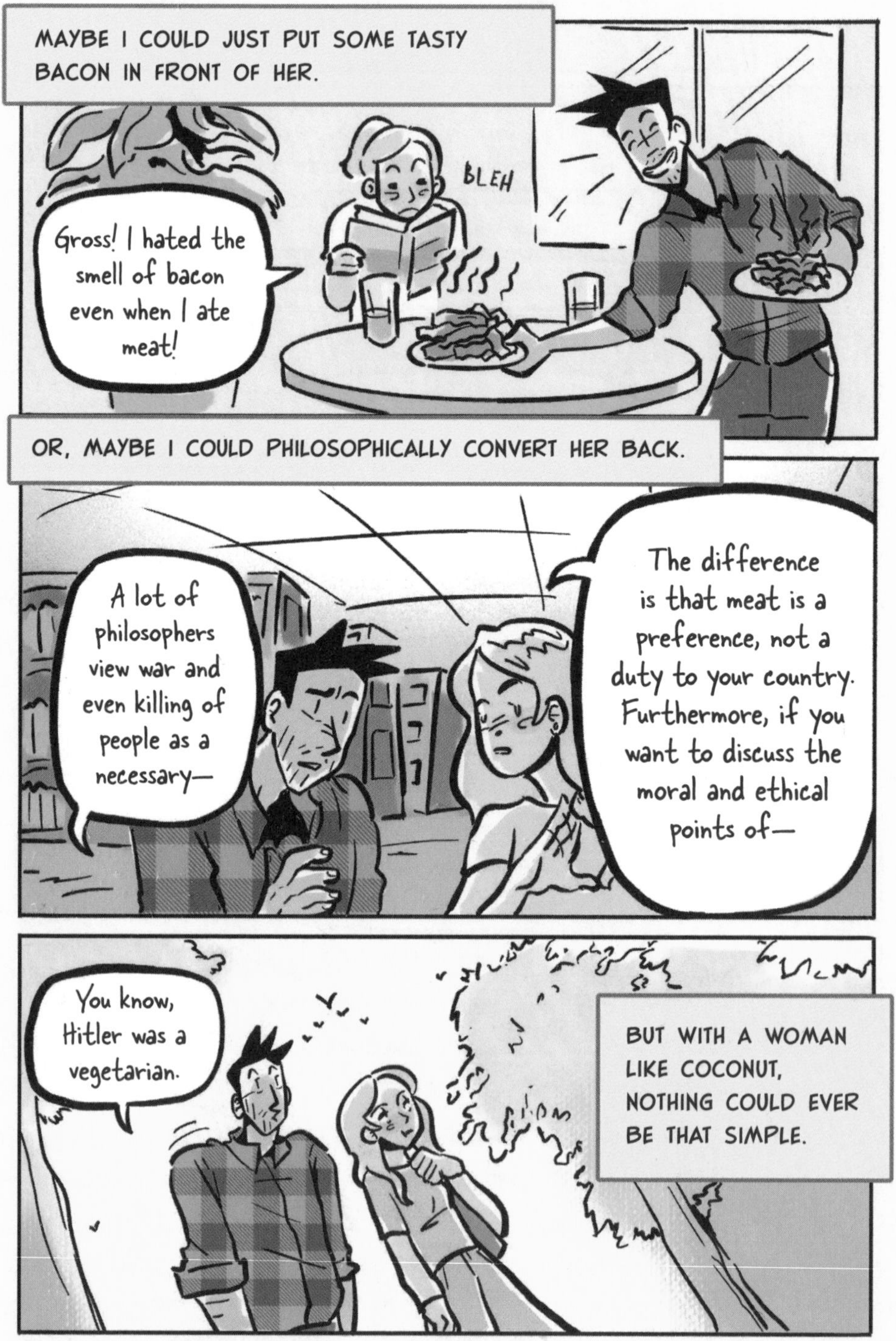
MAYBE I COULD JUST PUT SOME TASTY BACON IN FRONT OF HER.
BLEH
Gross! I hated the smell of bacon even when I ate meat!
OR, MAYBE I COULD PHILOSOPHICALLY CONVERT HER BACK.
A lot of philosophers view war and even killing of people as a necessary—
The difference is that meat is a preference, not a duty to your country. Furthermore, if you want to discuss the moral and ethical points of—
You know, Hitler was a vegetarian.
BUT WITH A WOMAN LIKE COCONUT, NOTHING COULD EVER BE THAT SIMPLE.

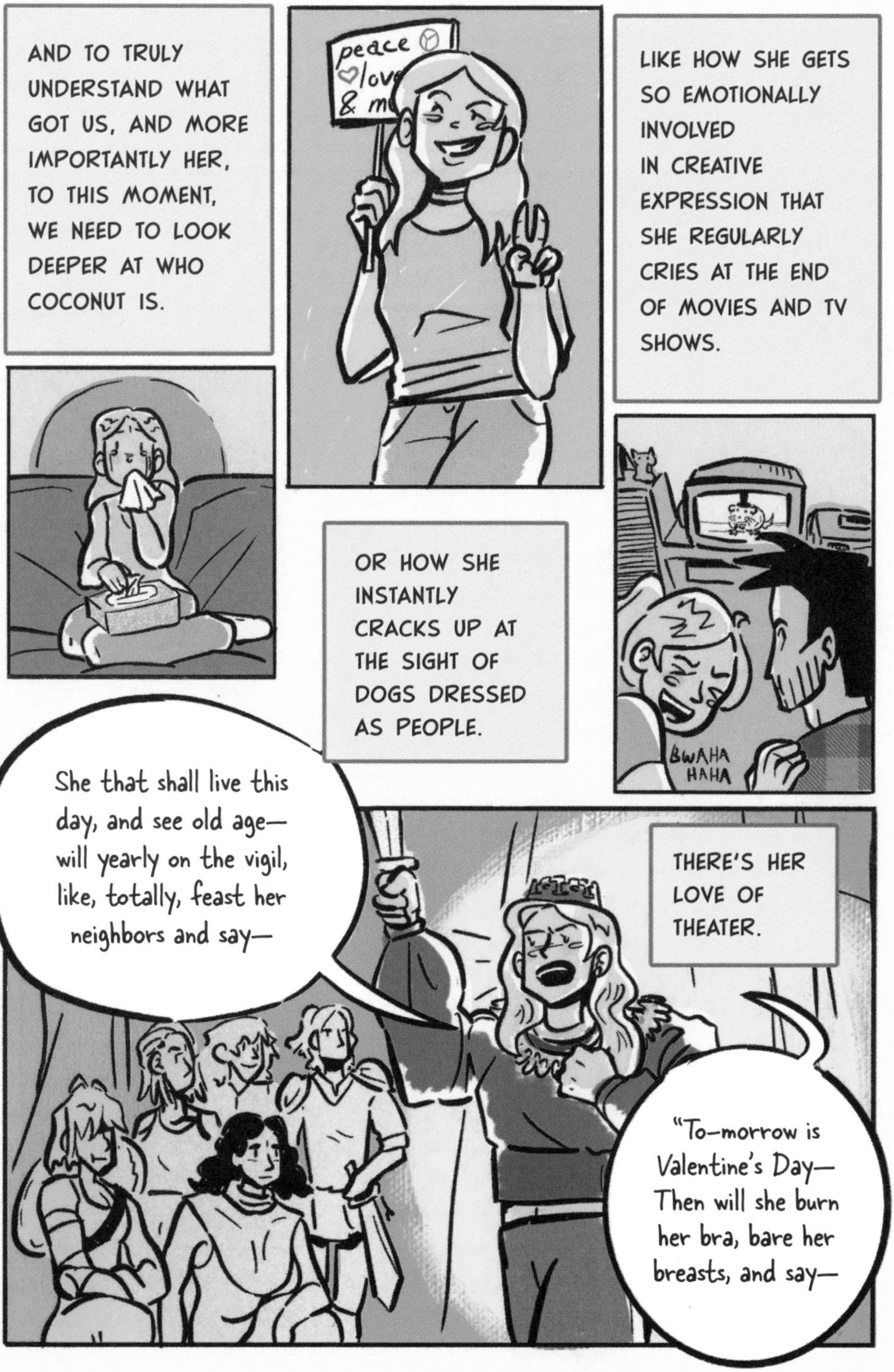
AND TO TRULY UNDERSTAND WHAT GOT US, AND MORE IMPORTANTLY HER, TO THIS MOMENT, WE NEED TO LOOK DEEPER AT WHO COCONUT IS.
peace ♡love & m
LIKE HOW SHE GETS SO EMOTIONALLY INVOLVED IN CREATIVE EXPRESSION THAT SHE REGULARLY CRIES AT THE END OF MOVIES AND TV SHOWS.
OR HOW SHE INSTANTLY CRACKS UP AT THE SIGHT OF DOGS DRESSED AS PEOPLE.
BWAHA HAHA
She that shall live this day, and see old age— will yearly on the vigil, like, totally, feast her neighbors and say—
THERE'S HER LOVE OF THEATER.
"To-morrow is Valentine's Day— Then will she burn her bra, bare her breasts, and say—

AND HOW SHE WORKED THREE SEPARATE JOBS WHILE PUTTING HERSELF THROUGH NURSING SCHOOL (AND COLLEGE FOR THE SECOND TIME) JUST SO THAT SHE COULD SPEND THE REST OF HER LIFE HELPING PEOPLE.

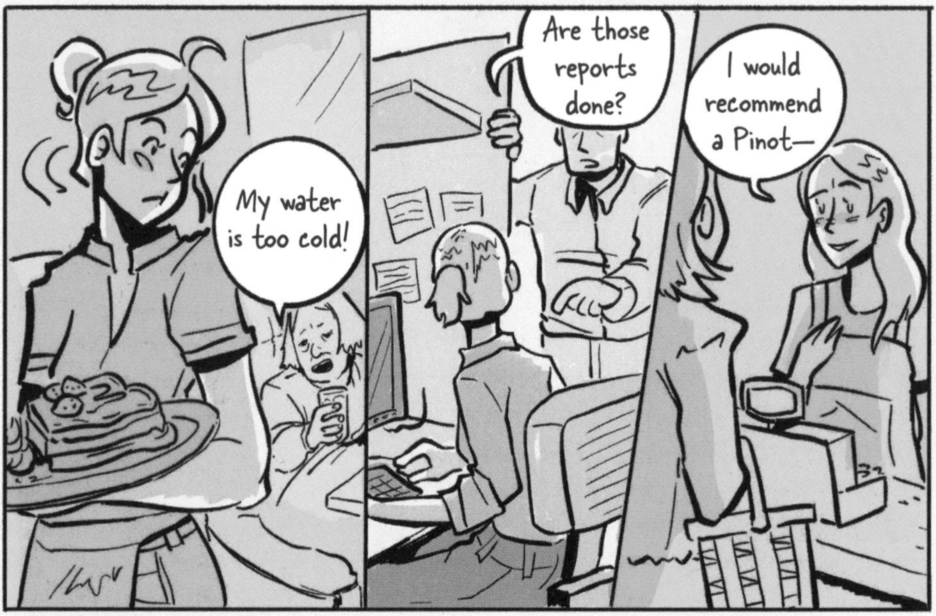
My water is too cold!
Are those reports done?
I would recommend a Pinot—

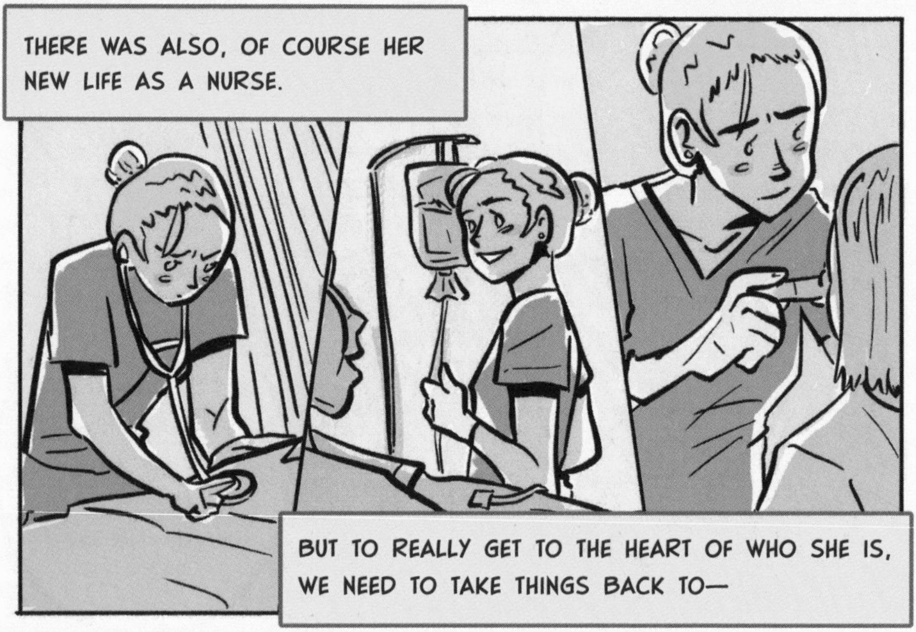
THERE WAS ALSO, OF COURSE HER NEW LIFE AS A NURSE.
BUT TO REALLY GET TO THE HEART OF WHO SHE IS, WE NEED TO TAKE THINGS BACK TO—

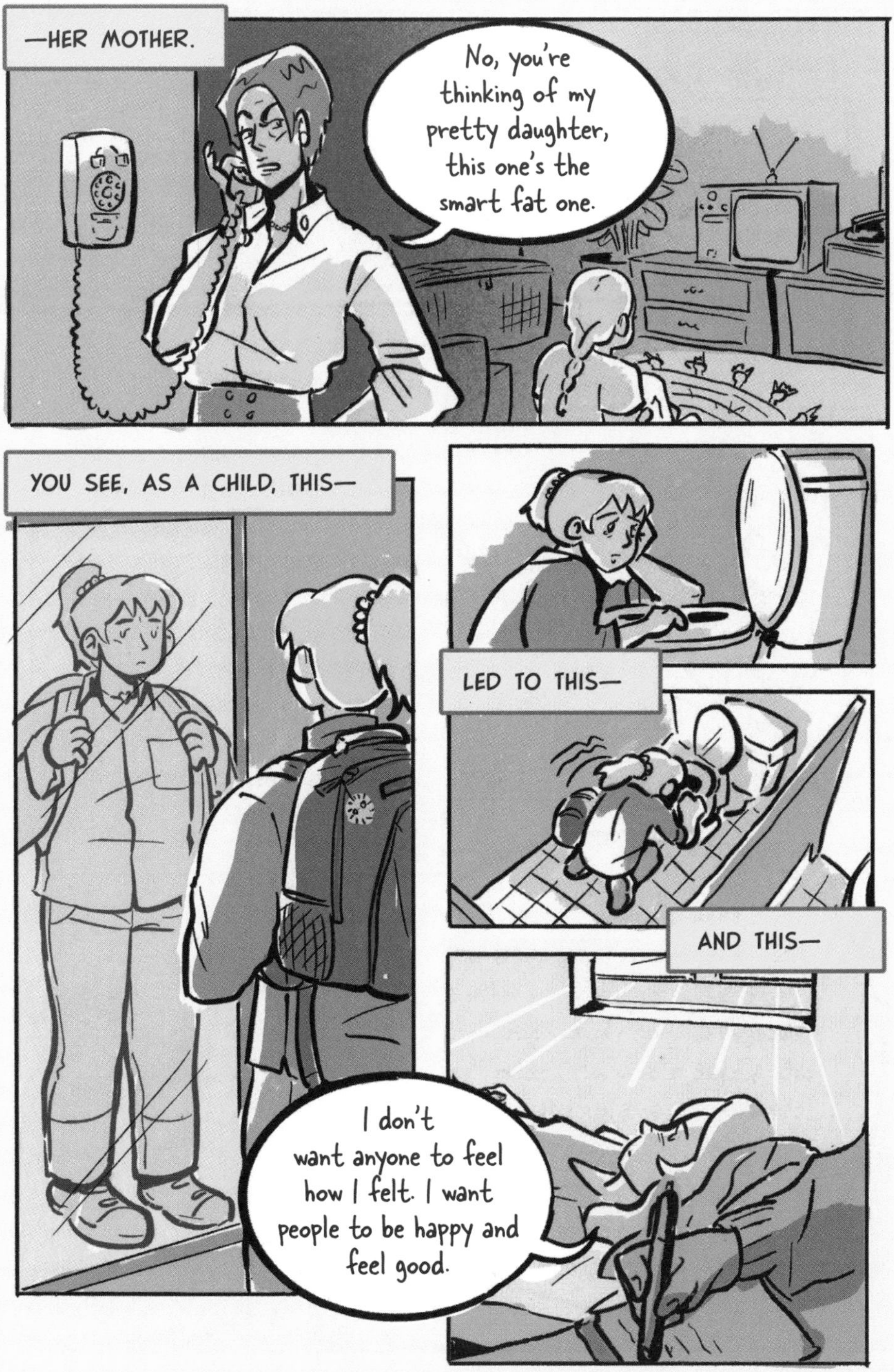
—HER MOTHER.
No, you're thinking of my pretty daughter, this one's the smart fat one.
YOU SEE, AS A CHILD, THIS—
LED TO THIS—
AND THIS—
I don't want anyone to feel how I felt. I want people to be happy and feel good.

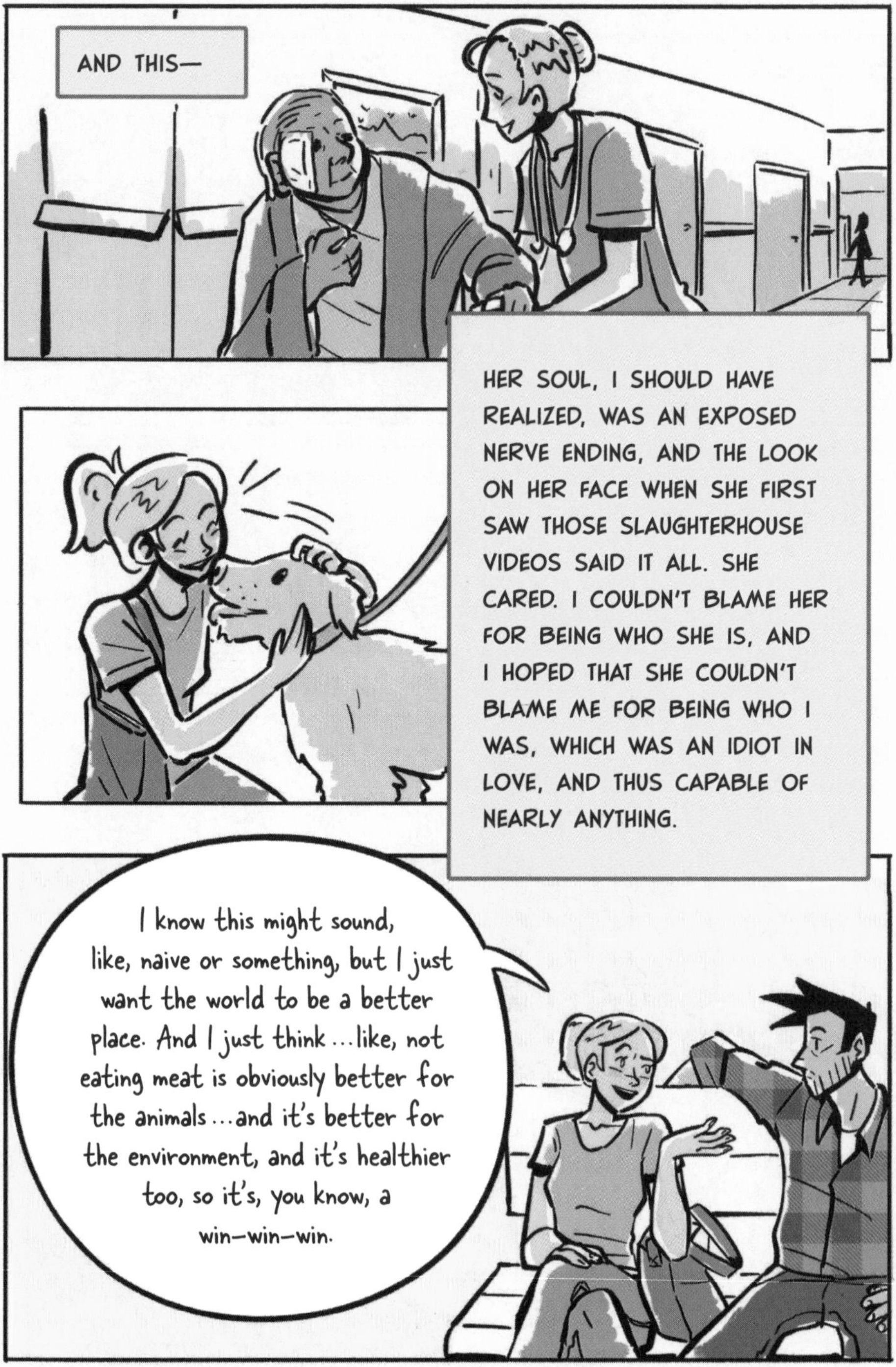
AND THIS—
HER SOUL, I SHOULD HAVE REALIZED, WAS AN EXPOSED NERVE ENDING, AND THE LOOK ON HER FACE WHEN SHE FIRST SAW THOSE SLAUGHTERHOUSE VIDEOS SAID IT ALL. SHE CARED. I COULDN'T BLAME HER FOR BEING WHO SHE IS, AND I HOPED THAT SHE COULDN'T BLAME ME FOR BEING WHO I WAS, WHICH WAS AN IDIOT IN LOVE, AND THUS CAPABLE OF NEARLY ANYTHING.
I know this might sound, like, naive or something, but I just want the world to be a better place. And I just think ...like, not eating meat is obviously better for the animals ...and it's better for the environment, and it's healthier too, so it's, you know, a win—win—win.

Animals Slaughtered in the U.S. Each Year

"A man can live and be healthy without killing animals for food; therefore, if he eats meat, he participates in taking animal life merely for the sake of his appetite."
~Leo Tolstoy

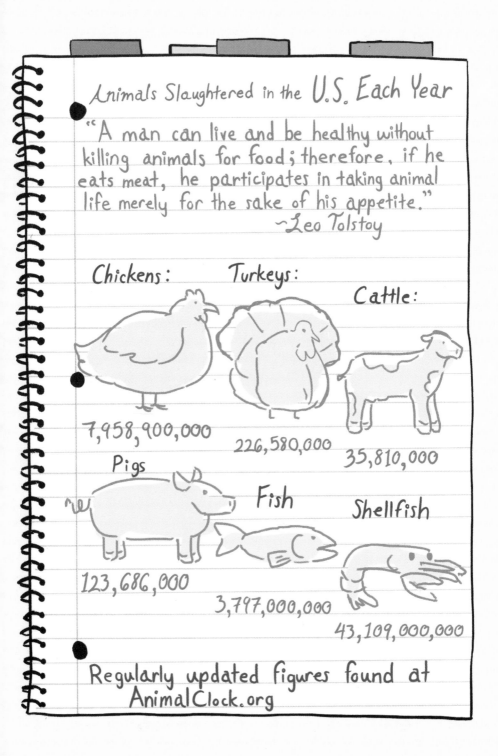

Chickens:

7,958,900,000

Turkeys:

226,580,000

Cattle:

35,810,000

Pigs

123,686,000

Fish

3,797,000,000

Shellfish

43,109,000,000

Regularly updated figures found at AnimalClock.org

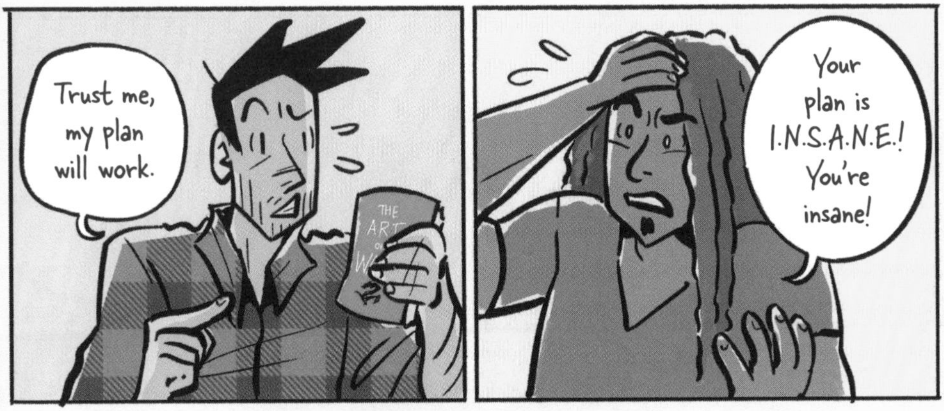
Trust me, my plan will work.
Your plan is I.N.S.A.N.E.! You're insane!

CHAPTER 4

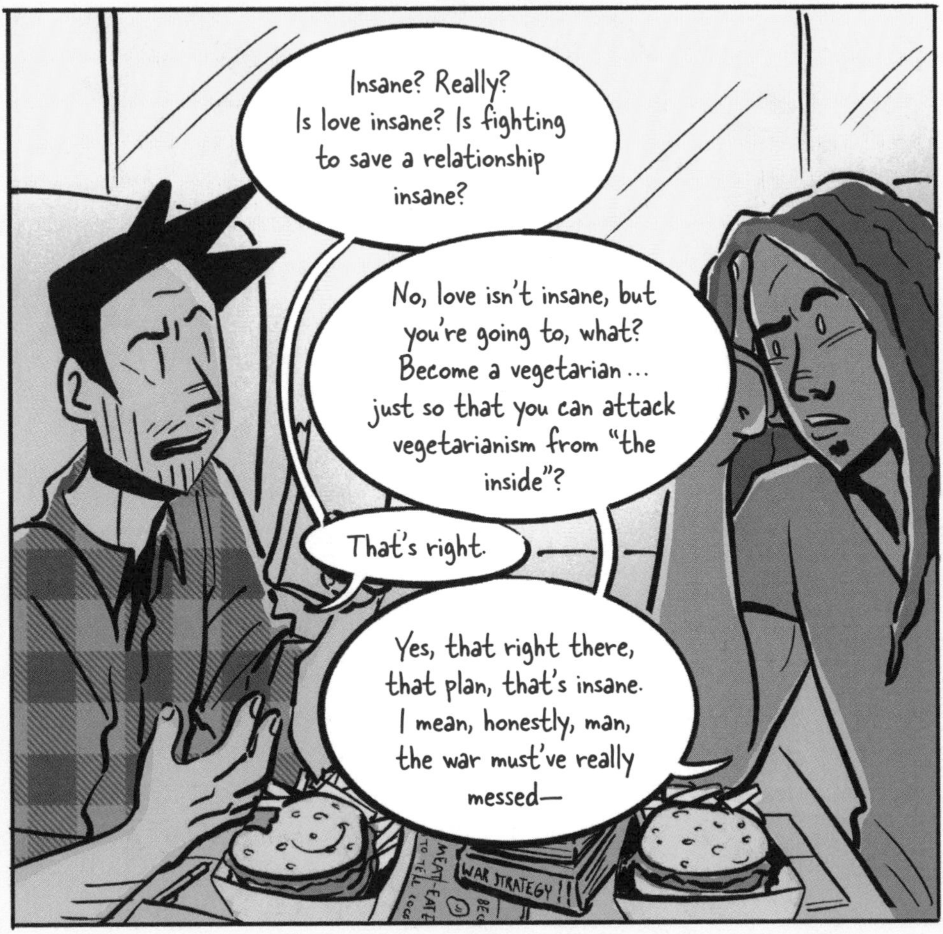
Insane? Really? Is love insane? Is fighting to save a relationship insane?
No, love isn't insane, but you're going to, what? Become a vegetarian... just so that you can attack vegetarianism from "the inside"?
That's right.
Yes, that right there, that plan, that's insane. I mean, honestly, man, the war must've really messed—
WAR STRATEGY!!

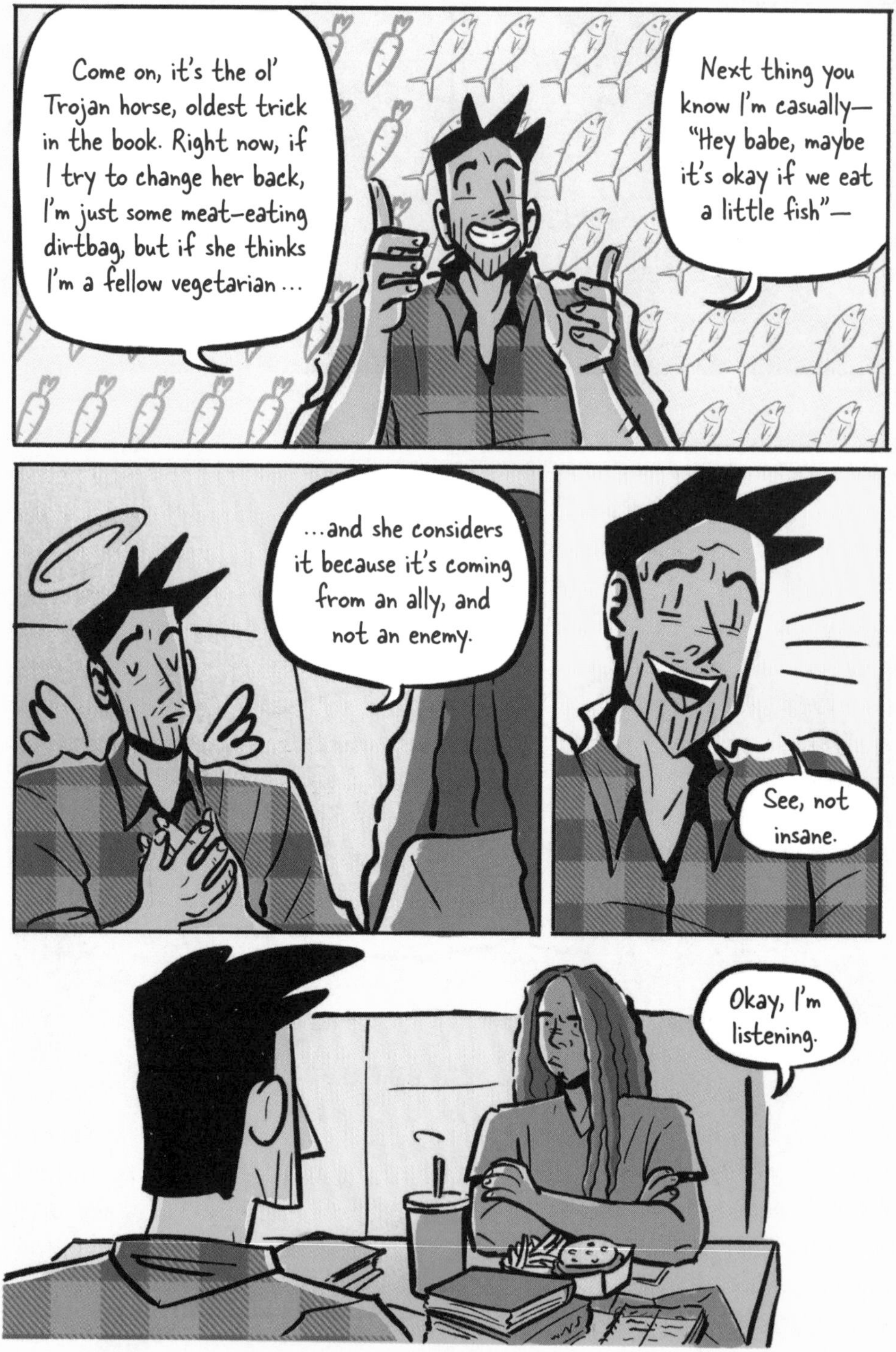
Come on, it's the ol' Trojan horse, oldest trick in the book. Right now, if I try to change her back, I'm just some meat-eating dirtbag, but if she thinks I'm a fellow vegetarian...
Next thing you know I'm casually— "Hey babe, maybe it's okay if we eat a little fish"—
...and she considers it because it's coming from an ally, and not an enemy.
See, not insane.
Okay, I'm listening.

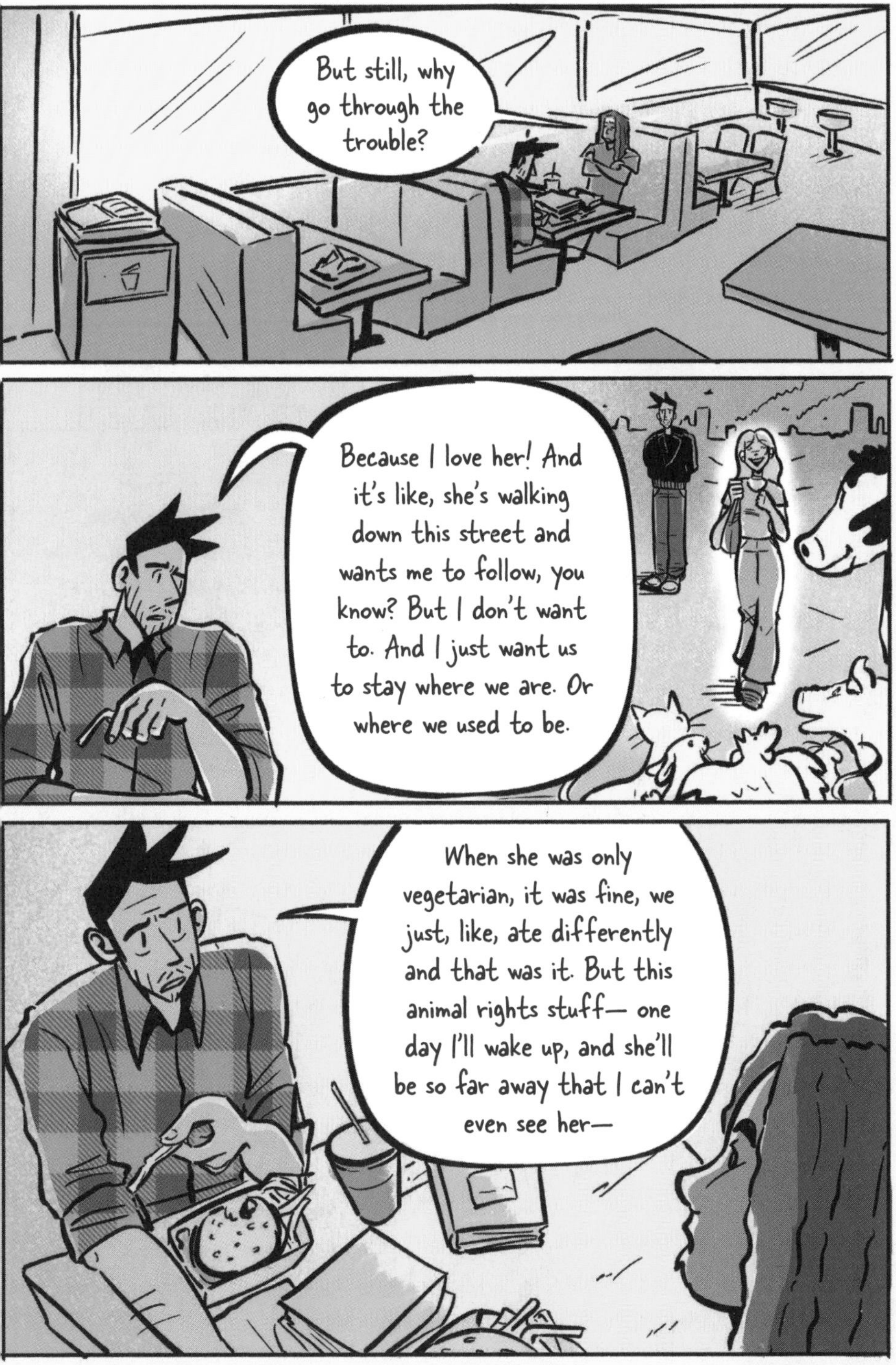

But still, why go through the trouble?
Because I love her! And it's like, she's walking down this street and wants me to follow, you know? But I don't want to. And I just want us to stay where we are. Or where we used to be.
When she was only vegetarian, it was fine, we just, like, ate differently and that was it. But this animal rights stuff— one day I'll wake up, and she'll be so far away that I can't even see her—

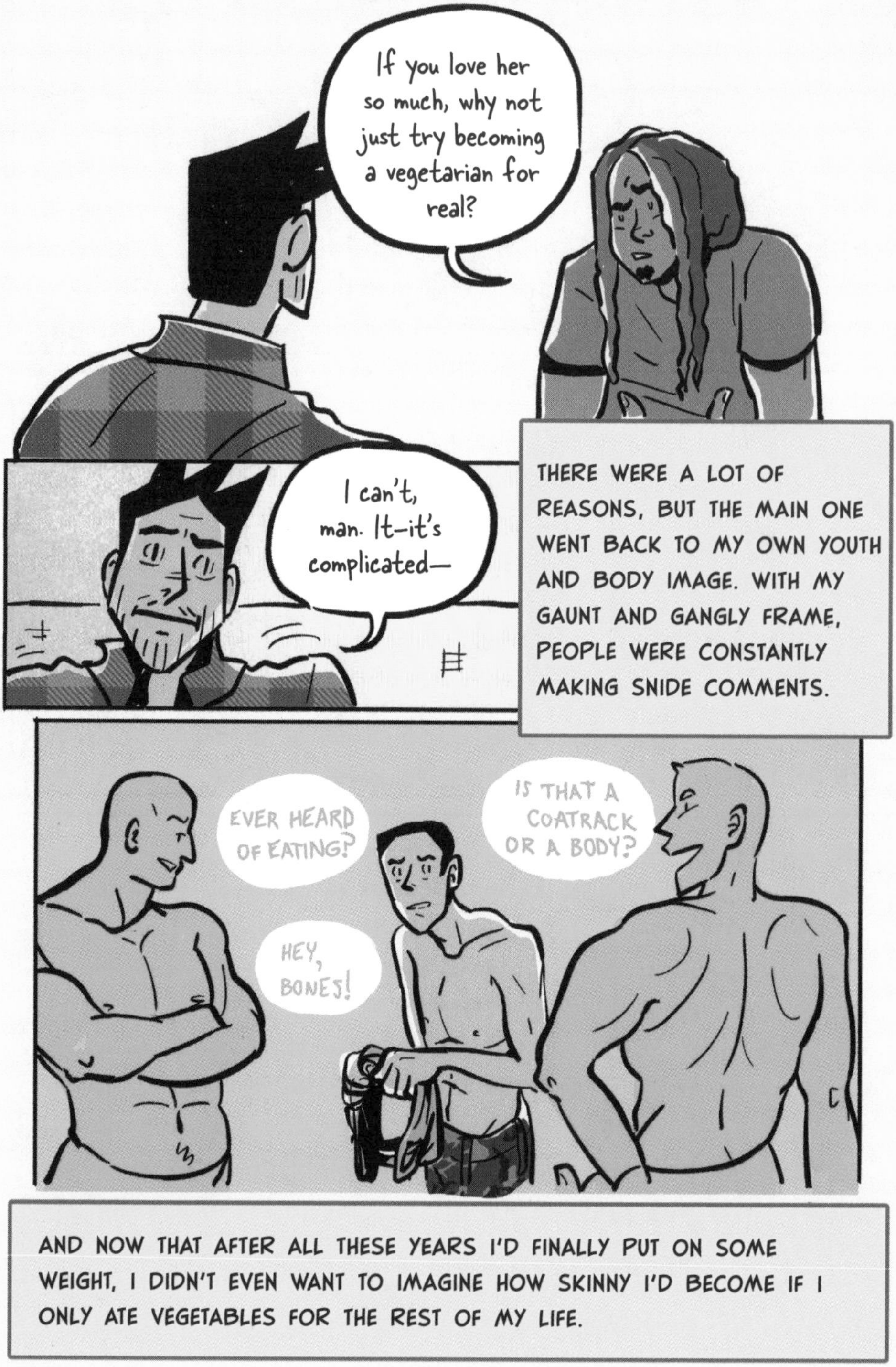

If you love her so much, why not just try becoming a vegetarian for real?
I can't, man. It-it's complicated—
THERE WERE A LOT OF REASONS, BUT THE MAIN ONE WENT BACK TO MY OWN YOUTH AND BODY IMAGE. WITH MY GAUNT AND GANGLY FRAME, PEOPLE WERE CONSTANTLY MAKING SNIDE COMMENTS.
EVER HEARD OF EATING?
IS THAT A COATRACK OR A BODY?
HEY, BONES!
AND NOW THAT AFTER ALL THESE YEARS I'D FINALLY PUT ON SOME WEIGHT, I DIDN'T EVEN WANT TO IMAGINE HOW SKINNY I'D BECOME IF I ONLY ATE VEGETABLES FOR THE REST OF MY LIFE.

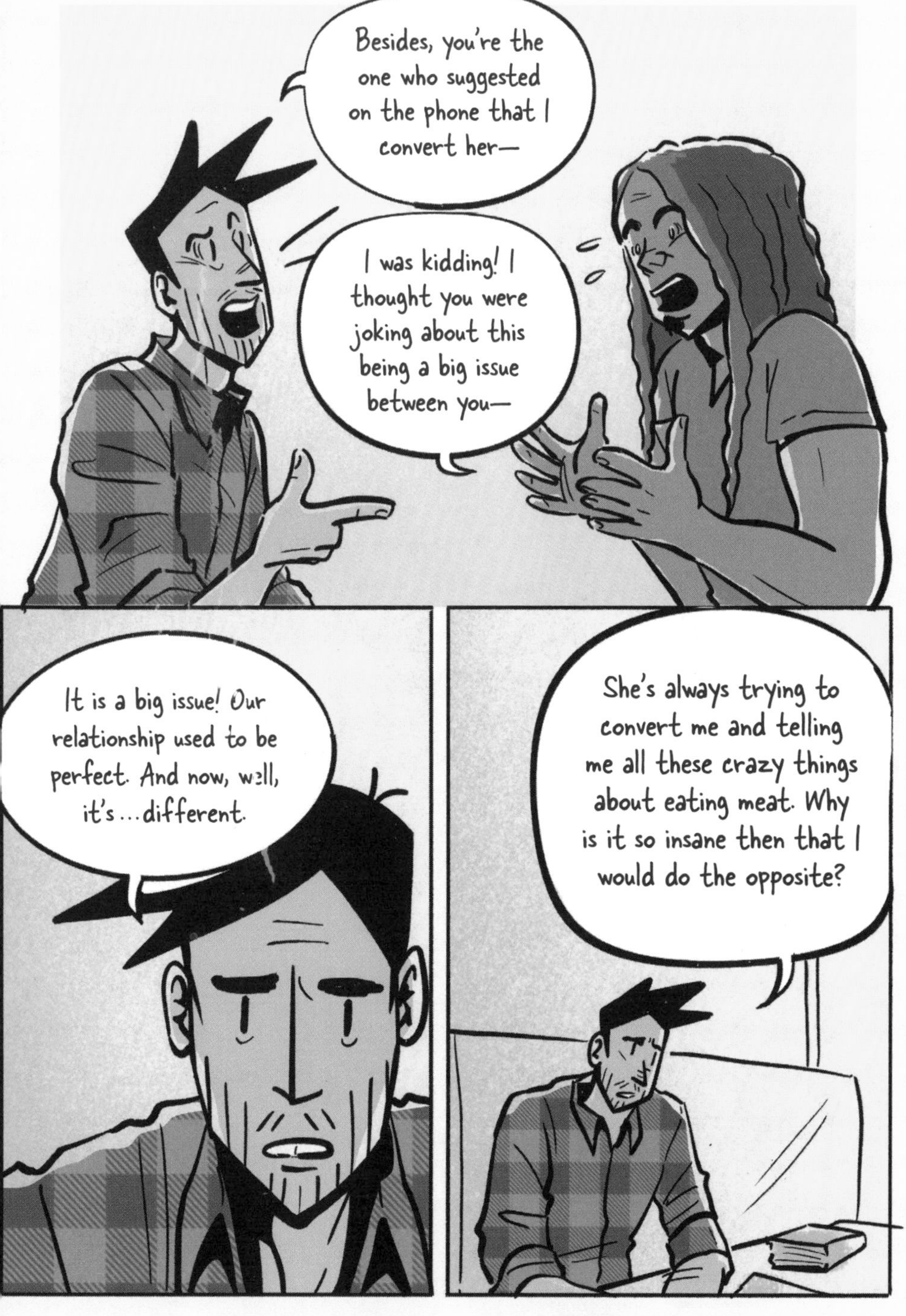
Besides, you're the one who suggested on the phone that I convert her—
I was kidding! I thought you were joking about this being a big issue between you—
It is a big issue! Our relationship used to be perfect. And now, well, it's...different.
She's always trying to convert me and telling me all these crazy things about eating meat. Why is it so insane then that I would do the opposite?

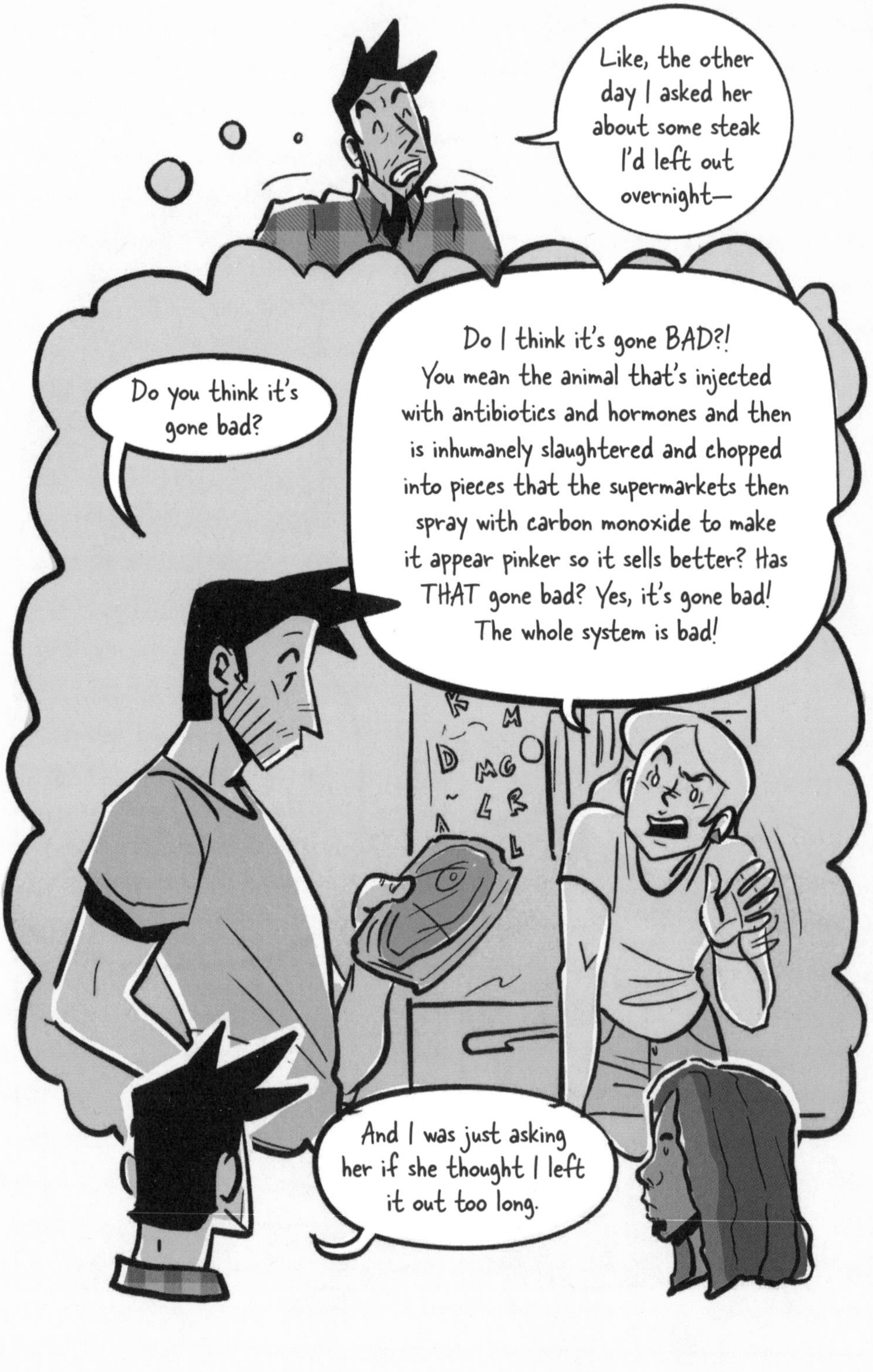
Like, the other day I asked her about some steak I'd left out overnight—
Do you think it's gone bad?
Do I think it's gone BAD?! You mean the animal that's injected with antibiotics and hormones and then is inhumanely slaughtered and chopped into pieces that the supermarkets then spray with carbon monoxide to make it appear pinker so it sells better? Has THAT gone bad? Yes, it's gone bad! The whole system is bad!
And I was just asking her if she thought I left it out too long.

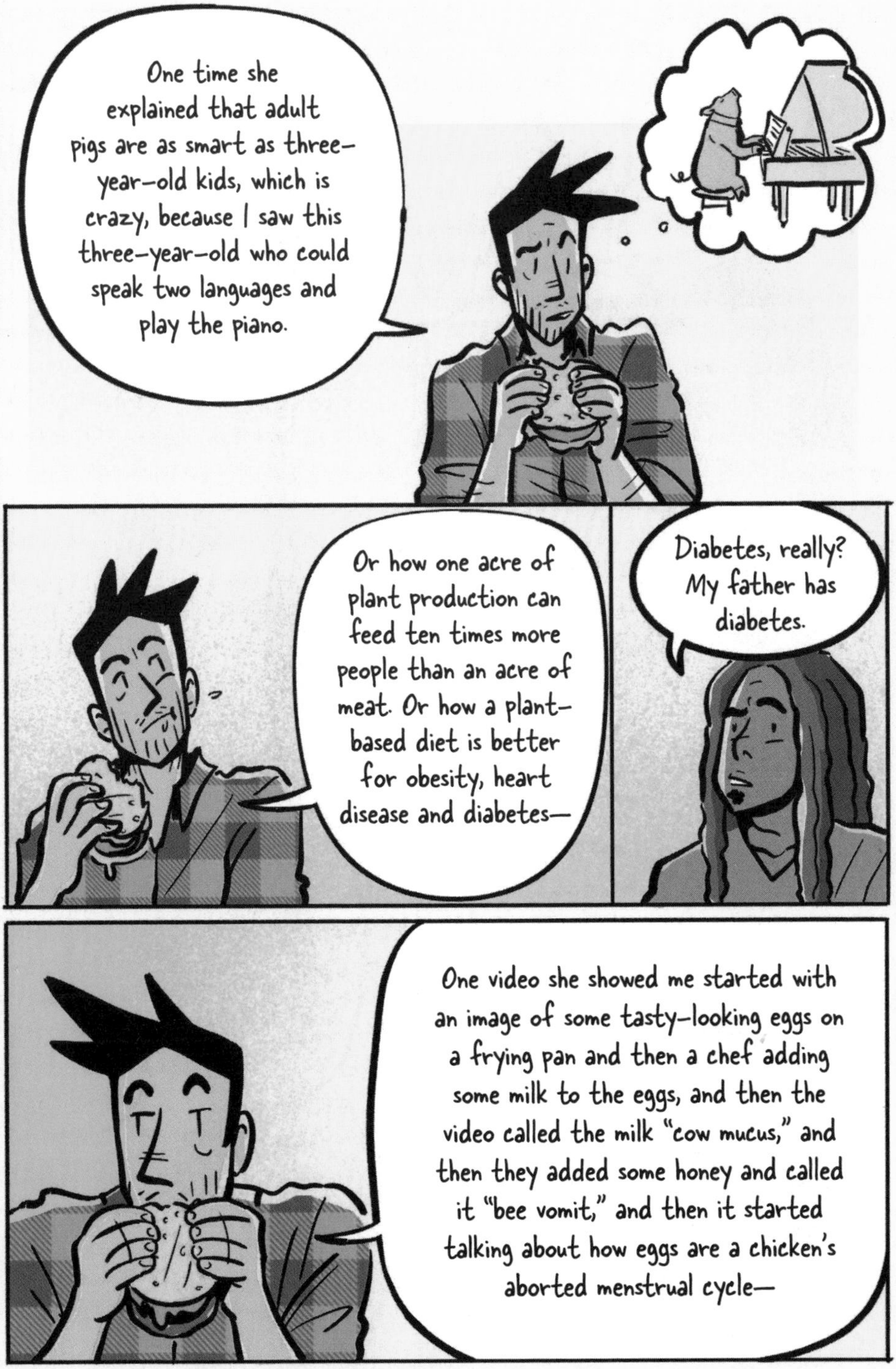
One time she explained that adult pigs are as smart as three-year-old kids, which is crazy, because I saw this three-year-old who could speak two languages and play the piano.
Or how one acre of plant production can feed ten times more people than an acre of meat. Or how a plant-based diet is better for obesity, heart disease and diabetes—
Diabetes, really? My father has diabetes.
One video she showed me started with an image of some tasty-looking eggs on a frying pan and then a chef adding some milk to the eggs, and then the video called the milk "cow mucus," and then they added some honey and called it "bee vomit," and then it started talking about how eggs are a chicken's aborted menstrual cycle—

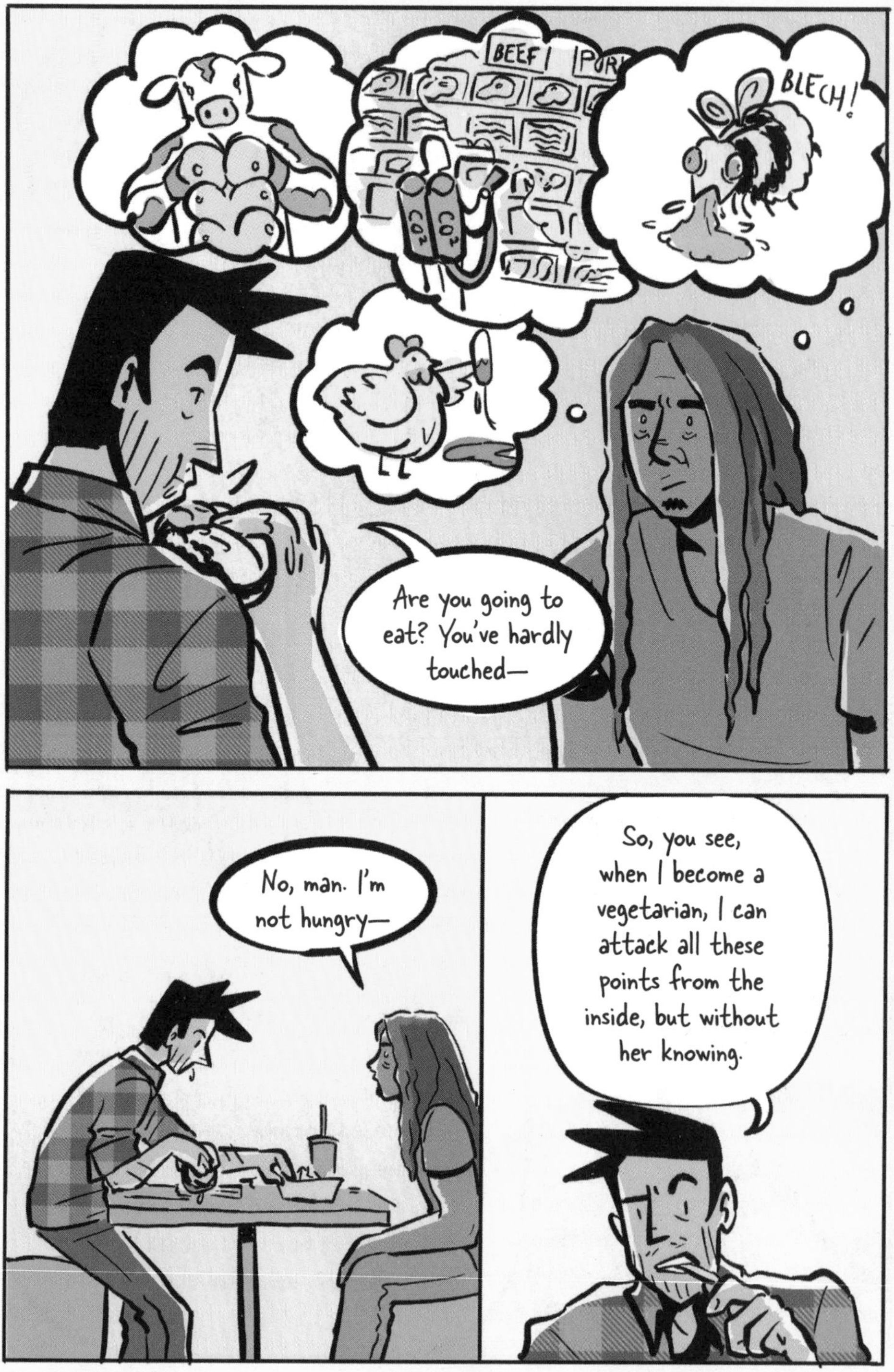
BEEF
PORK
CO2
CO2
BLECH!
Are you going to eat? You've hardly touched—
No, man. I'm not hungry—
So, you see, when I become a vegetarian, I can attack all these points from the inside, but without her knowing.

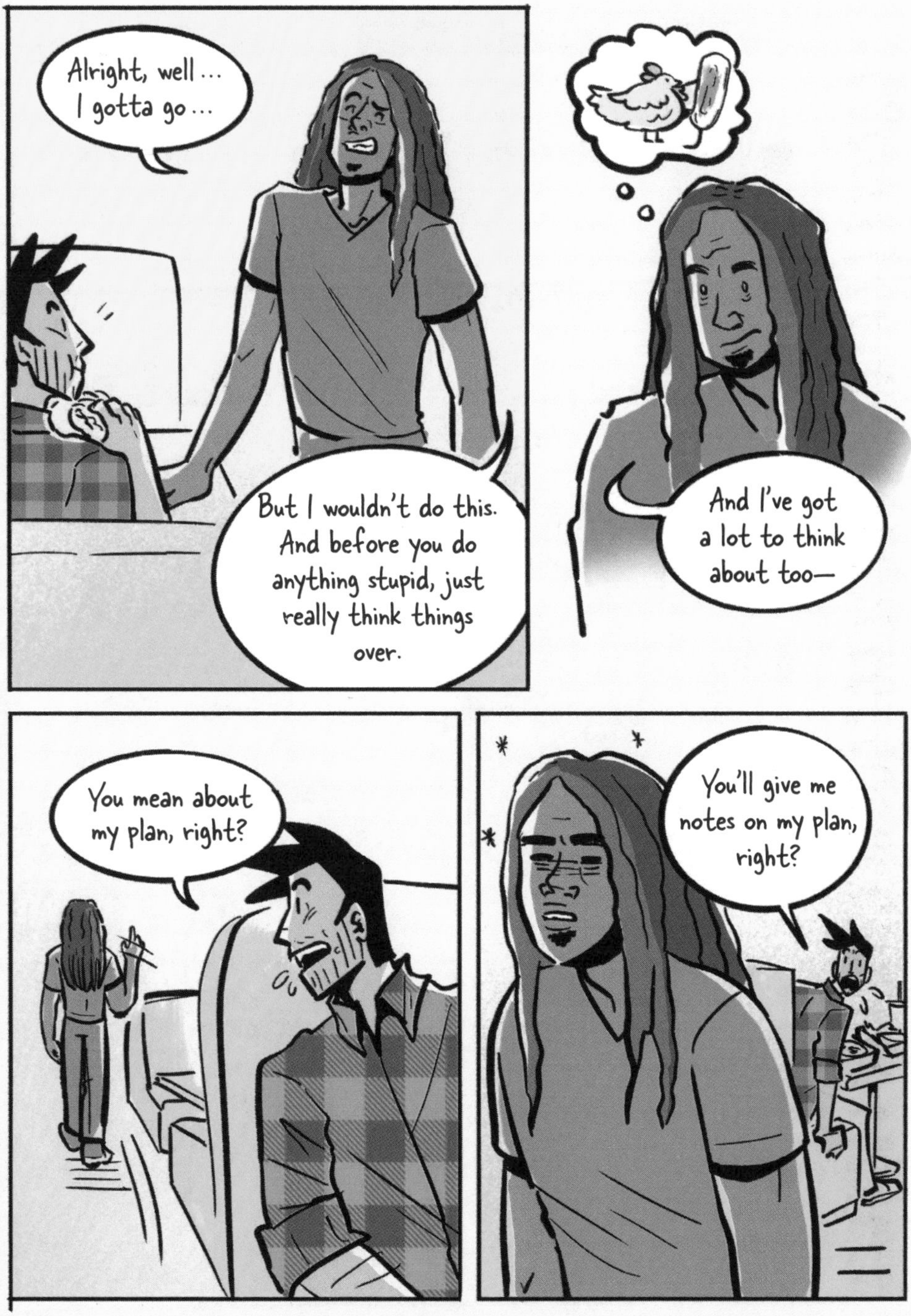
Alright, well ...
I gotta go ...
But I wouldn't do this. And before you do anything stupid, just really think things over.
And I've got a lot to think about too—
You mean about my plan, right?
You'll give me notes on my plan, right?

Vegetarian Sources of Protein

Edamame
1 cup = 18 grams of protein

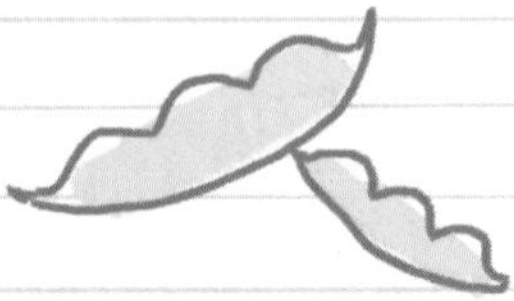

Black Beans
1 cup = 16 grams of protein

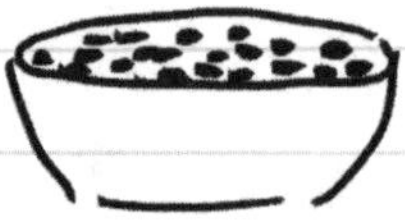

Green Peas
1 cup = 8 grams of protein

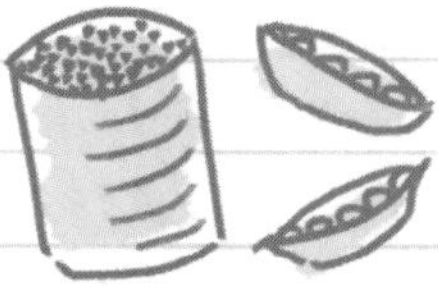

Chickpeas
1 cup = 14 grams of protein

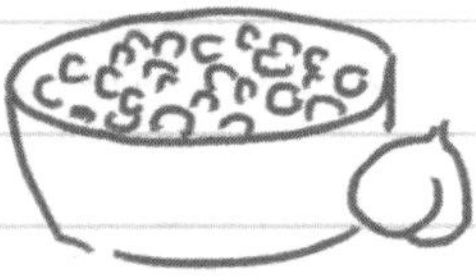

Spinach
1 cup = 6 grams of protein

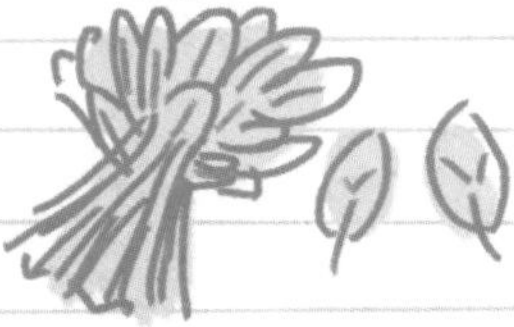

Lentils
1 cup = 17 grams of protein

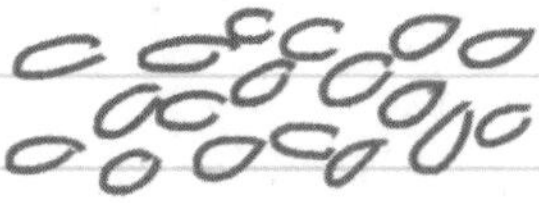

Broccoli
1 cup = 5 grams of proteins

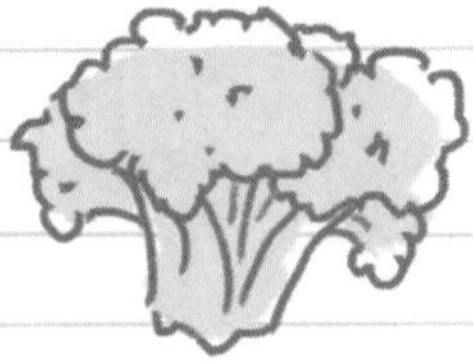

BEFORE WE GET INTO THE INTRICACIES OF OPERATION TOFU HORSE, YOU SHOULD KNOW THAT AT THIS POINT THERE WAS STILL NOTHING BUT LOVE IN THE RELATIONSHIP, THUS WHY WE SO BADLY WANTED TO CHANGE ONE ANOTHER.

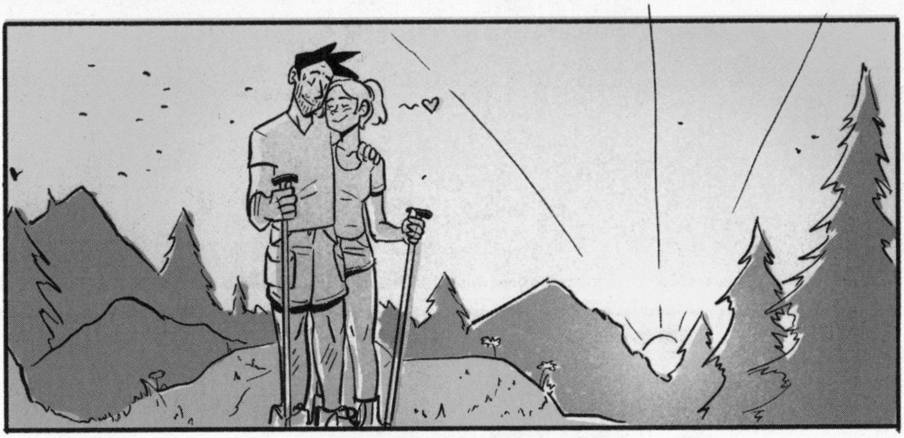

CHAPTER 5

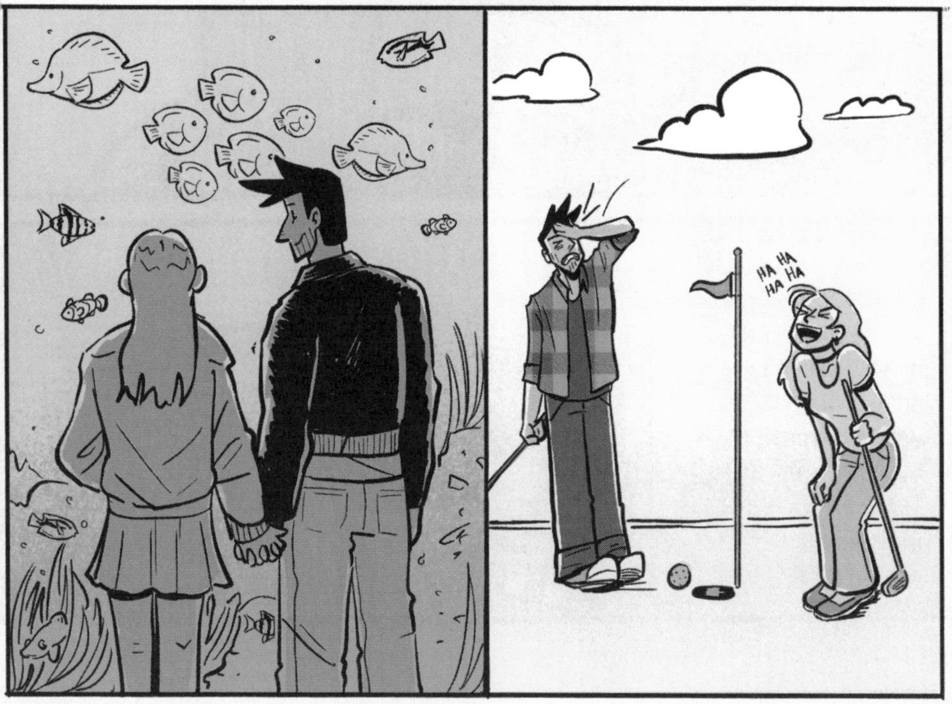
HA HA
HA HA

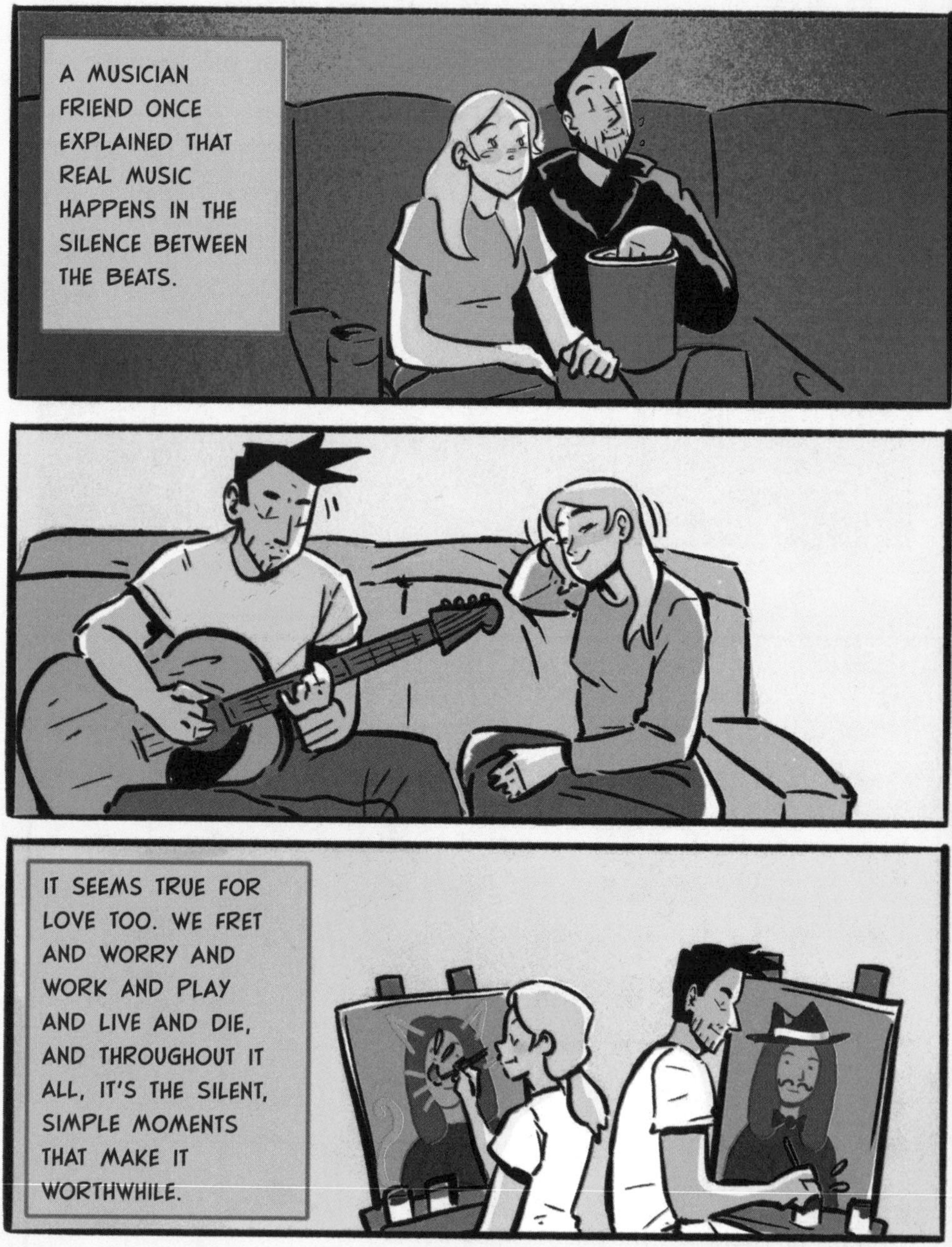
A MUSICIAN FRIEND ONCE EXPLAINED THAT REAL MUSIC HAPPENS IN THE SILENCE BETWEEN THE BEATS.
IT SEEMS TRUE FOR LOVE TOO. WE FRET AND WORRY AND WORK AND PLAY AND LIVE AND DIE, AND THROUGHOUT IT ALL, IT'S THE SILENT, SIMPLE MOMENTS THAT MAKE IT WORTHWHILE.

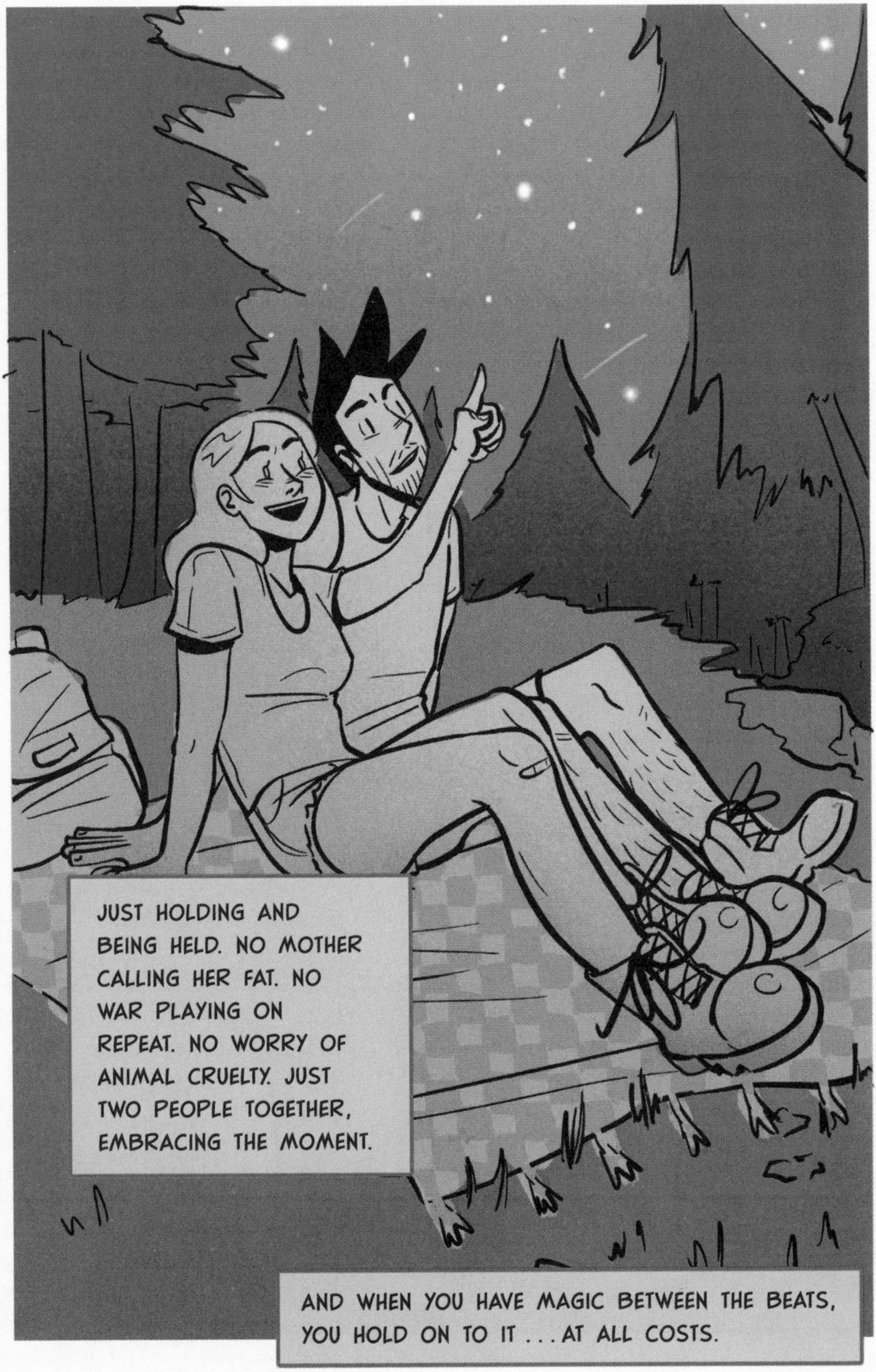
JUST HOLDING AND BEING HELD. NO MOTHER CALLING HER FAT. NO WAR PLAYING ON REPEAT. NO WORRY OF ANIMAL CRUELTY. JUST TWO PEOPLE TOGETHER, EMBRACING THE MOMENT.
AND WHEN YOU HAVE MAGIC BETWEEN THE BEATS, YOU HOLD ON TO IT . . . AT ALL COSTS.

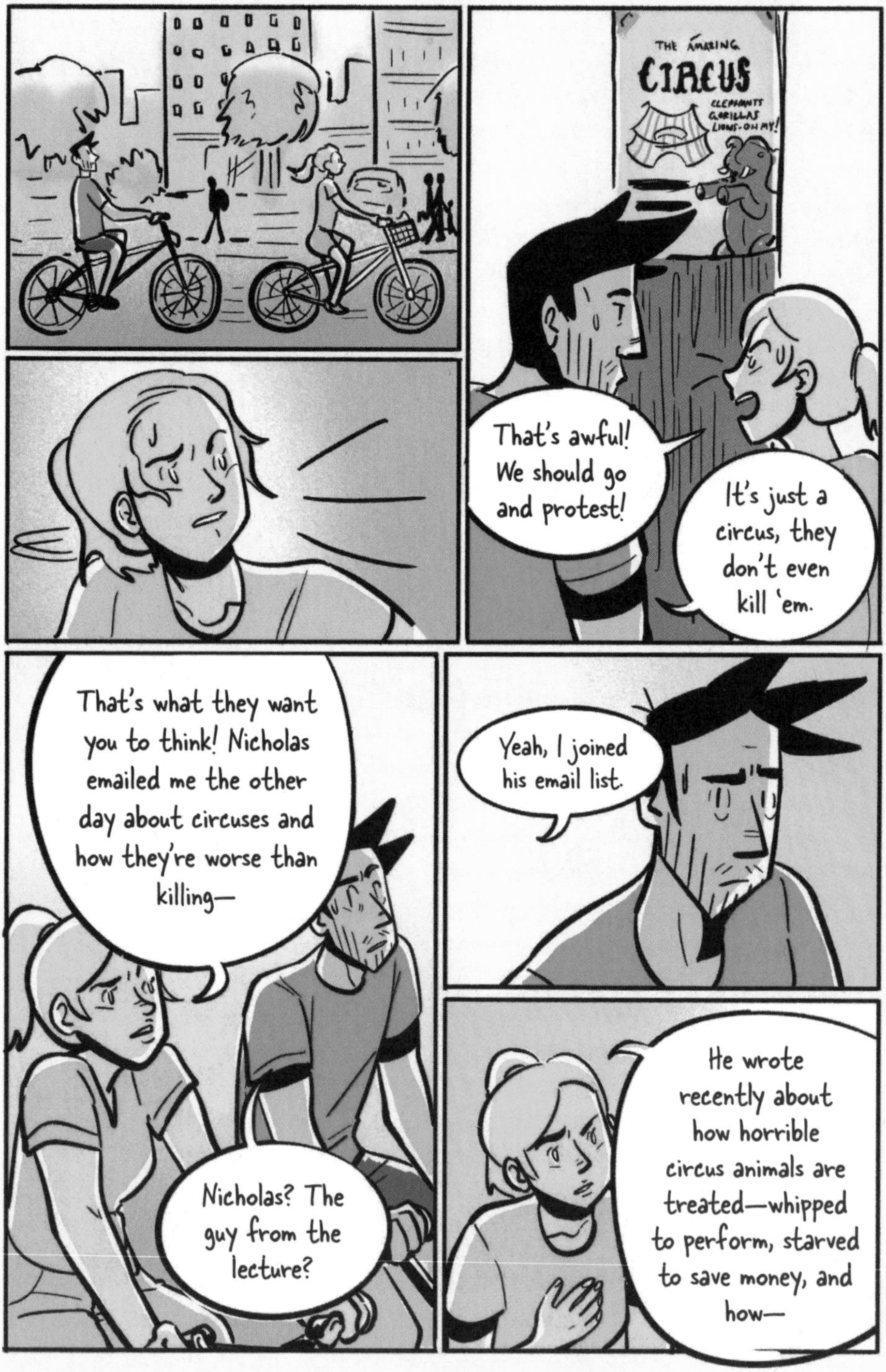
THE AMAZING
CIRCUS
ELEPHANTS GORILLAS LIONS-OH MY!
That's awful! We should go and protest!
It's just a circus, they don't even kill 'em.
That's what they want you to think! Nicholas emailed me the other day about circuses and how they're worse than killing—
Nicholas? The guy from the lecture?
Yeah, I joined his email list.
He wrote recently about how horrible circus animals are treated—whipped to perform, starved to save money, and how—

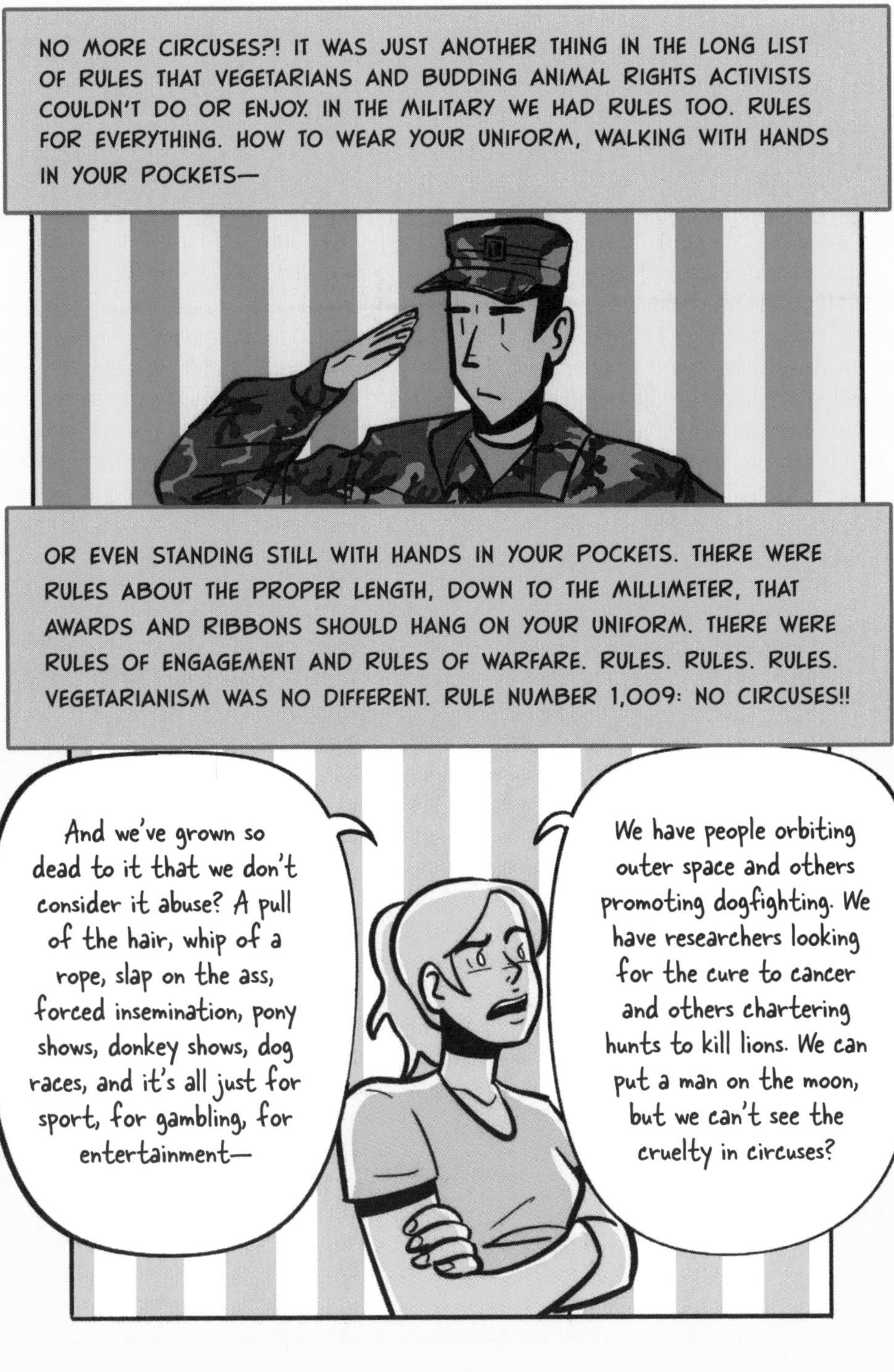
NO MORE CIRCUSES?! IT WAS JUST ANOTHER THING IN THE LONG LIST OF RULES THAT VEGETARIANS AND BUDDING ANIMAL RIGHTS ACTIVISTS COULDN'T DO OR ENJOY. IN THE MILITARY WE HAD RULES TOO. RULES FOR EVERYTHING. HOW TO WEAR YOUR UNIFORM, WALKING WITH HANDS IN YOUR POCKETS—
OR EVEN STANDING STILL WITH HANDS IN YOUR POCKETS. THERE WERE RULES ABOUT THE PROPER LENGTH, DOWN TO THE MILLIMETER, THAT AWARDS AND RIBBONS SHOULD HANG ON YOUR UNIFORM. THERE WERE RULES OF ENGAGEMENT AND RULES OF WARFARE. RULES. RULES. RULES. VEGETARIANISM WAS NO DIFFERENT. RULE NUMBER 1,009: NO CIRCUSES!!
And we've grown so dead to it that we don't consider it abuse? A pull of the hair, whip of a rope, slap on the ass, forced insemination, pony shows, donkey shows, dog races, and it's all just for sport, for gambling, for entertainment—
We have people orbiting outer space and others promoting dogfighting. We have researchers looking for the cure to cancer and others chartering hunts to kill lions. We can put a man on the moon, but we can't see the cruelty in circuses?

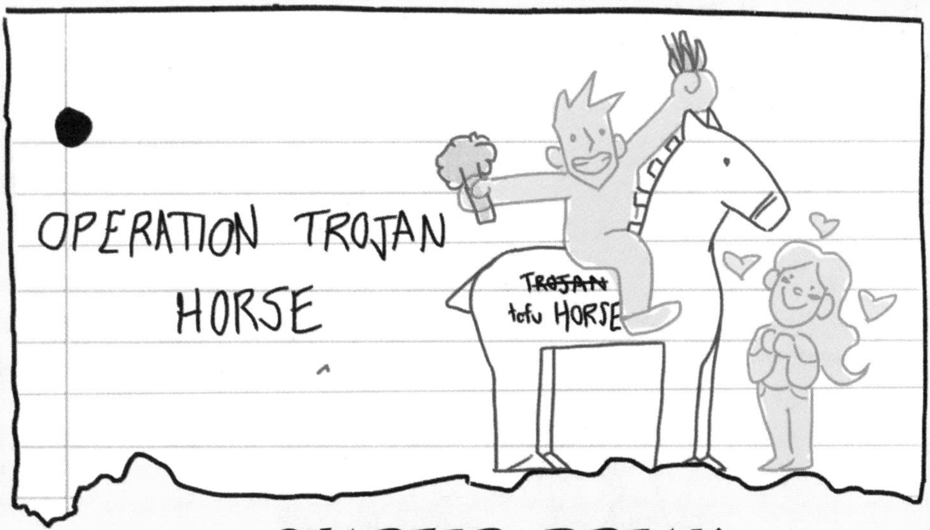
OPERATION TROJAN HORSE
~~TROJAN~~ tofu HORSE

CHAPTER BREAK

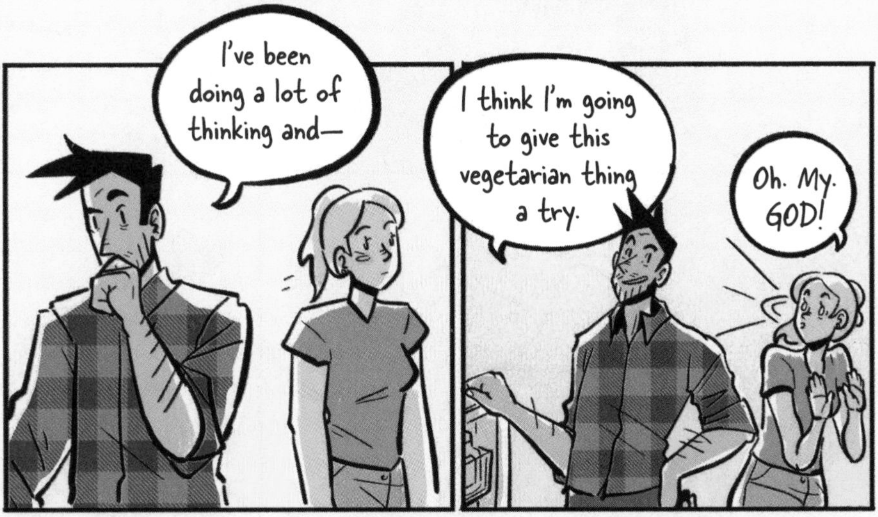
I've been doing a lot of thinking and—
I think I'm going to give this vegetarian thing a try.
Oh. My. GOD!

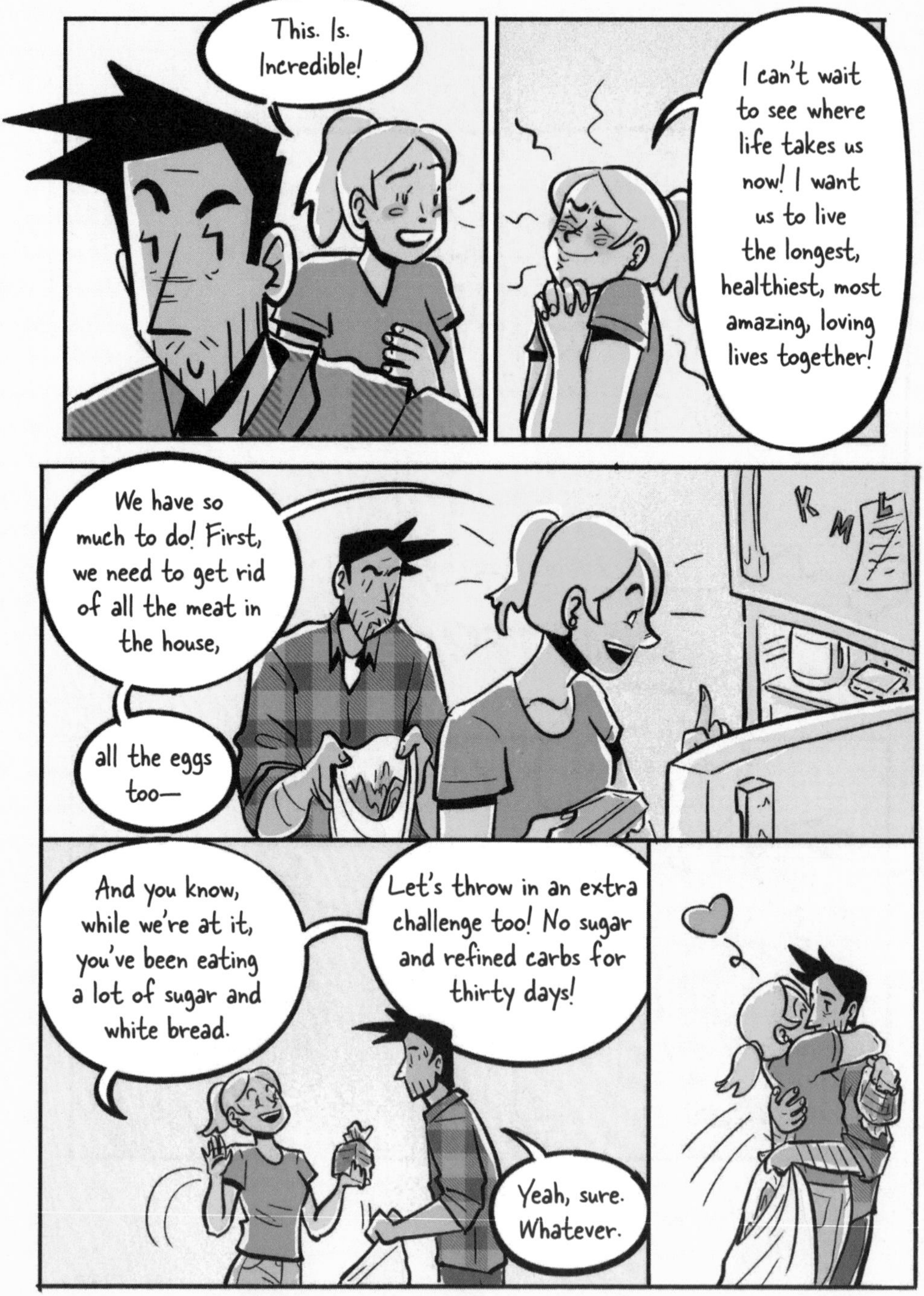
This. Is. Incredible!
I can't wait to see where life takes us now! I want us to live the longest, healthiest, most amazing, loving lives together!
We have so much to do! First, we need to get rid of all the meat in the house,
all the eggs too—
And you know, while we're at it, you've been eating a lot of sugar and white bread.
Let's throw in an extra challenge too! No sugar and refined carbs for thirty days!
Yeah, sure. Whatever.

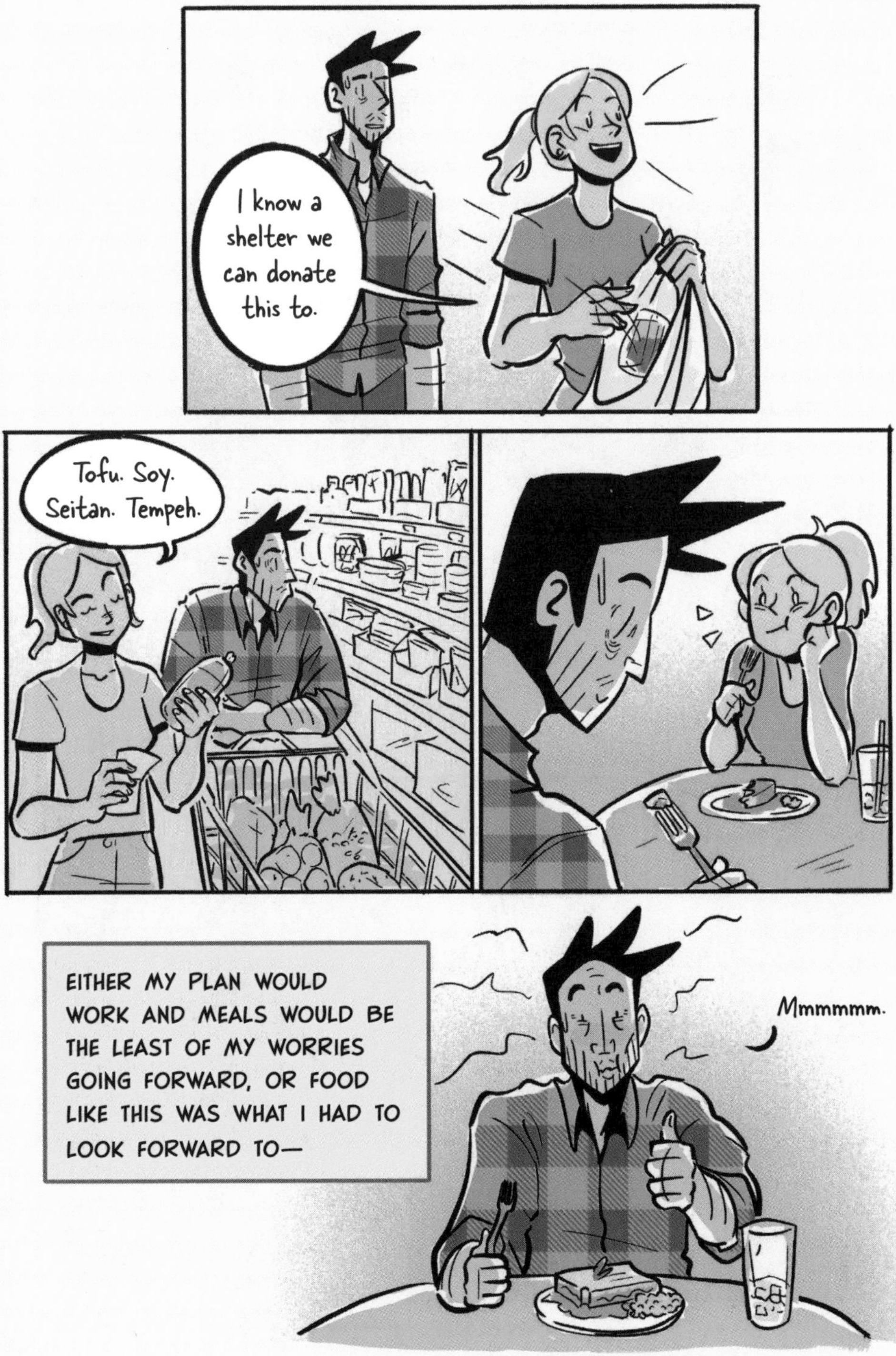
I know a shelter we can donate this to.
Tofu. Soy. Seitan. Tempeh.
EITHER MY PLAN WOULD WORK AND MEALS WOULD BE THE LEAST OF MY WORRIES GOING FORWARD, OR FOOD LIKE THIS WAS WHAT I HAD TO LOOK FORWARD TO—
Mmmmmm.

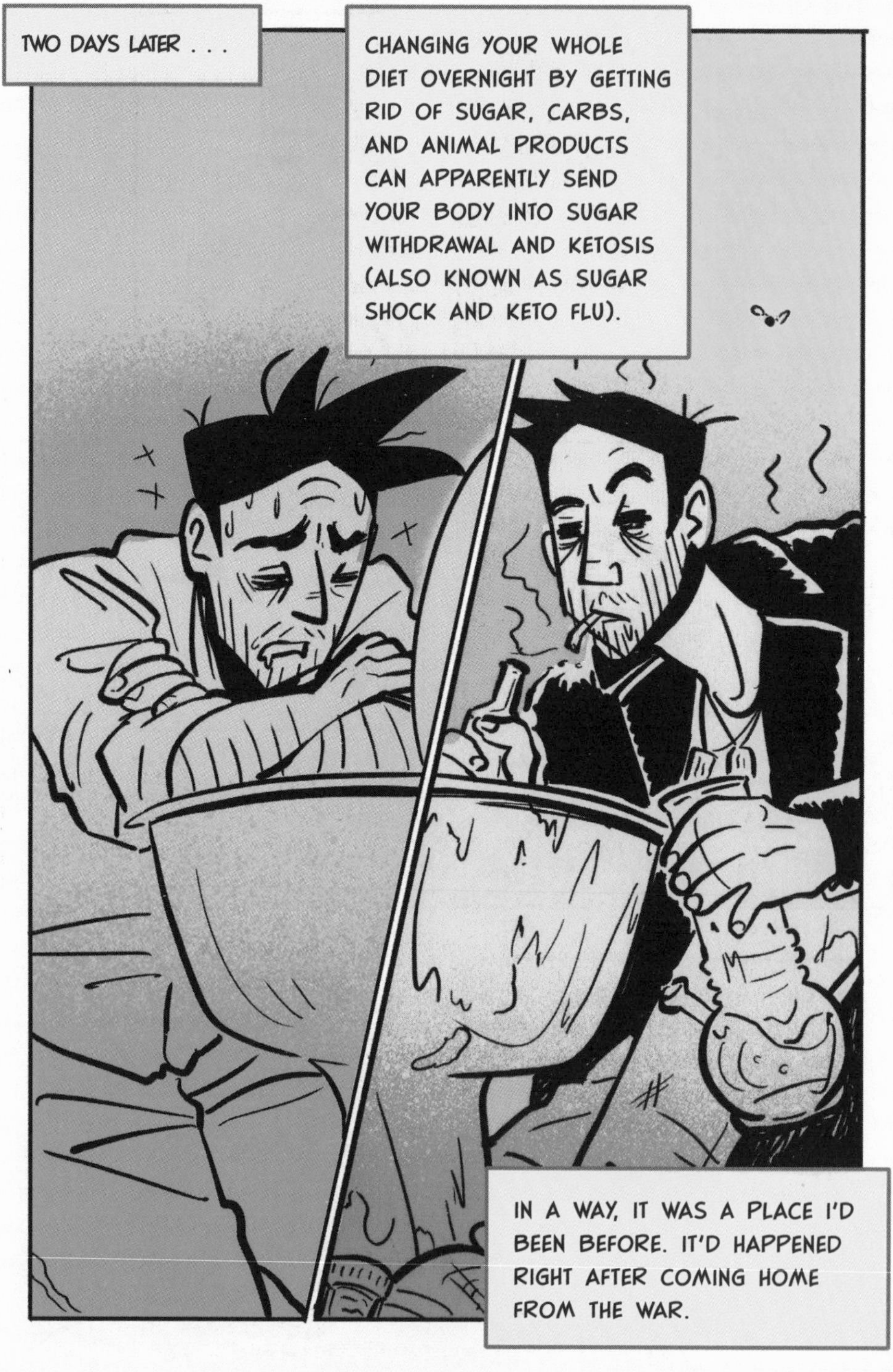

TWO DAYS LATER . . .
CHANGING YOUR WHOLE DIET OVERNIGHT BY GETTING RID OF SUGAR, CARBS, AND ANIMAL PRODUCTS CAN APPARENTLY SEND YOUR BODY INTO SUGAR WITHDRAWAL AND KETOSIS (ALSO KNOWN AS SUGAR SHOCK AND KETO FLU).
IN A WAY, IT WAS A PLACE I'D BEEN BEFORE. IT'D HAPPENED RIGHT AFTER COMING HOME FROM THE WAR.

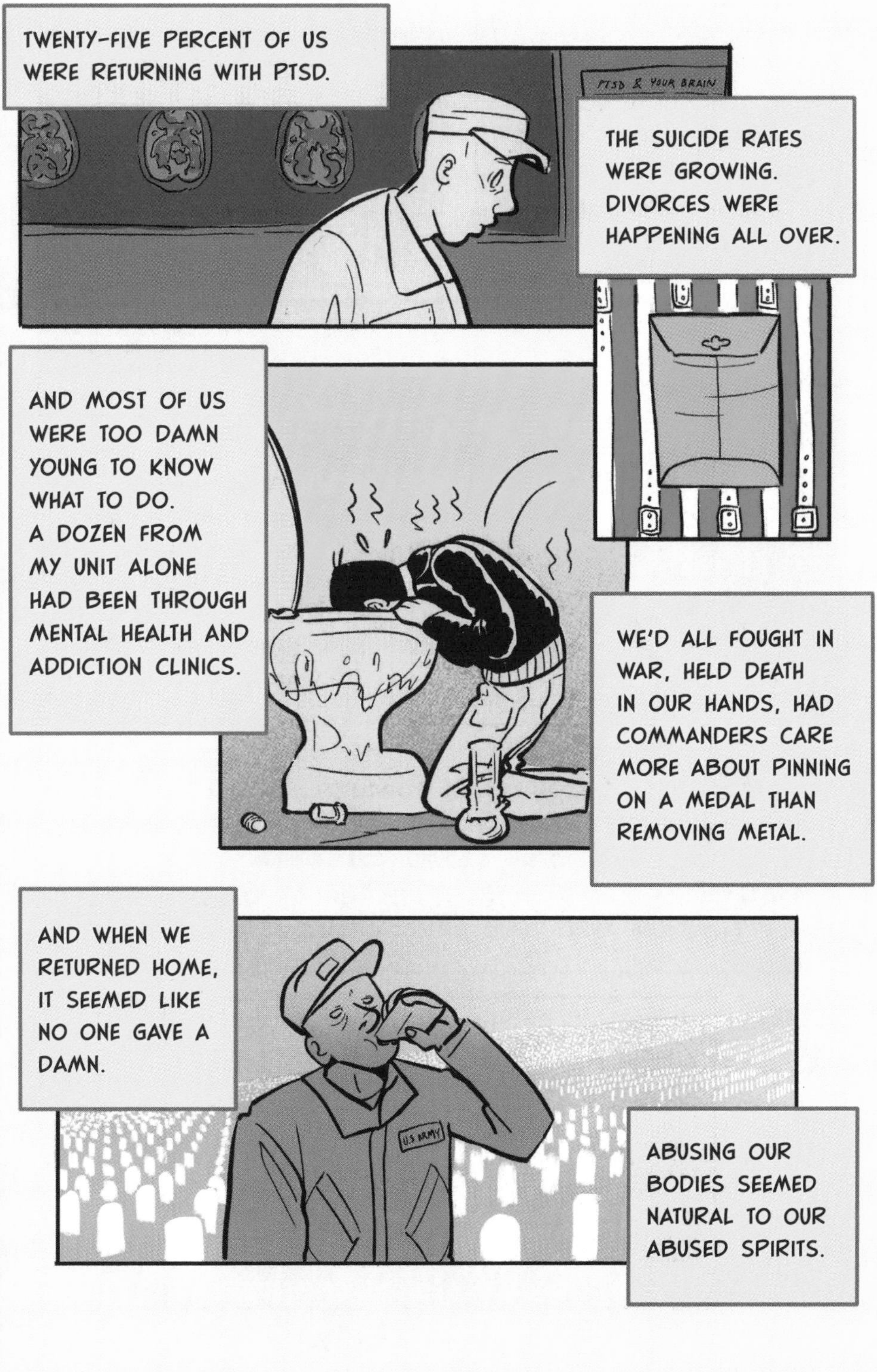
TWENTY-FIVE PERCENT OF US WERE RETURNING WITH PTSD.
PTSD & YOUR BRAIN
THE SUICIDE RATES WERE GROWING. DIVORCES WERE HAPPENING ALL OVER.
AND MOST OF US WERE TOO DAMN YOUNG TO KNOW WHAT TO DO. A DOZEN FROM MY UNIT ALONE HAD BEEN THROUGH MENTAL HEALTH AND ADDICTION CLINICS.
WE'D ALL FOUGHT IN WAR, HELD DEATH IN OUR HANDS, HAD COMMANDERS CARE MORE ABOUT PINNING ON A MEDAL THAN REMOVING METAL.
AND WHEN WE RETURNED HOME, IT SEEMED LIKE NO ONE GAVE A DAMN.
U.S ARMY
ABUSING OUR BODIES SEEMED NATURAL TO OUR ABUSED SPIRITS.

I HATED WHEN CIVILIANS FELT THE NEED TO SHARE THEIR OWN STORIES ABOUT COMING CLOSE TO DEATH: A CAR ACCIDENT, A HEALTH SCARE, A FRIEND PASSING AWAY, AND HOW THEY THEN FOUND GOD, OR A NEW LEASE ON LIFE.

BECAUSE WHAT THEY NEVER REALIZED WAS THAT IN WAR, SOMETHING LIKE THAT HAPPENED TEN TIMES A DAY: BOMBS FALLING, SHOTS FIRED, DEAD AND DYING IN YOUR HANDS. WELCOME TO MONDAY.

"LOVE LIFE, ENJOY LIFE." OR "LIFE IS POINTLESS, SCREW LIFE."
AFTER THE HUNDREDTH MOMENT AT WAR, YOU THROW THE FLOWER DOWN, BURN THE WHOLE BUSH TO THE GROUND. YOU SCREAM.
A NEW LEASE ON LIFE?
YEAH. I'VE HAD ONE THREE TIMES TODAY ALREADY.

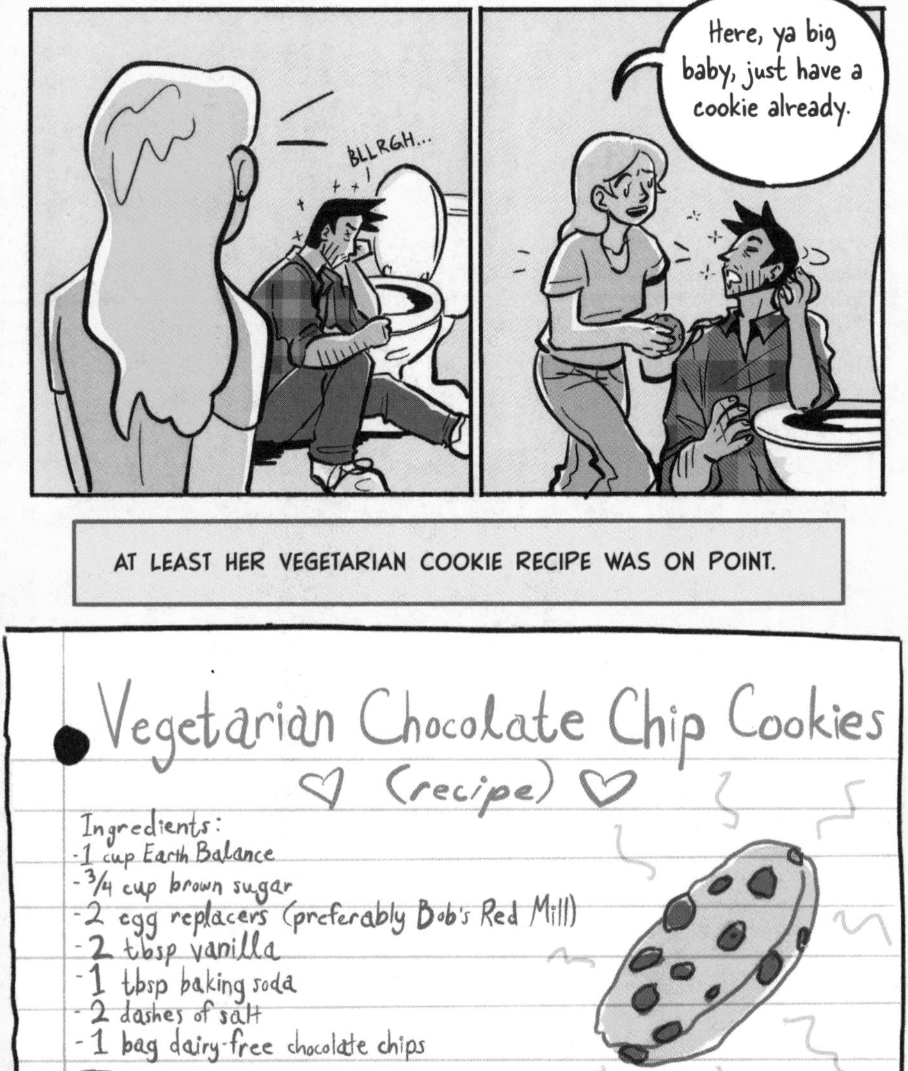
BLLRGH...
Here, ya big baby, just have a cookie already.
AT LEAST HER VEGETARIAN COOKIE RECIPE WAS ON POINT.
Vegetarian Chocolate Chip Cookies
(recipe)
Ingredients:
-1 cup Earth Balance
-3/4 cup brown sugar
-2 egg replacers (preferably Bob's Red Mill)
-2 tbsp vanilla
-1 tbsp baking soda
-2 dashes of salt
-1 bag dairy-free chocolate chips
Instructions
Preheat oven to 370°. Combine flour, baking soda & salt. In separate bowls beat sugar and butter until creamy. Add egg replacer and vanilla. Add dry mix. Add Chocolate Chips. Scoop onto baking sheet. Bake 9-11 min or until golden brown

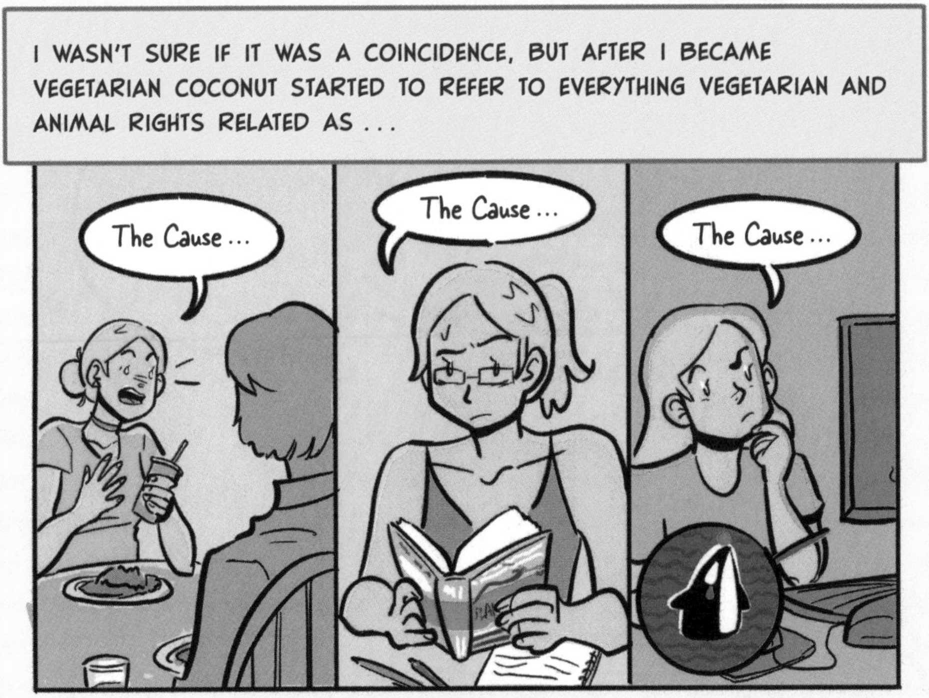
I WASN'T SURE IF IT WAS A COINCIDENCE, BUT AFTER I BECAME VEGETARIAN COCONUT STARTED TO REFER TO EVERYTHING VEGETARIAN AND ANIMAL RIGHTS RELATED AS . . .
The Cause . . .
The Cause . . .
The Cause . . .

CHAPTER 6

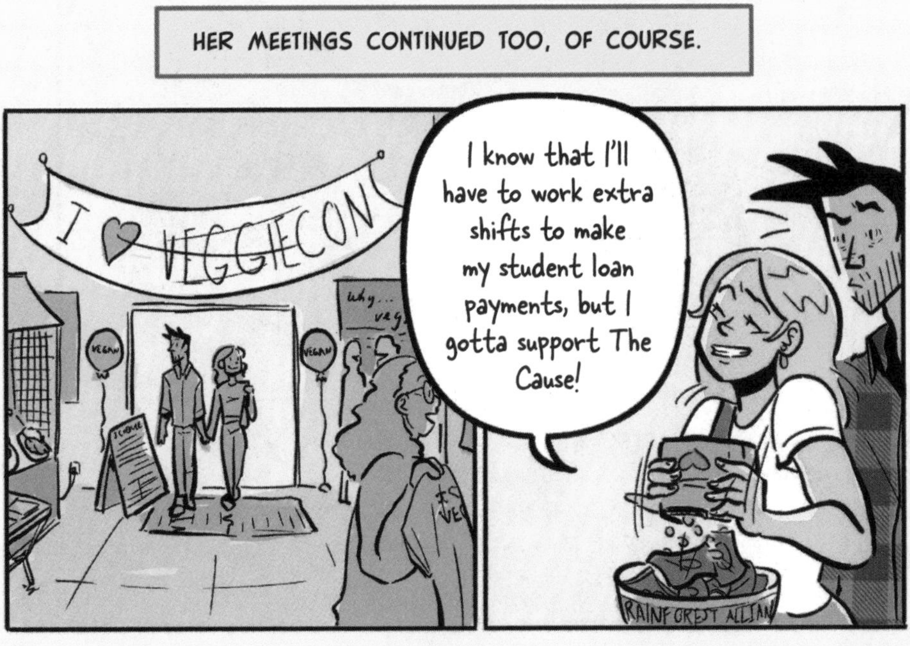
HER MEETINGS CONTINUED TOO, OF COURSE.
I ♥ VEGGIECON
I know that I'll have to work extra shifts to make my student loan payments, but I gotta support The Cause!

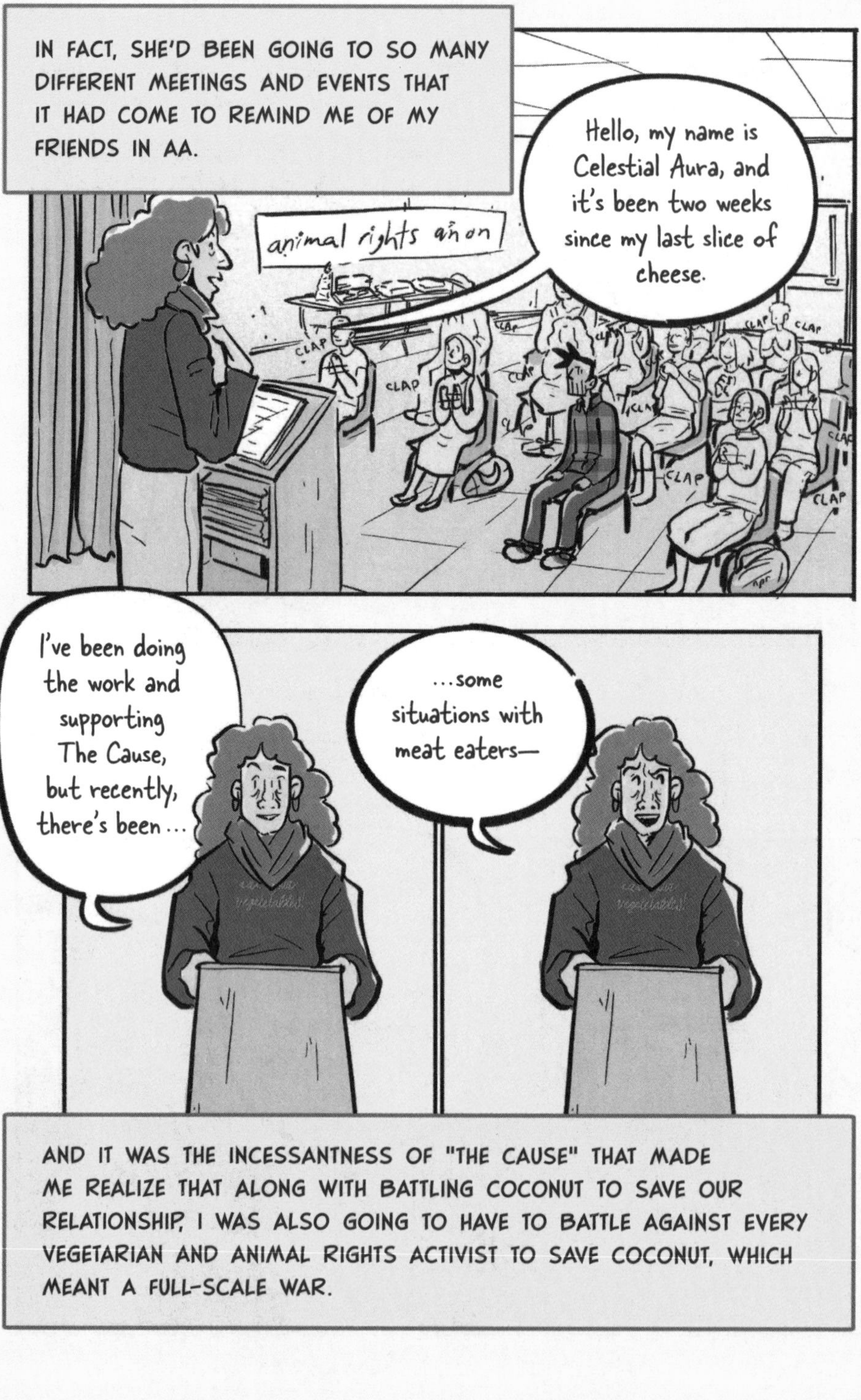
IN FACT, SHE'D BEEN GOING TO SO MANY DIFFERENT MEETINGS AND EVENTS THAT IT HAD COME TO REMIND ME OF MY FRIENDS IN AA.
animal rights anon
Hello, my name is Celestial Aura, and it's been two weeks since my last slice of cheese.
CLAP
CLAP
CLAP
CLAP
CLAP
CLAP
I've been doing the work and supporting The Cause, but recently, there's been ...
...some situations with meat eaters—
AND IT WAS THE INCESSANTNESS OF "THE CAUSE" THAT MADE ME REALIZE THAT ALONG WITH BATTLING COCONUT TO SAVE OUR RELATIONSHIP, I WAS ALSO GOING TO HAVE TO BATTLE AGAINST EVERY VEGETARIAN AND ANIMAL RIGHTS ACTIVIST TO SAVE COCONUT, WHICH MEANT A FULL-SCALE WAR.

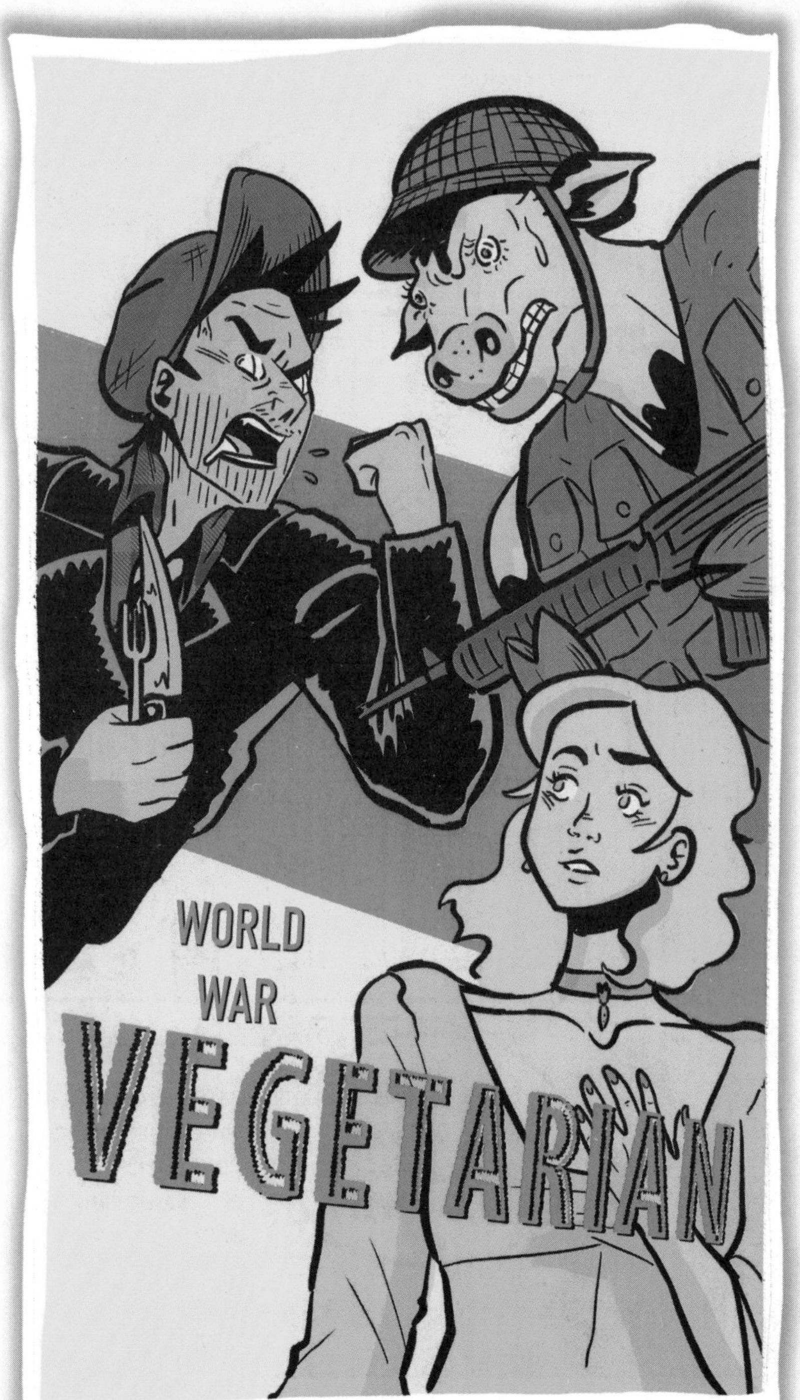
WORLD
WAR
VEGETARIAN

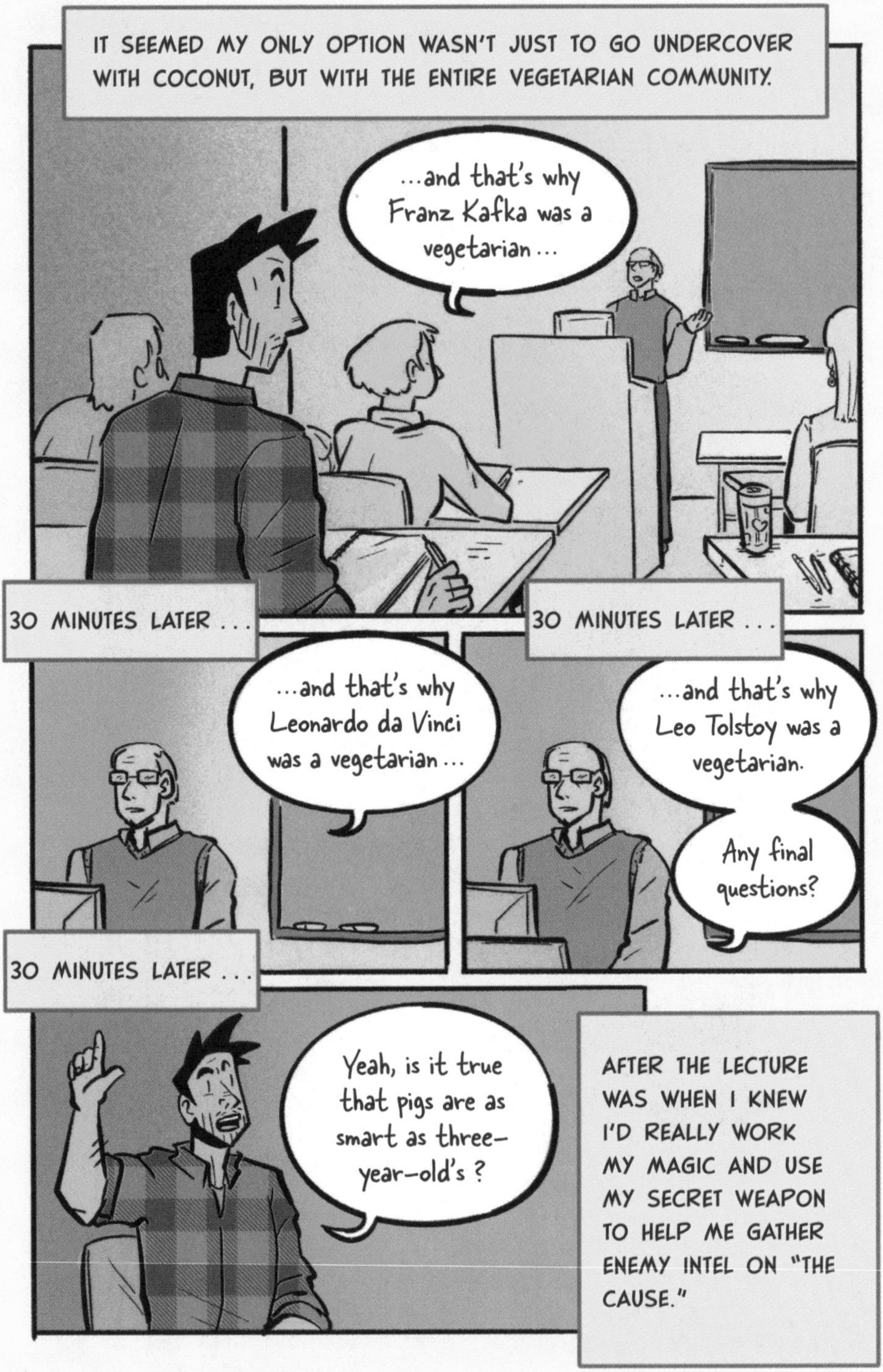
IT SEEMED MY ONLY OPTION WASN'T JUST TO GO UNDERCOVER WITH COCONUT, BUT WITH THE ENTIRE VEGETARIAN COMMUNITY.
...and that's why Franz Kafka was a vegetarian...
30 MINUTES LATER . . .
...and that's why Leonardo da Vinci was a vegetarian...
30 MINUTES LATER . . .
...and that's why Leo Tolstoy was a vegetarian.
Any final questions?
30 MINUTES LATER . . .
Yeah, is it true that pigs are as smart as three-year-old's ?
AFTER THE LECTURE WAS WHEN I KNEW I'D REALLY WORK MY MAGIC AND USE MY SECRET WEAPON TO HELP ME GATHER ENEMY INTEL ON "THE CAUSE."

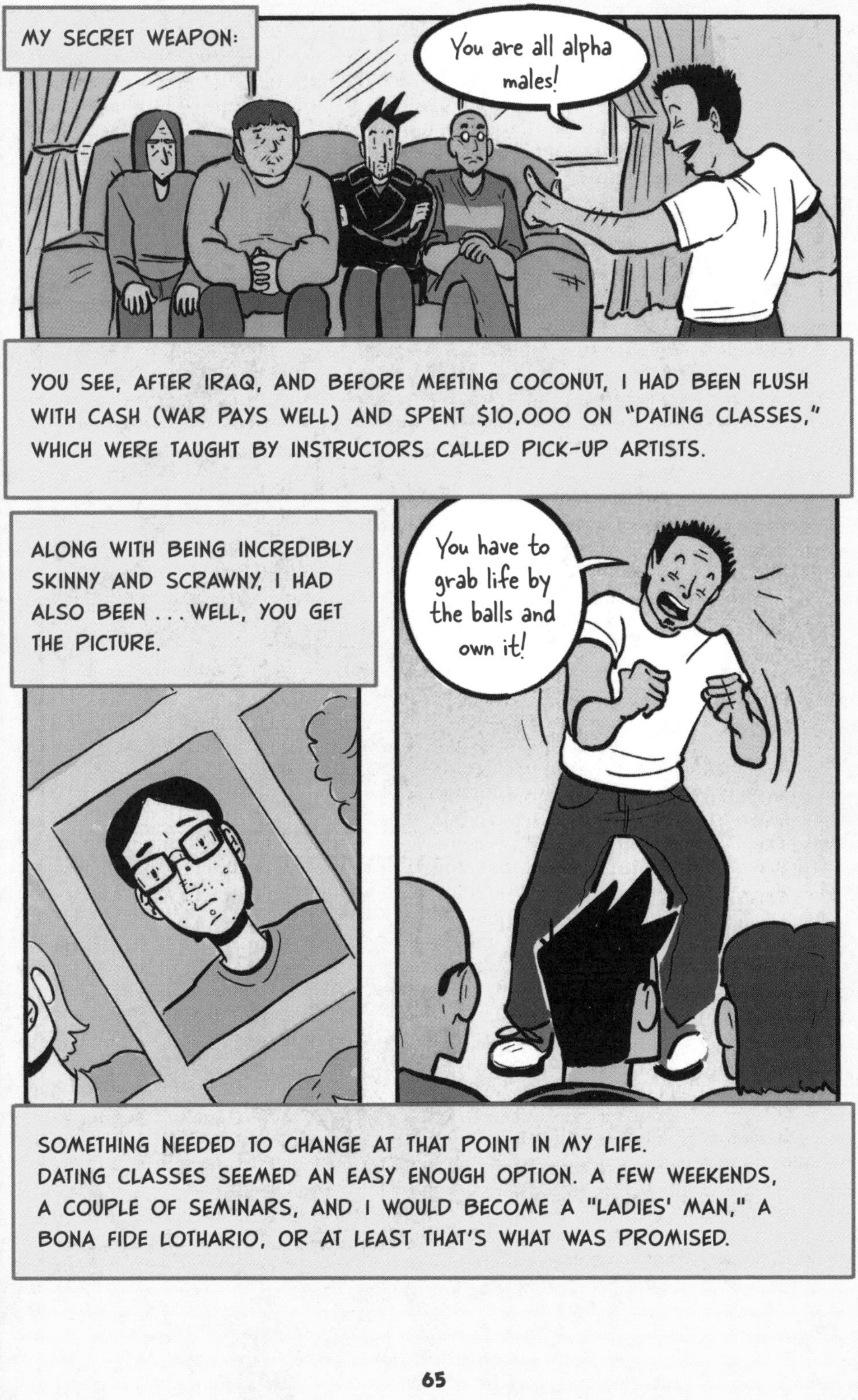
MY SECRET WEAPON:
You are all alpha males!
YOU SEE, AFTER IRAQ, AND BEFORE MEETING COCONUT, I HAD BEEN FLUSH WITH CASH (WAR PAYS WELL) AND SPENT $10,000 ON "DATING CLASSES," WHICH WERE TAUGHT BY INSTRUCTORS CALLED PICK-UP ARTISTS.
ALONG WITH BEING INCREDIBLY SKINNY AND SCRAWNY, I HAD ALSO BEEN . . . WELL, YOU GET THE PICTURE.
You have to grab life by the balls and own it!
SOMETHING NEEDED TO CHANGE AT THAT POINT IN MY LIFE. DATING CLASSES SEEMED AN EASY ENOUGH OPTION. A FEW WEEKENDS, A COUPLE OF SEMINARS, AND I WOULD BECOME A "LADIES' MAN," A BONA FIDE LOTHARIO, OR AT LEAST THAT'S WHAT WAS PROMISED.

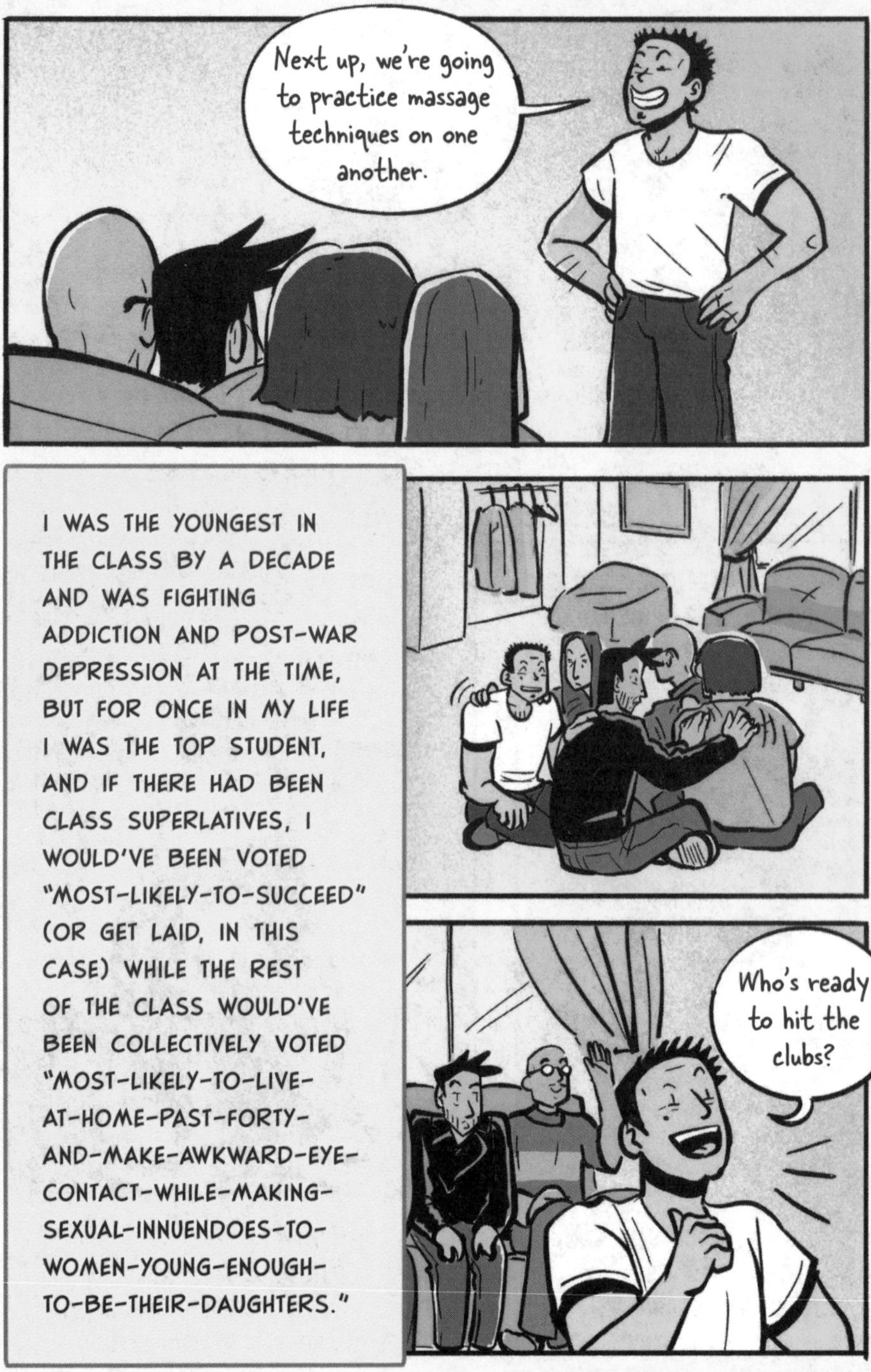
Next up, we're going to practice massage techniques on one another.
I WAS THE YOUNGEST IN THE CLASS BY A DECADE AND WAS FIGHTING ADDICTION AND POST-WAR DEPRESSION AT THE TIME, BUT FOR ONCE IN MY LIFE I WAS THE TOP STUDENT, AND IF THERE HAD BEEN CLASS SUPERLATIVES, I WOULD'VE BEEN VOTED "MOST-LIKELY-TO-SUCCEED" (OR GET LAID, IN THIS CASE) WHILE THE REST OF THE CLASS WOULD'VE BEEN COLLECTIVELY VOTED "MOST-LIKELY-TO-LIVE-AT-HOME-PAST-FORTY-AND-MAKE-AWKWARD-EYE-CONTACT-WHILE-MAKING-SEXUAL-INNUENDOES-TO-WOMEN-YOUNG-ENOUGH-TO-BE-THEIR-DAUGHTERS."
Who's ready to hit the clubs?

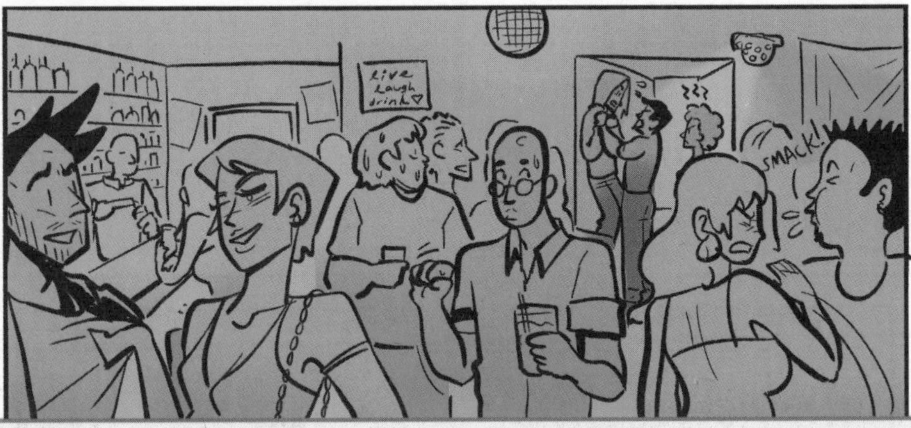
Live
Laugh
drink♡
SMACK!

SOMEHOW, THE CLASSES ACTUALLY WORKED FOR ME, TO AN EXTENT. THEY TAUGHT ME TO STOP BEING AFRAID OF REJECTION, AND TO TREAT A WOMAN I WAS INTERESTED IN AS A POTENTIAL FRIEND RATHER THAN A ROMANTIC PARTNER (PROFOUND, I KNOW, BUT IT HELPED).

THEY EVEN TAUGHT ME ABOUT BODY LANGUAGE, TONE OF VOICE, AND THE PSYCHOLOGICAL COMPLEXITIES OF APPROACHING GROUPS OF PEOPLE AND LEADING THE CONVERSATION AND DYNAMIC WHEREVER I WANTED.

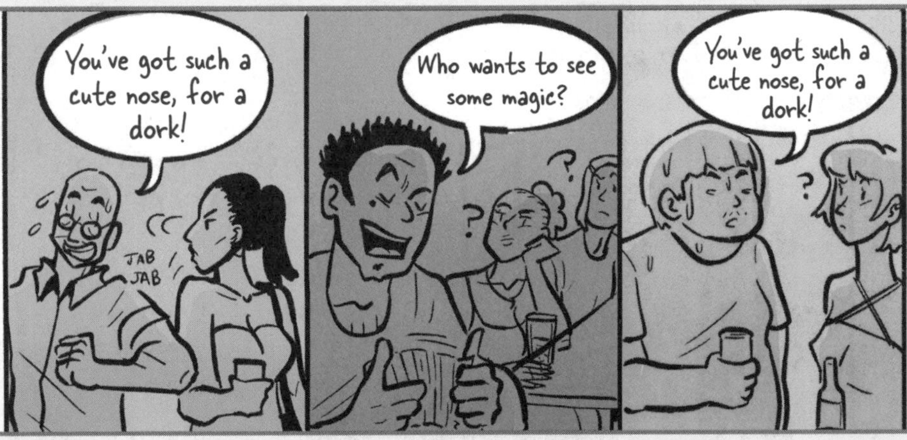
You've got such a cute nose, for a dork!
JAB JAB
Who wants to see some magic?
You've got such a cute nose, for a dork!

THERE WERE SOME THINGS FROM THE CLASSES THAT DIDN'T WORK OUT—THE MAGIC TRICKS, HEAD GAMES, AND MEMORIZED ROUTINES—BUT I WAS ABLE TO SEPARATE ENOUGH OF THE GOOD FROM THE BAD.

EVEN YEARS LATER, I STILL FELT CONFIDENT THAT I COULD APPROACH AND CONTROL THE DYNAMIC OF ANY GROUP, AND I KNEW THAT WOULD BE MY SECRET WEAPON TONIGHT.

THE TRICK TO IT, THE TEN-THOUSAND-DOLLAR SECRET TO APPROACHING A GROUP OF PEOPLE, THE THING THAT EVERY SO-CALLED PICK UP ARTIST IS SUPPOSED TO KNOW, IS THAT YOU MUST ALWAYS START IT CASUAL, AS THOUGH YOU JUST NEED A QUICK ANSWER TO A QUESTION AND AREN'T LOOKING TO "HIT ON" THEM OR ANYTHING ELSE.

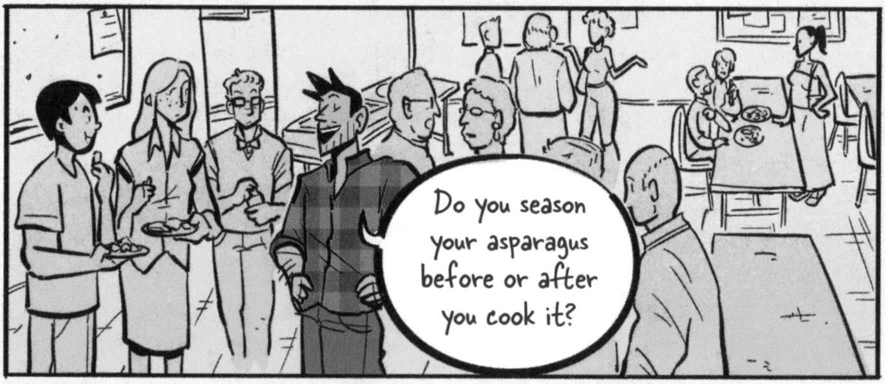
Do you season your asparagus before or after you cook it?

NEXT YOU SHARE AN INTERESTING ANECDOTE TO BUILD RAPPORT.

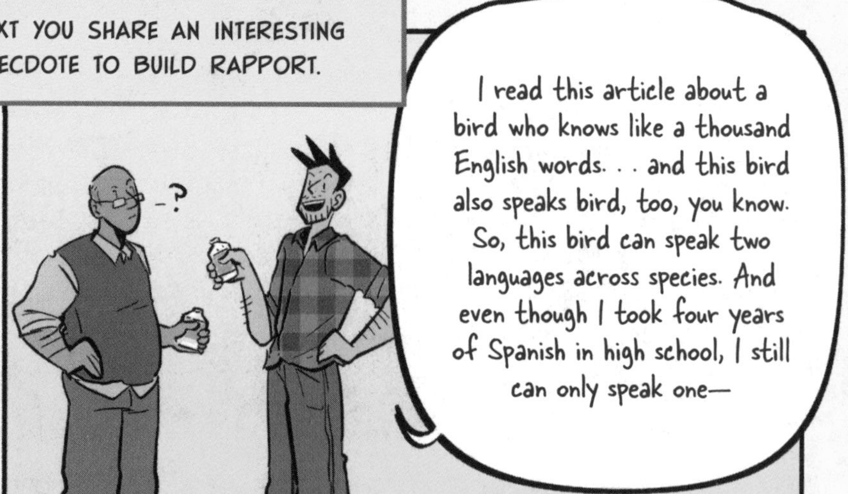
-?
I read this article about a bird who knows like a thousand English words. . . and this bird also speaks bird, too, you know. So, this bird can speak two languages across species. And even though I took four years of Spanish in high school, I still can only speak one—

WHILE YOU'RE TALKING, YOU ALSO WANT TO MIRROR GESTICULATIONS AND BODY LANGUAGE, WHICH IS A PSYCHOLOGICAL TECHNIQUE TO GET SOMEONE TO LIKE YOU (THEY THINK THEY'RE TALKING TO THEMSELVES). AND THEN AFTER YOU'VE CREATED A CONNECTION, YOU BRING THINGS AROUND TOWARD YOUR OBJECTIVE—

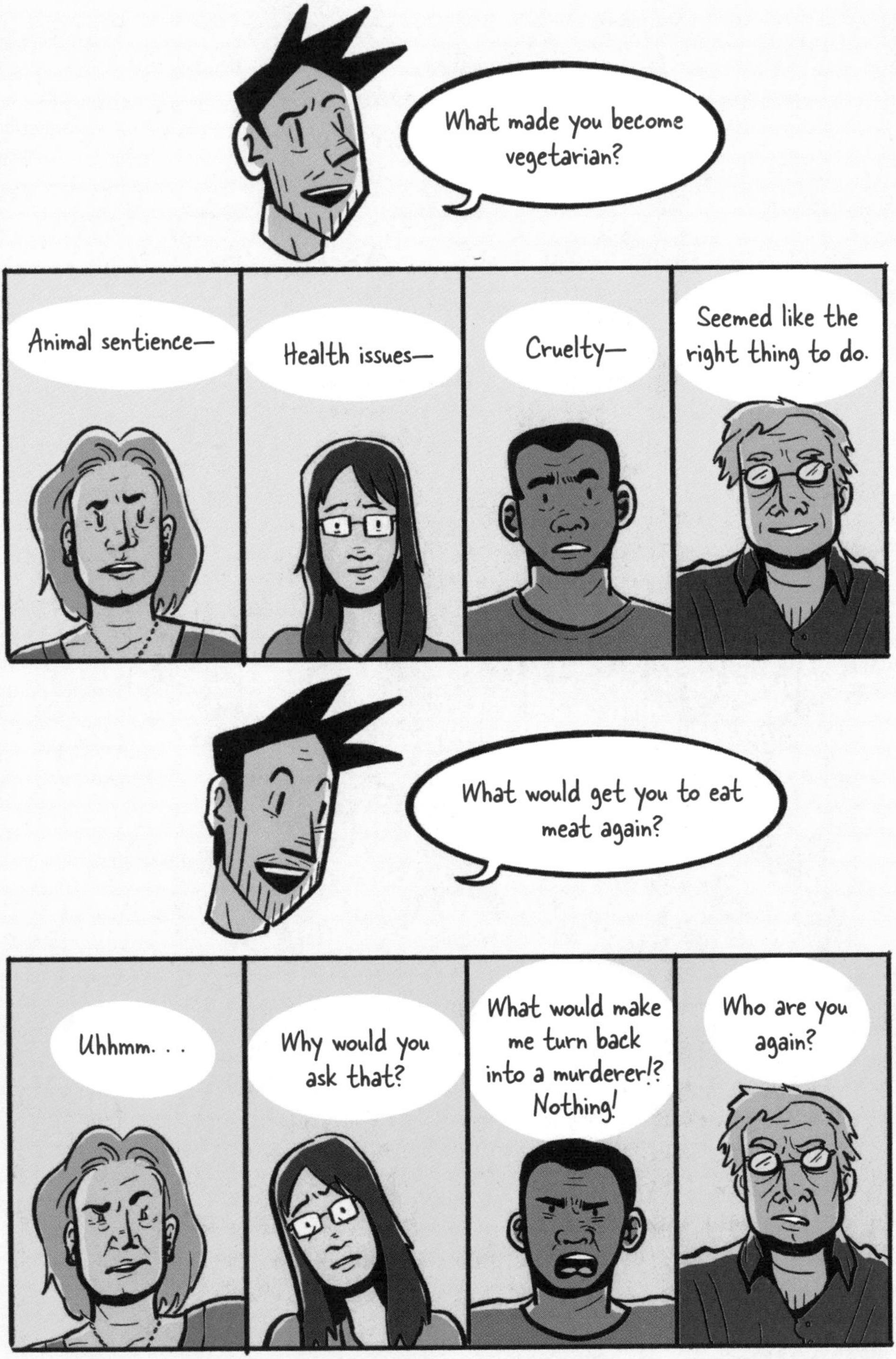
What made you become vegetarian?
Animal sentience—
Health issues—
Cruelty—
Seemed like the right thing to do.
What would get you to eat meat again?
Uhhmm. . .
Why would you ask that?
What would make me turn back into a murderer!? Nothing!
Who are you again?

IN A WAY, IT WAS THE DATING CLASSES THAT HELPED ME QUIT MY ADDICTIONS. THEY GAVE ME A SENSE OF PURPOSE AND A MISSION TO ACCOMPLISH, SOMETHING I DIDN'T EVEN KNOW I'D MISSED SINCE BEING HOME.

BUT FOR ALL THE DATING CLASSES, AND THE THOUSANDS OF DOLLARS I SPENT ON THEM, NONE OF IT CAME WITH ADVICE ABOUT ACTUALLY BEING IN A RELATIONSHIP. ONE CLASS HAD US SPEND AN HOUR PRACTICING THE BEST WAY TO MAKE EYE CONTACT. ANOTHER HAD US SPEND TWO HOURS WALKING UP AND SIMPLY SAYING "HI" TO ONE ANOTHER. BUT ADVICE ON BEING IN A HEALTHY RELATIONSHIP? OR DEALING WITH A DIFFICULTY THAT MAY ARISE—LIKE A DIFFERENCE IN CONVICTIONS OR LIFESTYLE OR DIET? NOTHING. NADA. ZILCH.
THERE WAS NO CLASS FOR THE JOURNEY I WAS NOW ON.

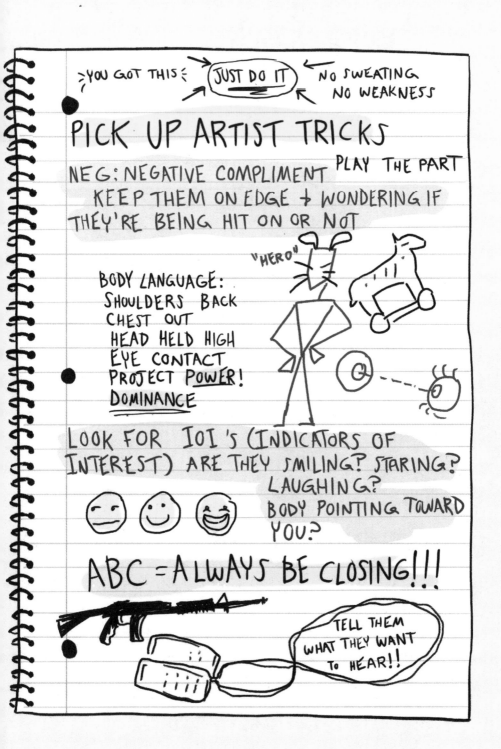

>YOU GOT THIS< (JUST DO IT) < NO SWEATING NO WEAKNESS

PICK UP ARTIST TRICKS

NEG: NEGATIVE COMPLIMENT — PLAY THE PART
KEEP THEM ON EDGE + WONDERING IF
THEY'RE BEING HIT ON OR NOT

"HERO"

BODY LANGUAGE:
SHOULDERS BACK
CHEST OUT
HEAD HELD HIGH
EYE CONTACT
PROJECT POWER!
DOMINANCE

LOOK FOR IOI's (INDICATORS OF
INTEREST) ARE THEY SMILING? STARING?
LAUGHING?
BODY POINTING TOWARD
YOU?

ABC = ALWAYS BE CLOSING!!!

TELL THEM WHAT THEY WANT TO HEAR!!

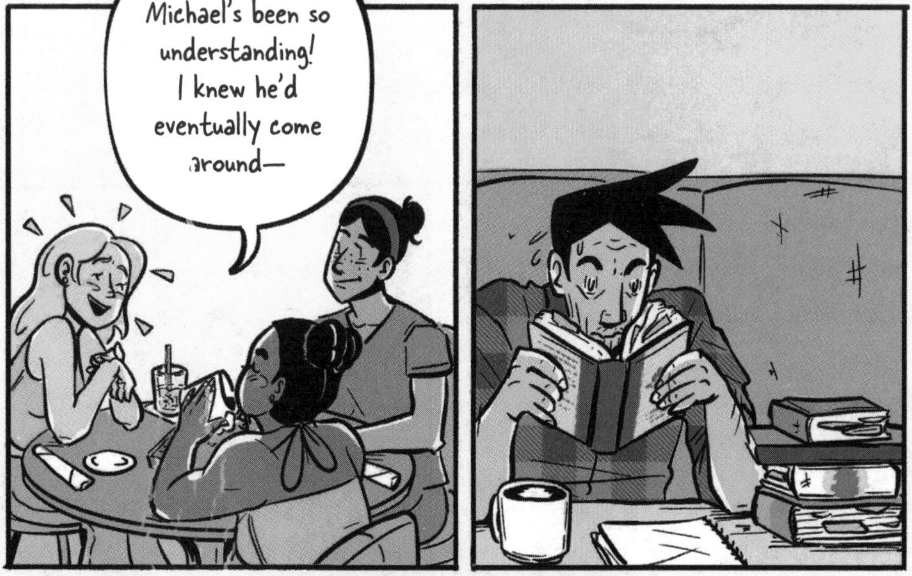
Michael's been so understanding! I knew he'd eventually come around—

CHAPTER 7

"LET YOUR PLANS BE DARK AND IMPENETRABLE AS NIGHT, AND WHEN YOU MOVE, FALL LIKE A THUNDERBOLT." —SUN TZU, *THE ART OF WAR*

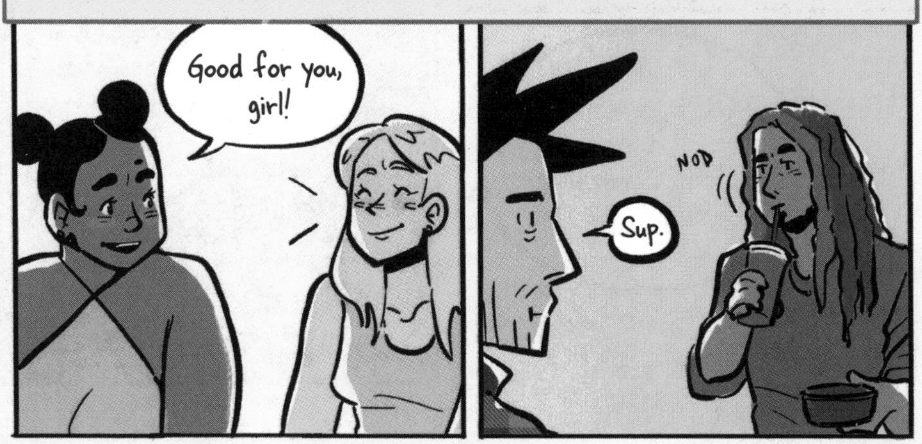
Good for you, girl!
NOD
Sup.

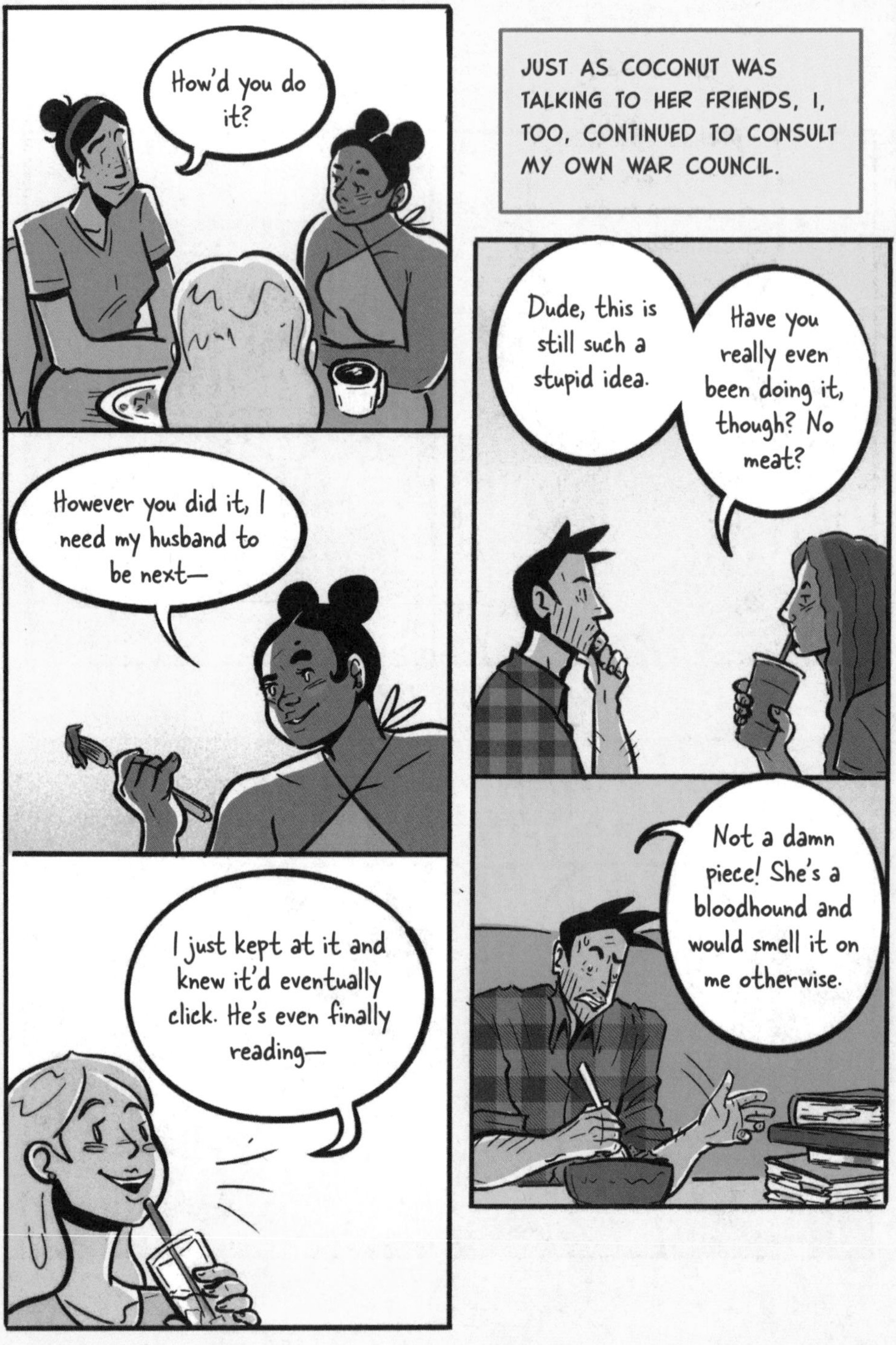
How'd you do it?
However you did it, I need my husband to be next—
I just kept at it and knew it'd eventually click. He's even finally reading—
JUST AS COCONUT WAS TALKING TO HER FRIENDS, I, TOO, CONTINUED TO CONSULT MY OWN WAR COUNCIL.
Dude, this is still such a stupid idea.
Have you really even been doing it, though? No meat?
Not a damn piece! She's a bloodhound and would smell it on me otherwise.

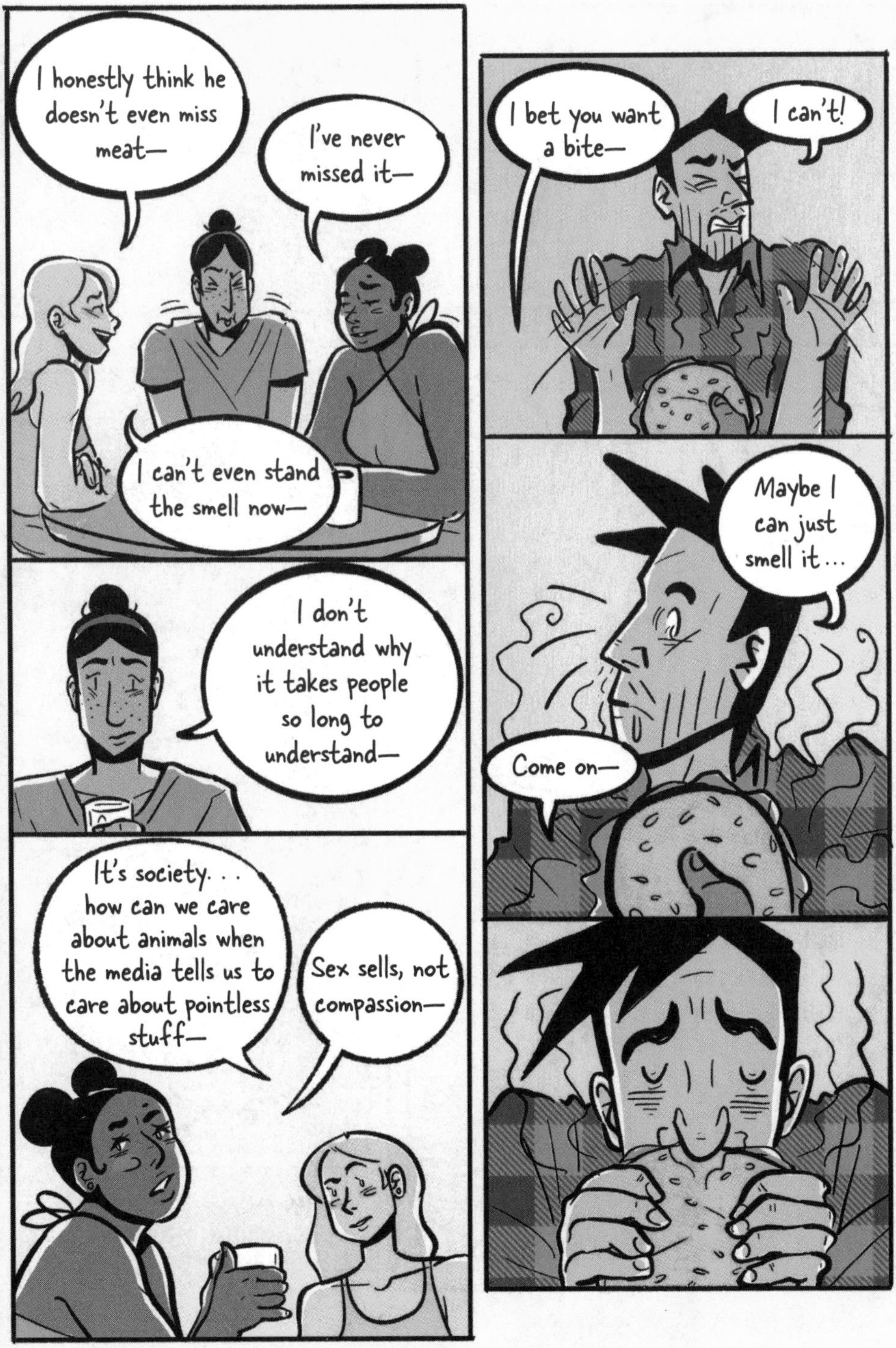
I honestly think he doesn't even miss meat—
I've never missed it—
I can't even stand the smell now—
I don't understand why it takes people so long to understand—
It's society. . . how can we care about animals when the media tells us to care about pointless stuff—
Sex sells, not compassion—
I bet you want a bite—
I can't!
Maybe I can just smell it...
Come on—

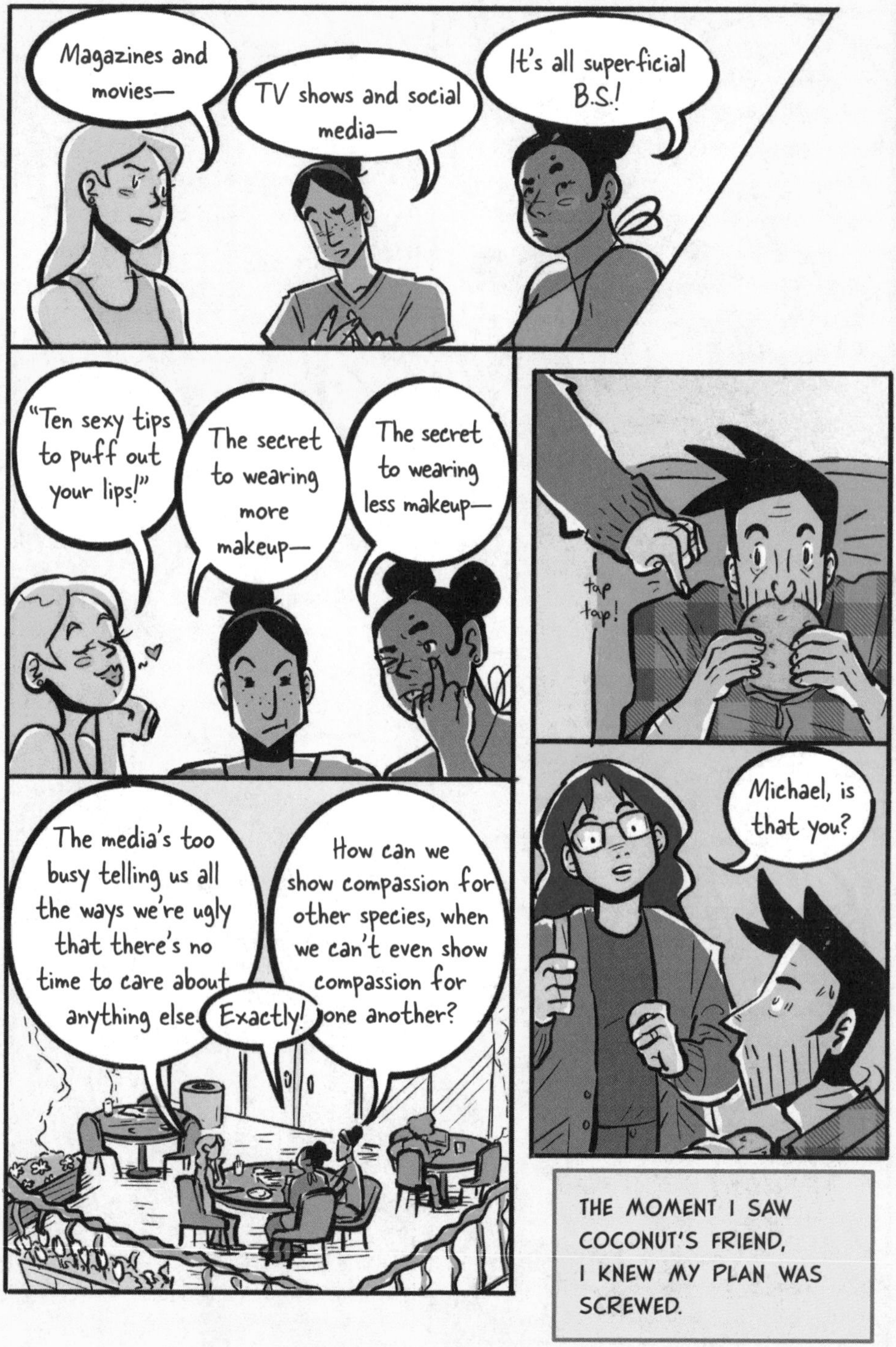

Magazines and movies—
TV shows and social media—
It's all superficial B.S.!
"Ten sexy tips to puff out your lips!"
The secret to wearing more makeup—
The secret to wearing less makeup—
tap tap!
The media's too busy telling us all the ways we're ugly that there's no time to care about anything else.
Exactly!
How can we show compassion for other species, when we can't even show compassion for one another?
Michael, is that you?
THE MOMENT I SAW COCONUT'S FRIEND, I KNEW MY PLAN WAS SCREWED.

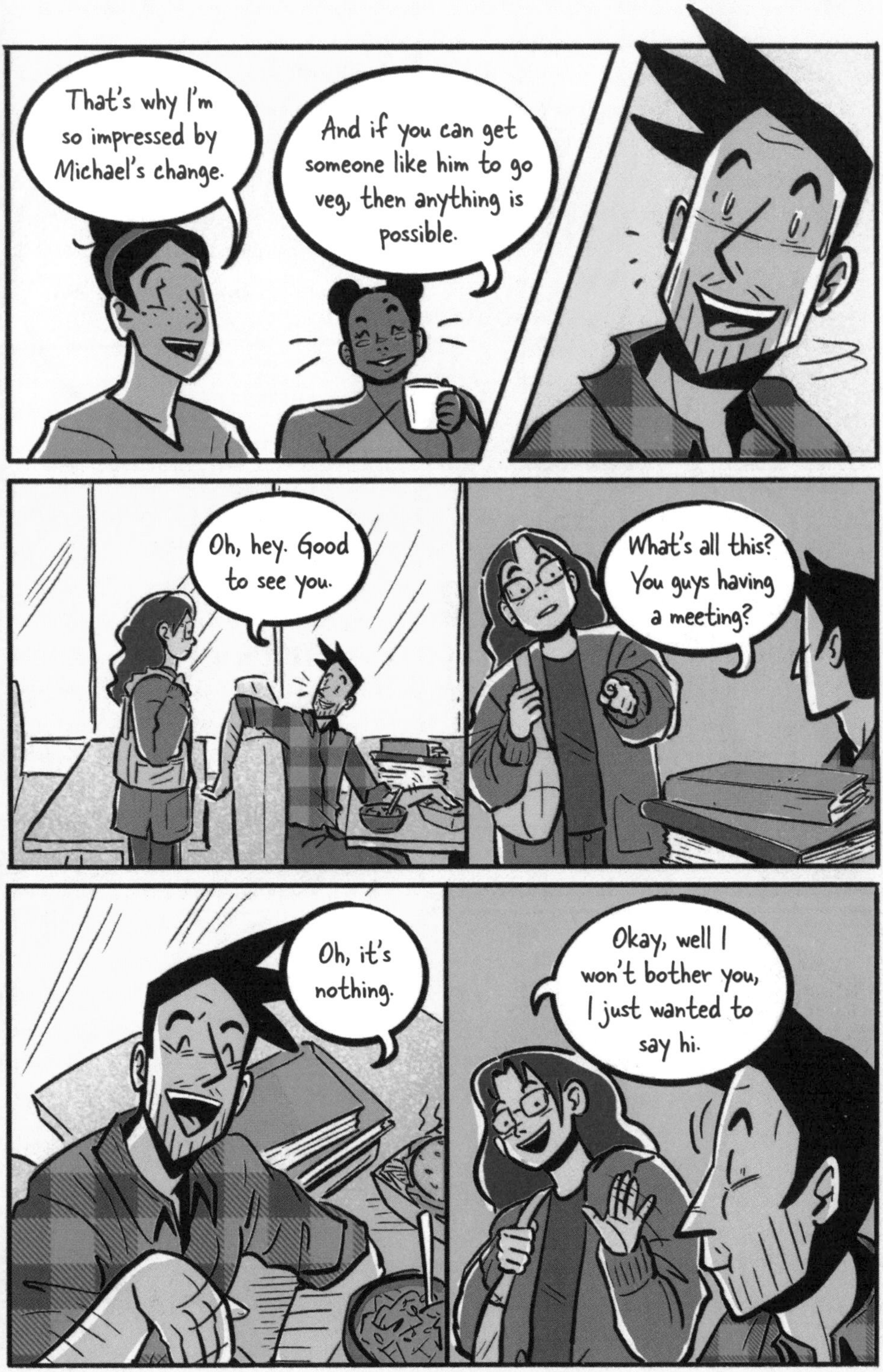

That's why I'm so impressed by Michael's change.
And if you can get someone like him to go veg, then anything is possible.
Oh, hey. Good to see you.
What's all this? You guys having a meeting?
Oh, it's nothing.
Okay, well I won't bother you, I just wanted to say hi.

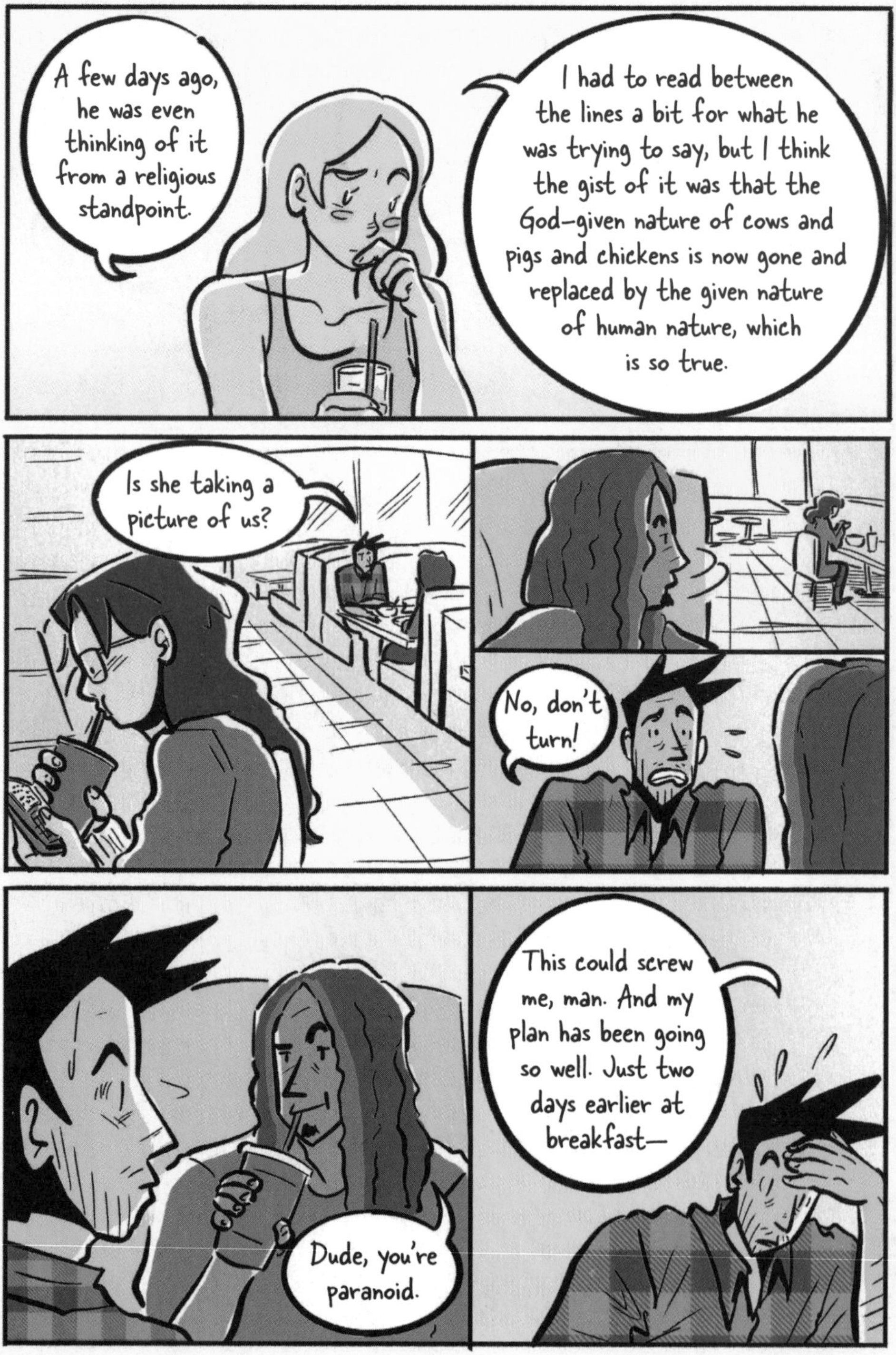
A few days ago, he was even thinking of it from a religious standpoint.
I had to read between the lines a bit for what he was trying to say, but I think the gist of it was that the God-given nature of cows and pigs and chickens is now gone and replaced by the given nature of human nature, which is so true.
Is she taking a picture of us?
No, don't turn!
Dude, you're paranoid.
This could screw me, man. And my plan has been going so well. Just two days earlier at breakfast—

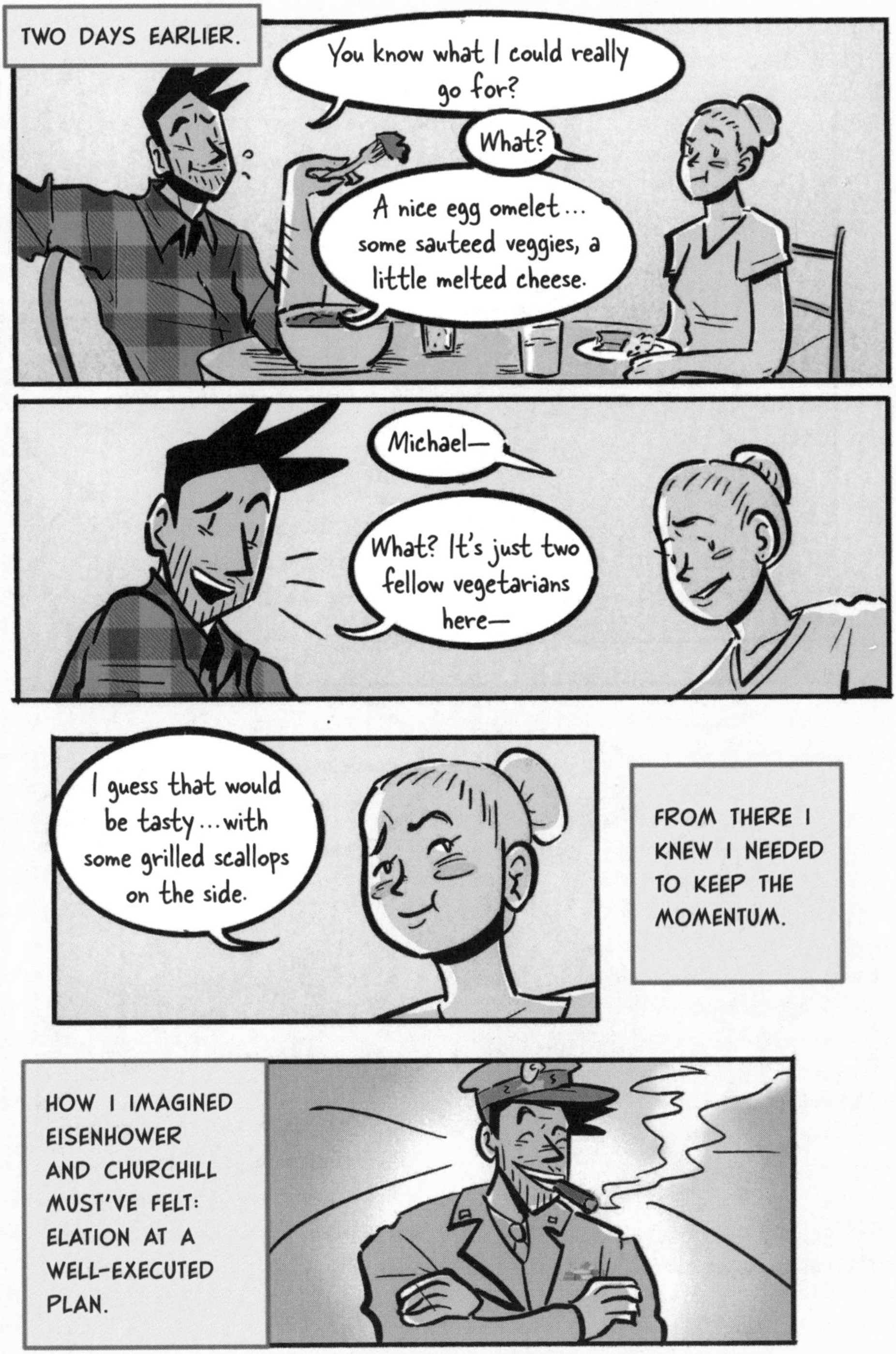

TWO DAYS EARLIER.
You know what I could really go for?
What?
A nice egg omelet... some sauteed veggies, a little melted cheese.
Michael—
What? It's just two fellow vegetarians here—
I guess that would be tasty...with some grilled scallops on the side.
FROM THERE I KNEW I NEEDED TO KEEP THE MOMENTUM.
HOW I IMAGINED EISENHOWER AND CHURCHILL MUST'VE FELT: ELATION AT A WELL-EXECUTED PLAN.

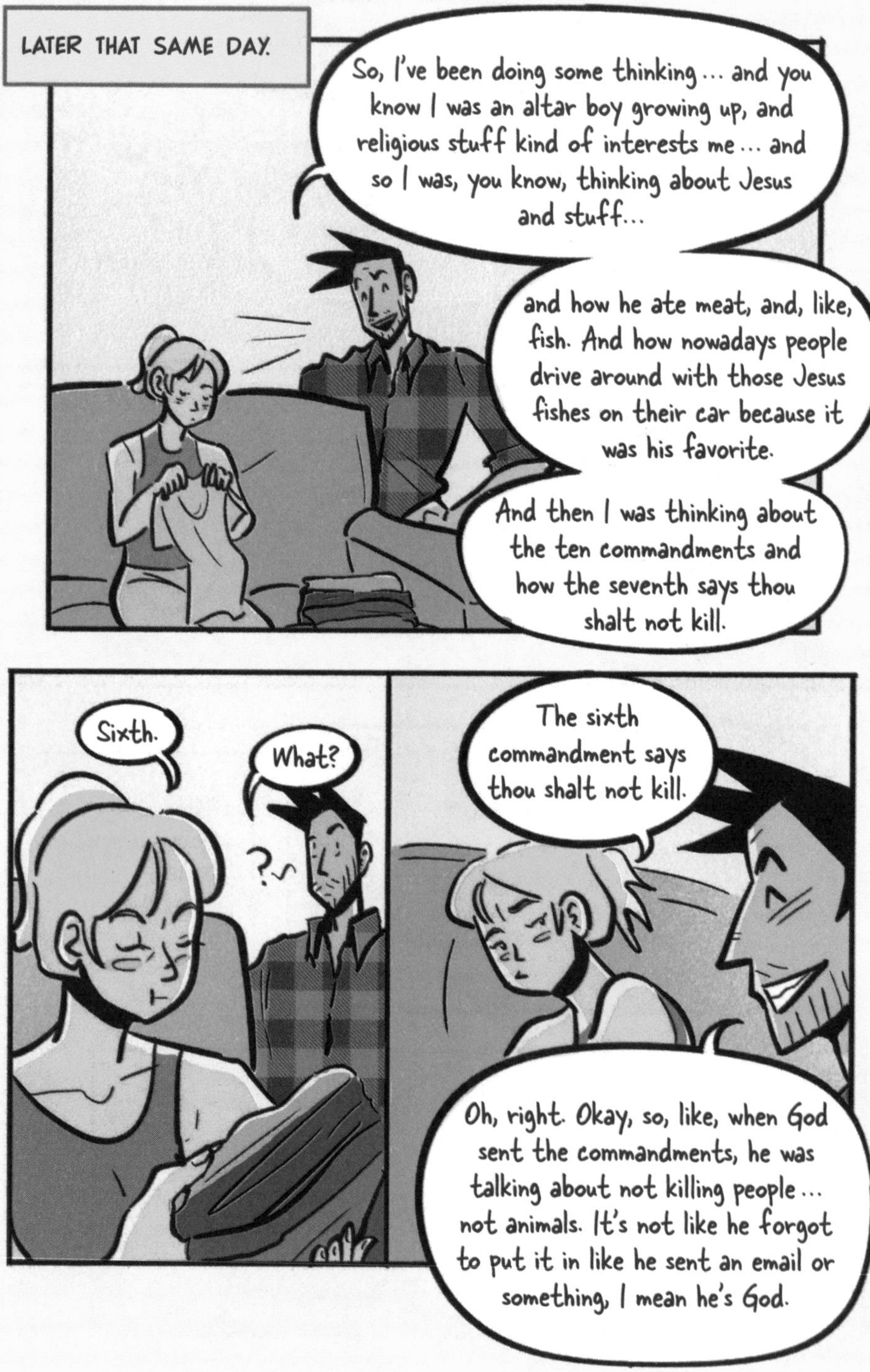

LATER THAT SAME DAY.
So, I've been doing some thinking... and you know I was an altar boy growing up, and religious stuff kind of interests me... and so I was, you know, thinking about Jesus and stuff...
and how he ate meat, and, like, fish. And how nowadays people drive around with those Jesus fishes on their car because it was his favorite.
And then I was thinking about the ten commandments and how the seventh says thou shalt not kill.
Sixth.
What?
?
The sixth commandment says thou shalt not kill.
Oh, right. Okay, so, like, when God sent the commandments, he was talking about not killing people... not animals. It's not like he forgot to put it in like he sent an email or something, I mean he's God.

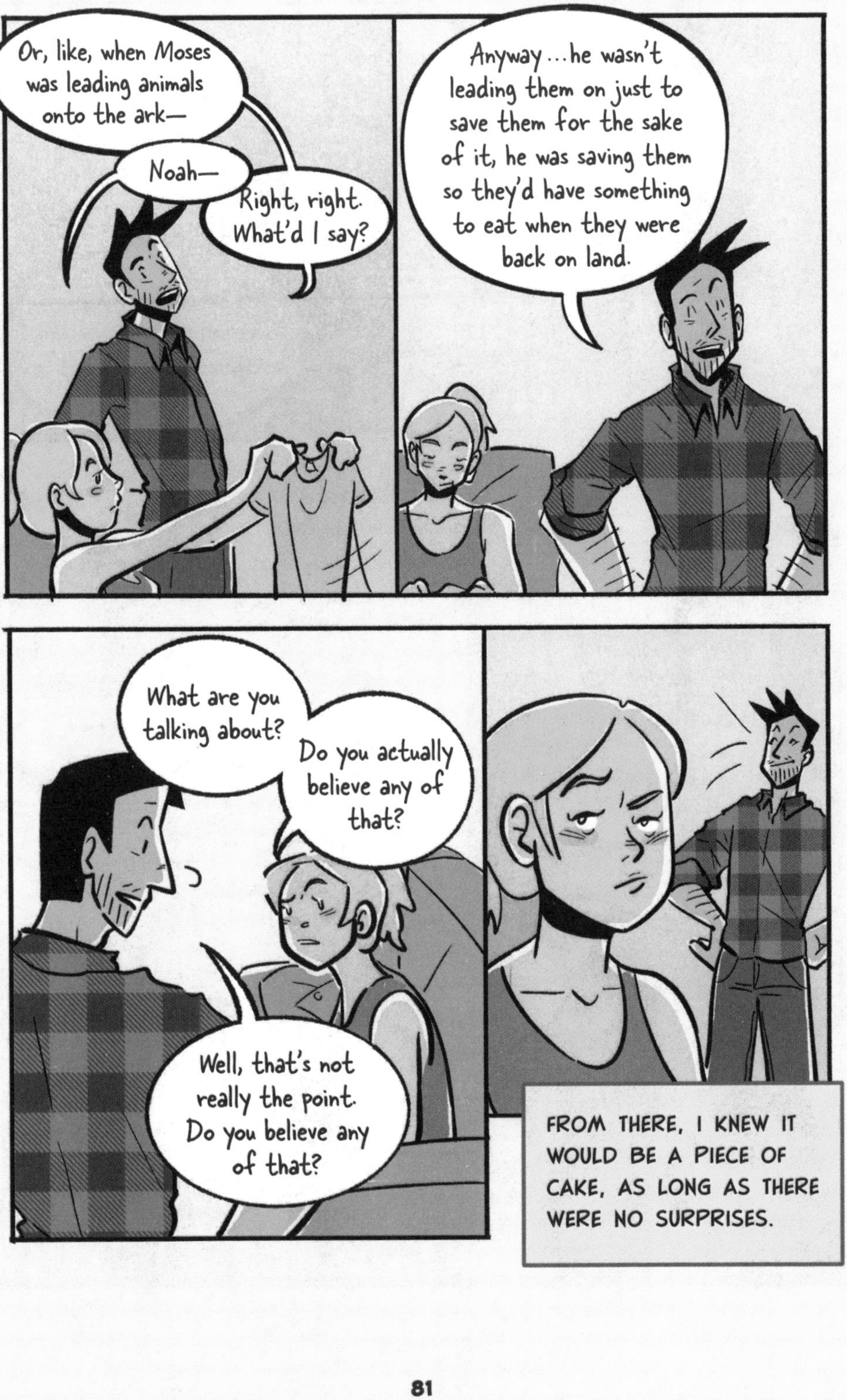

Or, like, when Moses was leading animals onto the ark—
Noah—
Right, right. What'd I say?
Anyway...he wasn't leading them on just to save them for the sake of it, he was saving them so they'd have something to eat when they were back on land.
What are you talking about?
Do you actually believe any of that?
Well, that's not really the point. Do you believe any of that?
FROM THERE, I KNEW IT WOULD BE A PIECE OF CAKE, AS LONG AS THERE WERE NO SURPRISES.

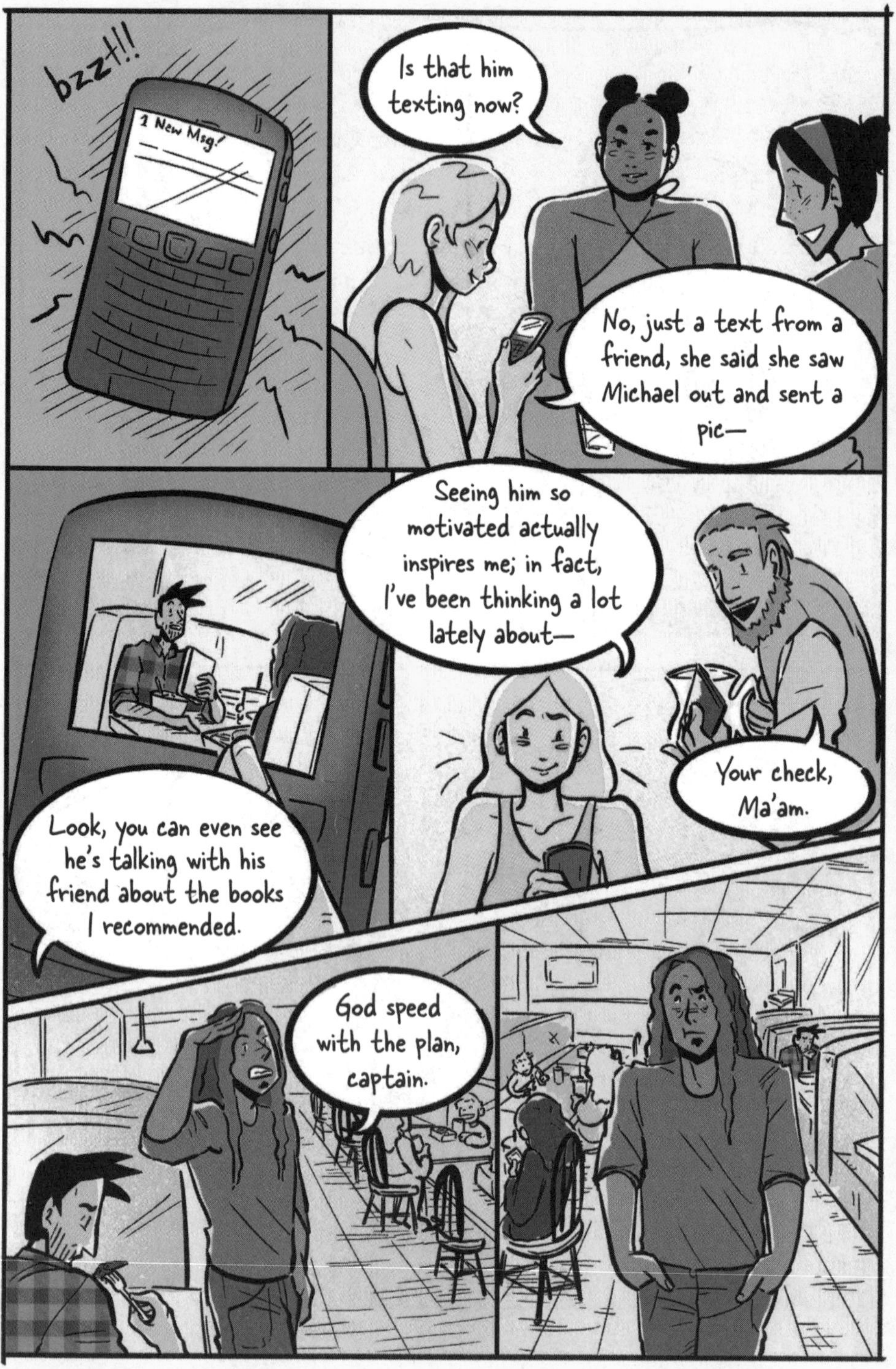
bzzt!!
1 New Msg!
Is that him texting now?
No, just a text from a friend, she said she saw Michael out and sent a pic—
Seeing him so motivated actually inspires me; in fact, I've been thinking a lot lately about—
Your check, Ma'am.
Look, you can even see he's talking with his friend about the books I recommended.
God speed with the plan, captain.

Religion and Animals

Many scholars believe that rituals developed by early hunters were the precursors to organized religion, which is why most major religions have restrictions, rules, ceremonies, or traditions surrounding food and the killing of animals.

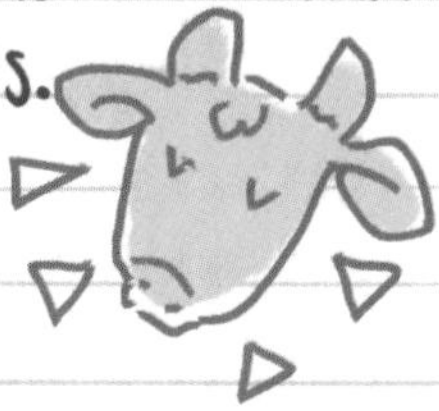

EX.

Hindus - NO meat, fish, eggs (cows are sacred)

Jews - No pig, rabbit, shellfish (Kosher)

Muslims - No pig, and other meat must be killed in a specific way (Halal).

Buddhists - Can eat meat, but only if they did not kill the animal

Christians - No restrictions?

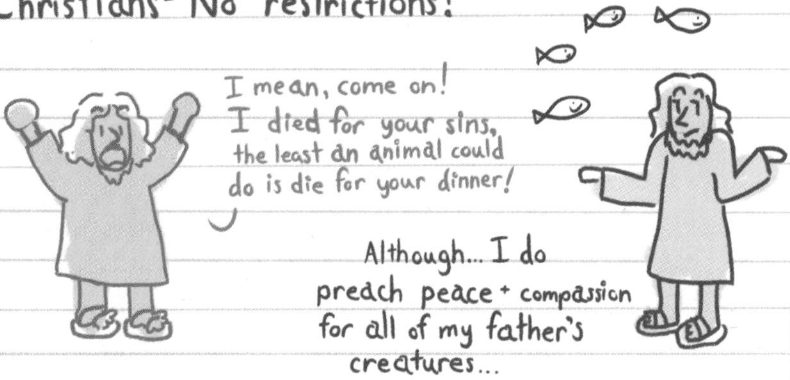

I mean, come on! I died for your sins, the least an animal could do is die for your dinner!
Although... I do preach peace + compassion for all of my father's creatures...

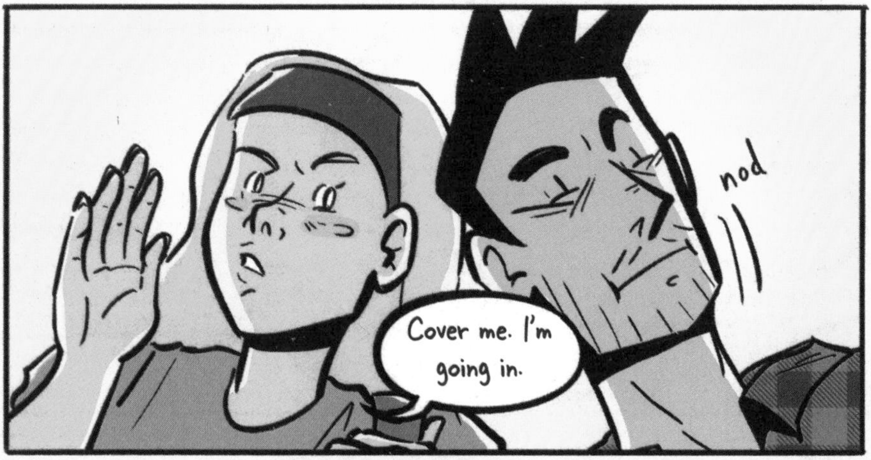
Cover me. I'm going in.
nod

CHAPTER 8

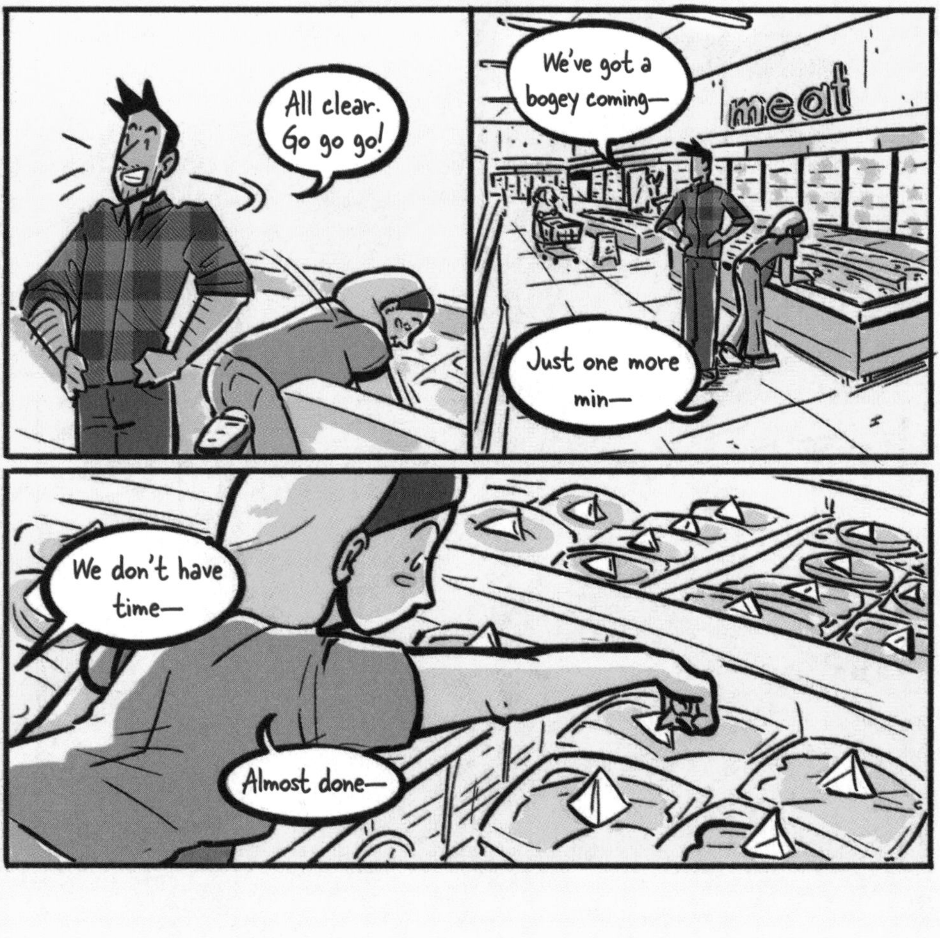
All clear. Go go go!
We've got a bogey coming—
meat
Just one more min—
We don't have time—
Almost done—

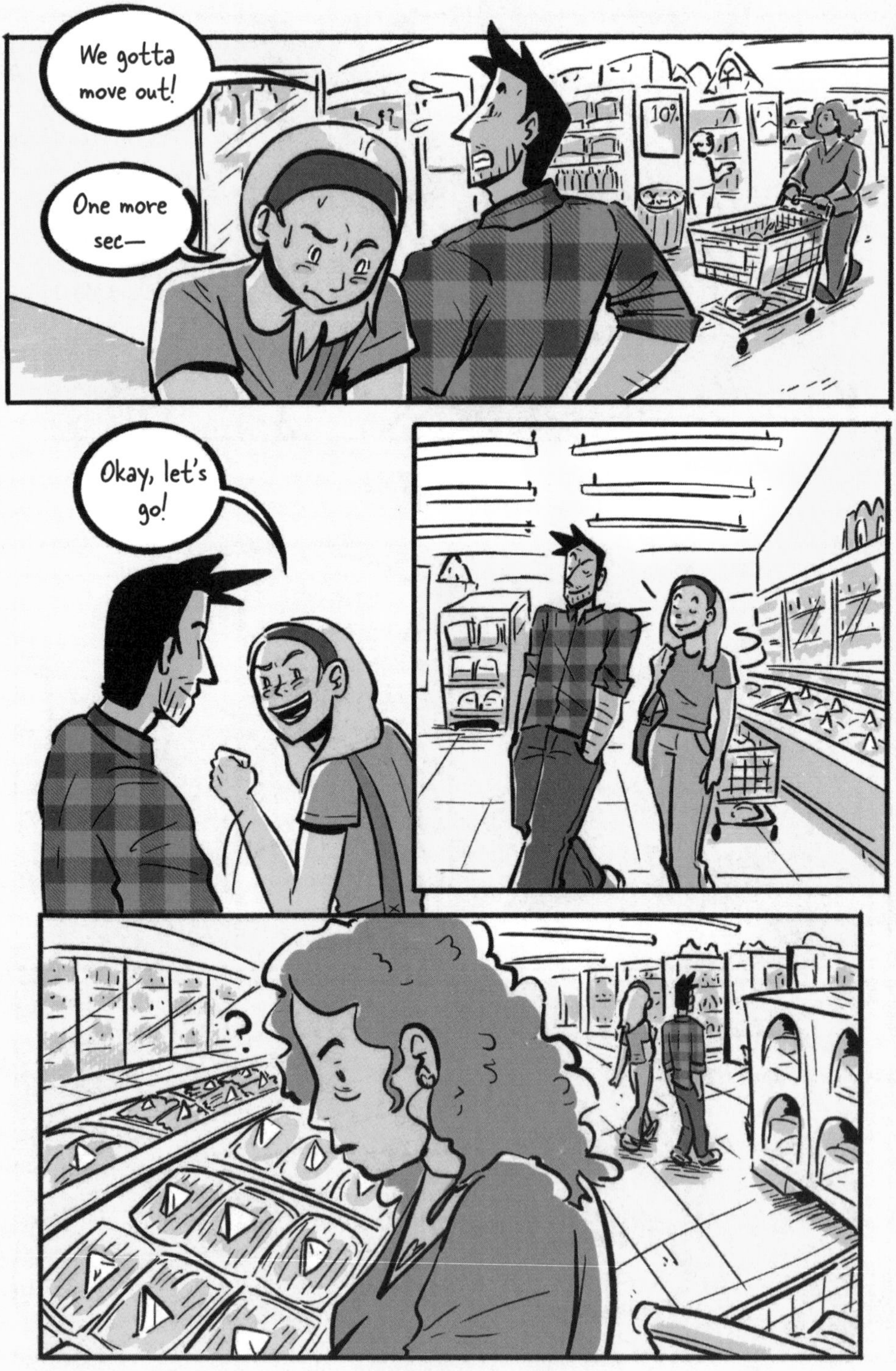
We gotta move out!
One more sec—
10%
Okay, let's go!
?

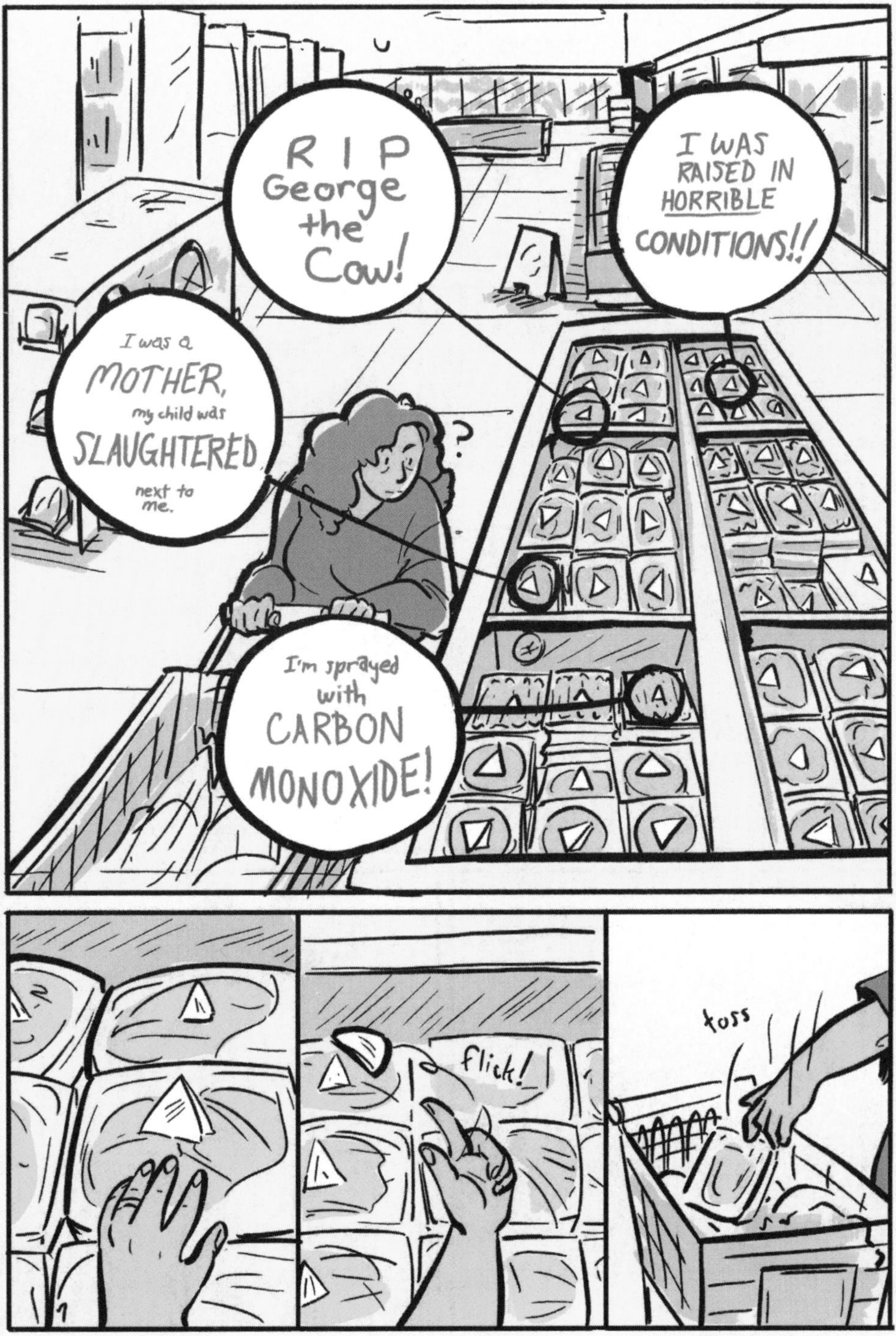

R I P George the Cow!
I WAS RAISED IN HORRIBLE CONDITIONS!!
I was a MOTHER, my child was SLAUGHTERED next to me.
?
I'm sprayed with CARBON MONOXIDE!
flick!
toss

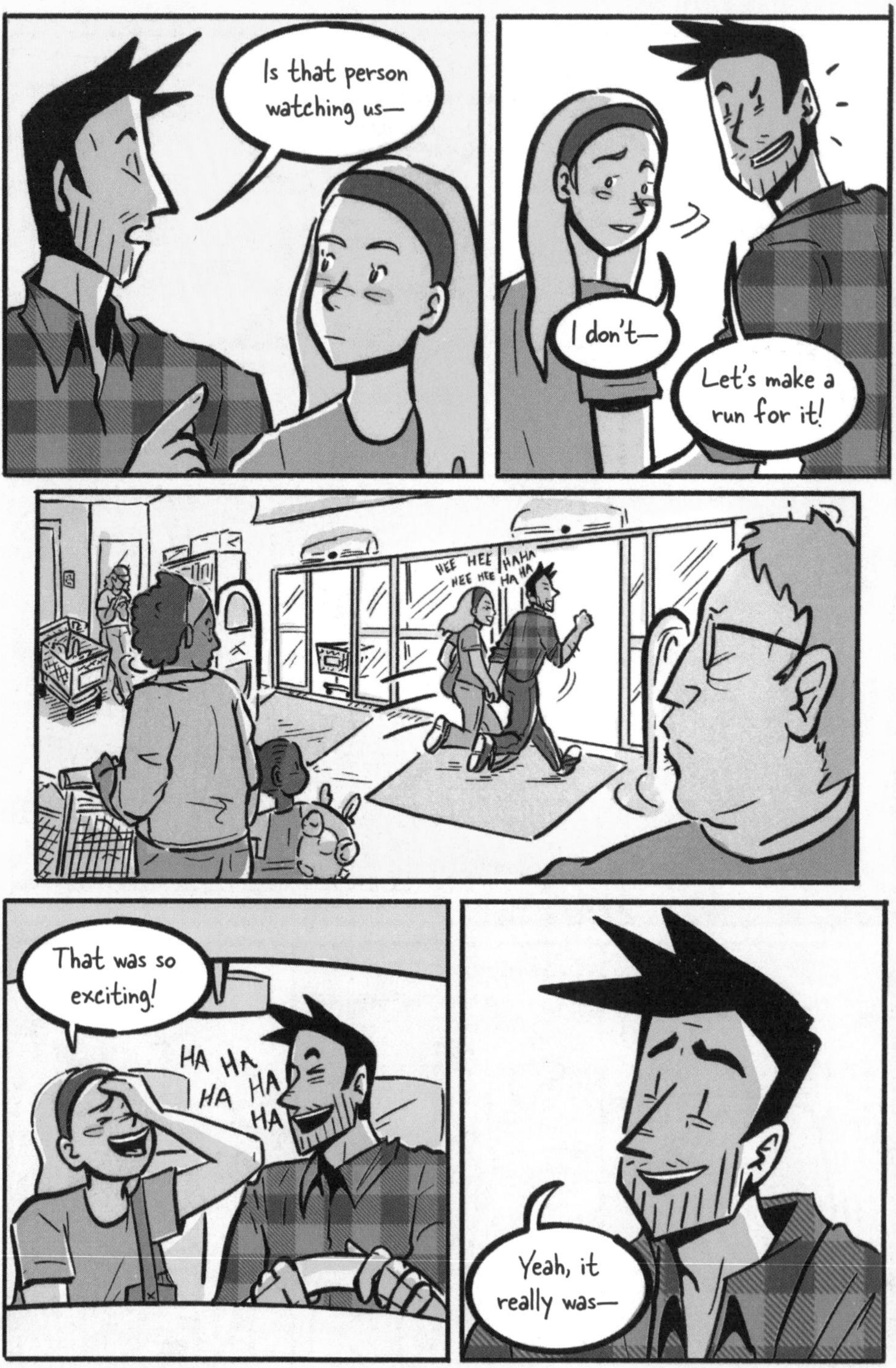
Is that person watching us—
I don't—
Let's make a run for it!
HEE HEE HAHA
HEE HEE HA HA
That was so exciting!
HA HA HA HA HA
Yeah, it really was—

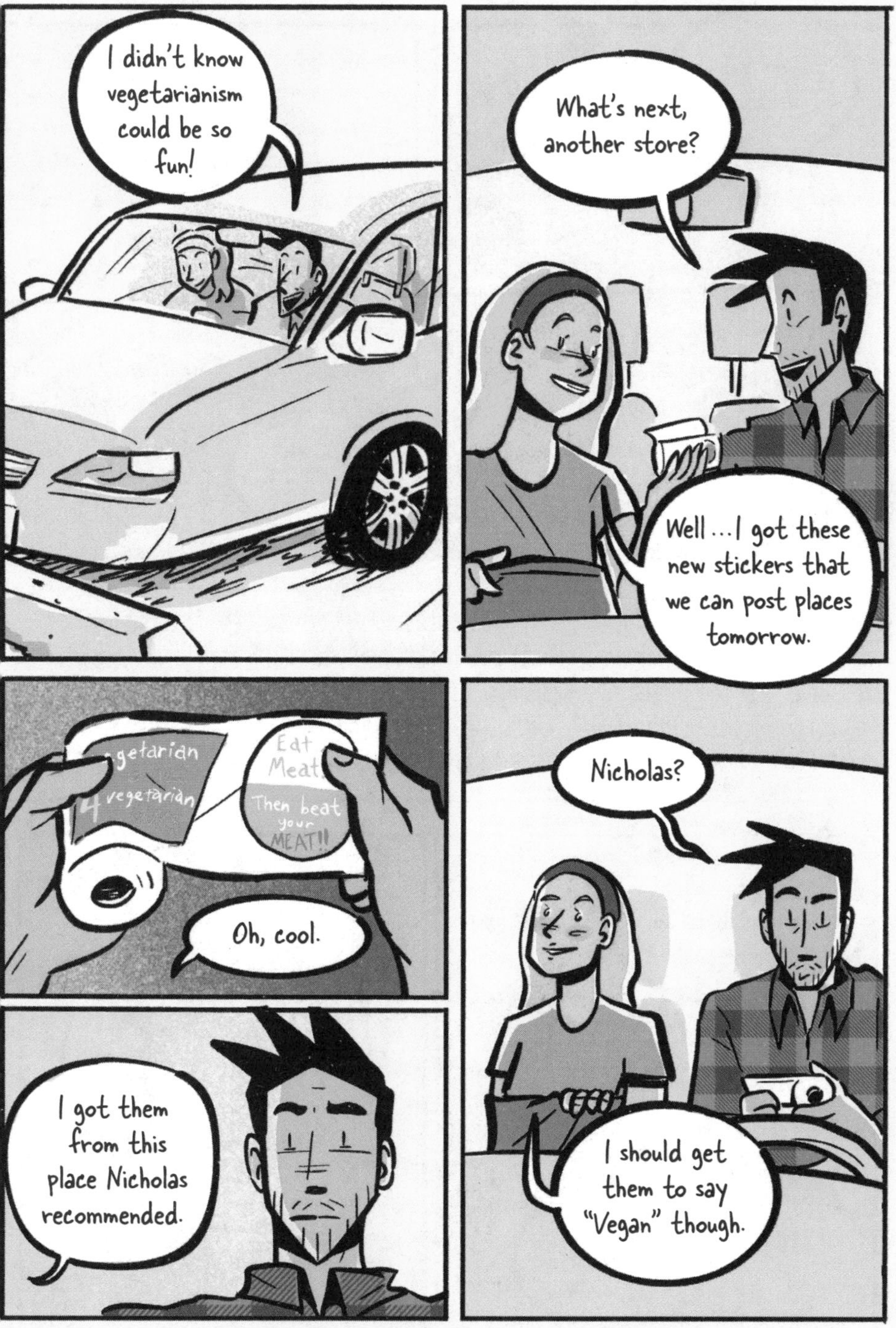

I didn't know vegetarianism could be so fun!
What's next, another store?
Well ... I got these new stickers that we can post places tomorrow.
4 vegetarian
Eat Meat
Then beat your MEAT!!
Oh, cool.
I got them from this place Nicholas recommended.
Nicholas?
I should get them to say "Vegan" though.

Vegan? What do you—
Well, I think I'm going to take the plunge into veganism.
Scratch Scratch
Oh, eh... cool.

VEGANISM: VEGETARIANISM'S HARDCORE YOUNGER SISTER. ALONG WITH NO MEAT, FISH, OR EGGS, IT ADDS NO DAIRY OF ANY KIND. NO MILK, YOGURT, BUTTER, CHEESE, NOTHING. EVEN HONEY IS OFF-LIMITS (BEES ARE ABUSED IN THE CULTIVATING OF IT). SOME PEOPLE ALSO TAKE IT TO MEAN THAT ALONG WITH NOT WEARING LEATHER, WOOL IS OFF-LIMITS TOO.

Seeing your change has just been so inspirational.
This is because of of me?

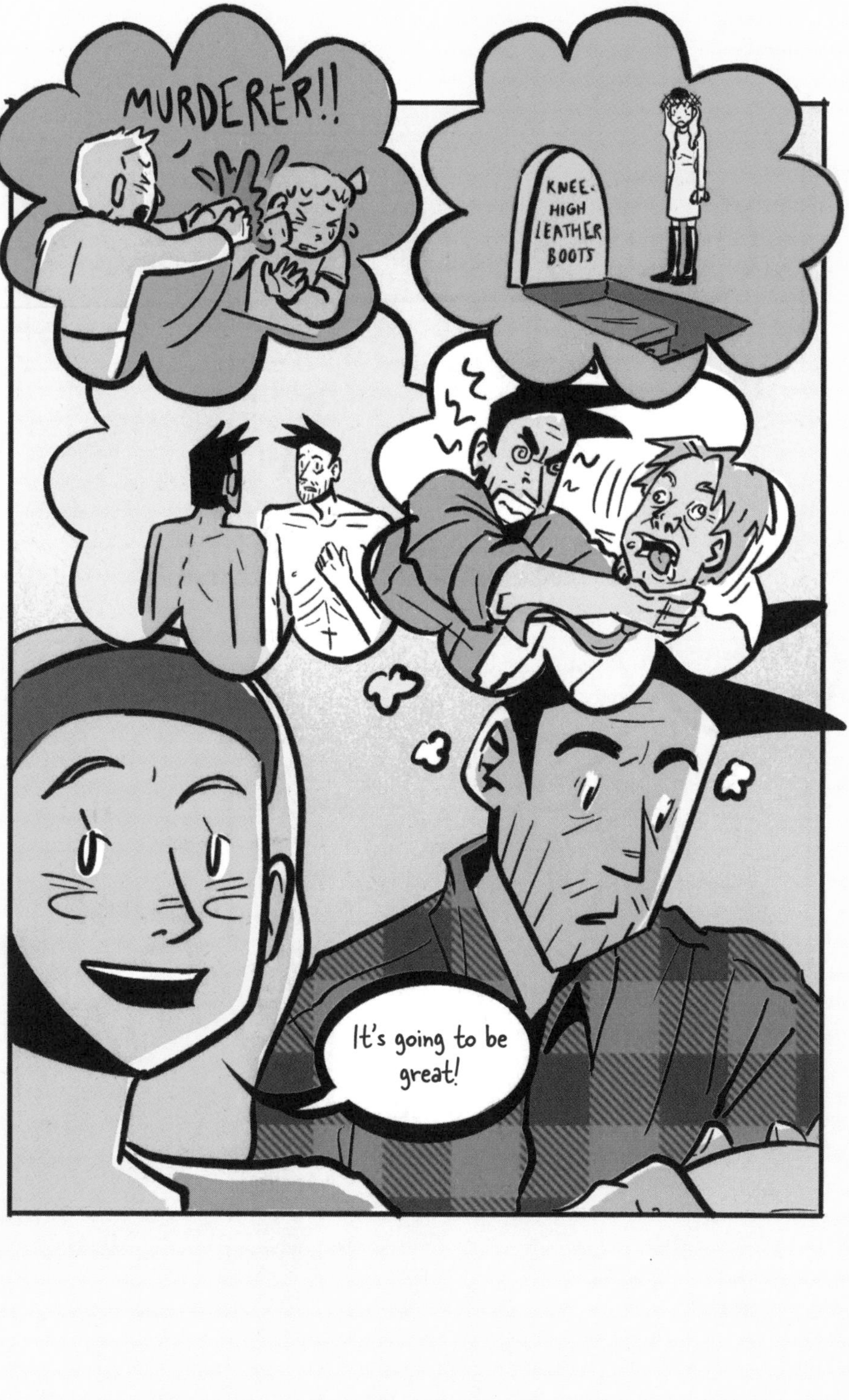
MURDERER!!
KNEE-HIGH LEATHER BOOTS
It's going to be great!

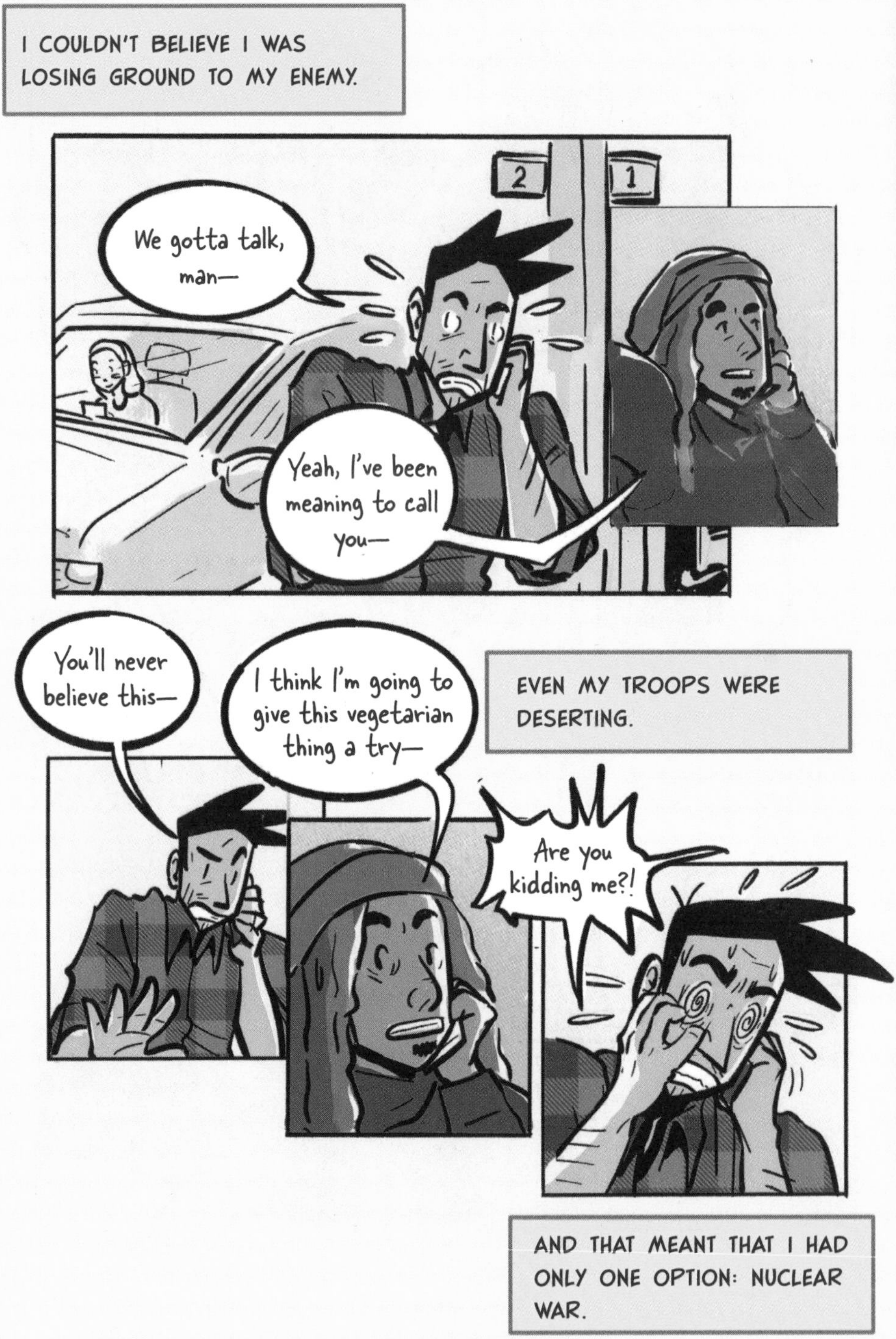
I COULDN'T BELIEVE I WAS LOSING GROUND TO MY ENEMY.
We gotta talk, man—
Yeah, I've been meaning to call you—
You'll never believe this—
I think I'm going to give this vegetarian thing a try—
EVEN MY TROOPS WERE DESERTING.
Are you kidding me?!
AND THAT MEANT THAT I HAD ONLY ONE OPTION: NUCLEAR WAR.

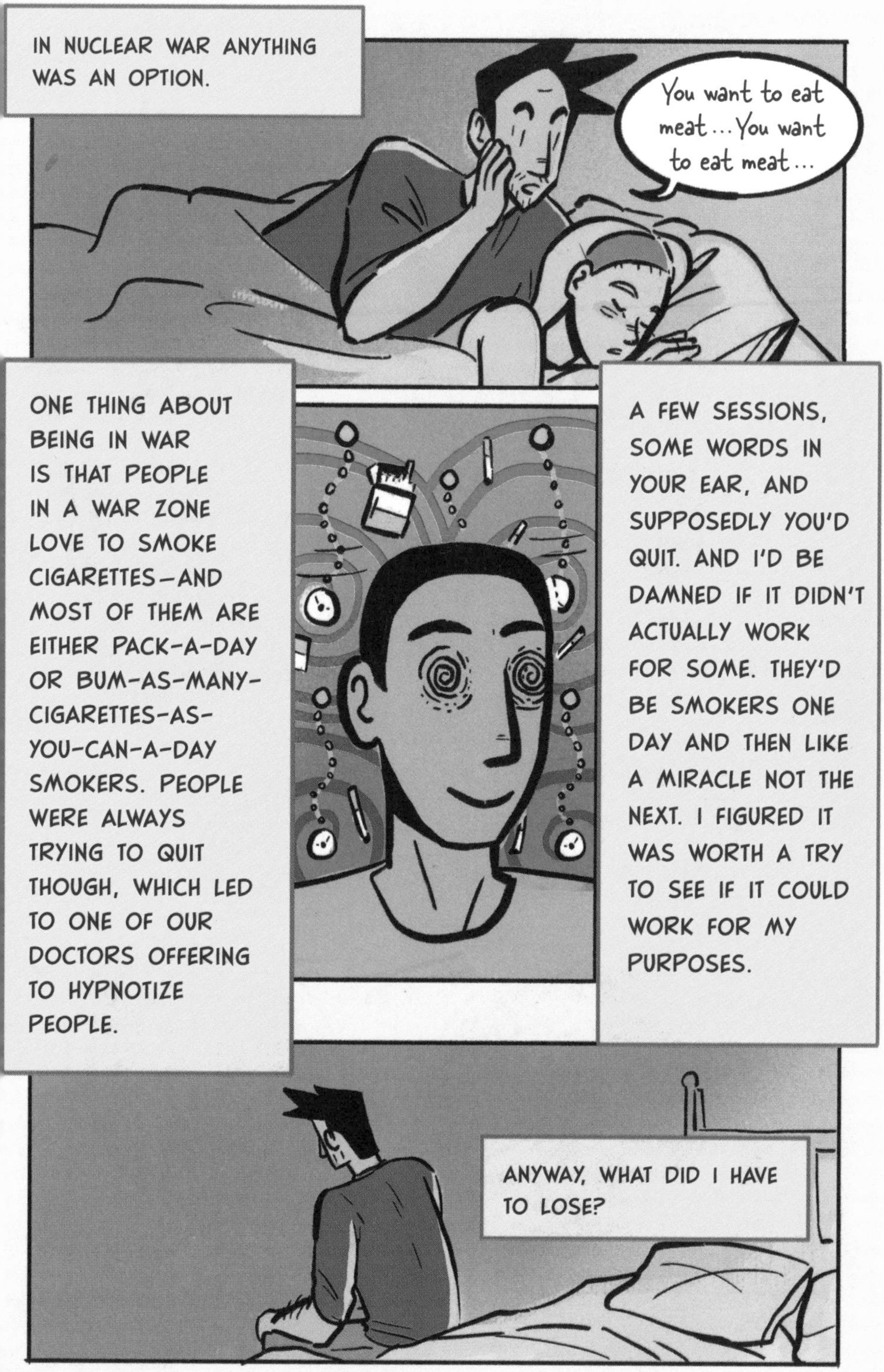
IN NUCLEAR WAR ANYTHING WAS AN OPTION.
You want to eat meat... You want to eat meat...
ONE THING ABOUT BEING IN WAR IS THAT PEOPLE IN A WAR ZONE LOVE TO SMOKE CIGARETTES—AND MOST OF THEM ARE EITHER PACK-A-DAY OR BUM-AS-MANY-CIGARETTES-AS-YOU-CAN-A-DAY SMOKERS. PEOPLE WERE ALWAYS TRYING TO QUIT THOUGH, WHICH LED TO ONE OF OUR DOCTORS OFFERING TO HYPNOTIZE PEOPLE.
A FEW SESSIONS, SOME WORDS IN YOUR EAR, AND SUPPOSEDLY YOU'D QUIT. AND I'D BE DAMNED IF IT DIDN'T ACTUALLY WORK FOR SOME. THEY'D BE SMOKERS ONE DAY AND THEN LIKE A MIRACLE NOT THE NEXT. I FIGURED IT WAS WORTH A TRY TO SEE IF IT COULD WORK FOR MY PURPOSES.
ANYWAY, WHAT DID I HAVE TO LOSE?

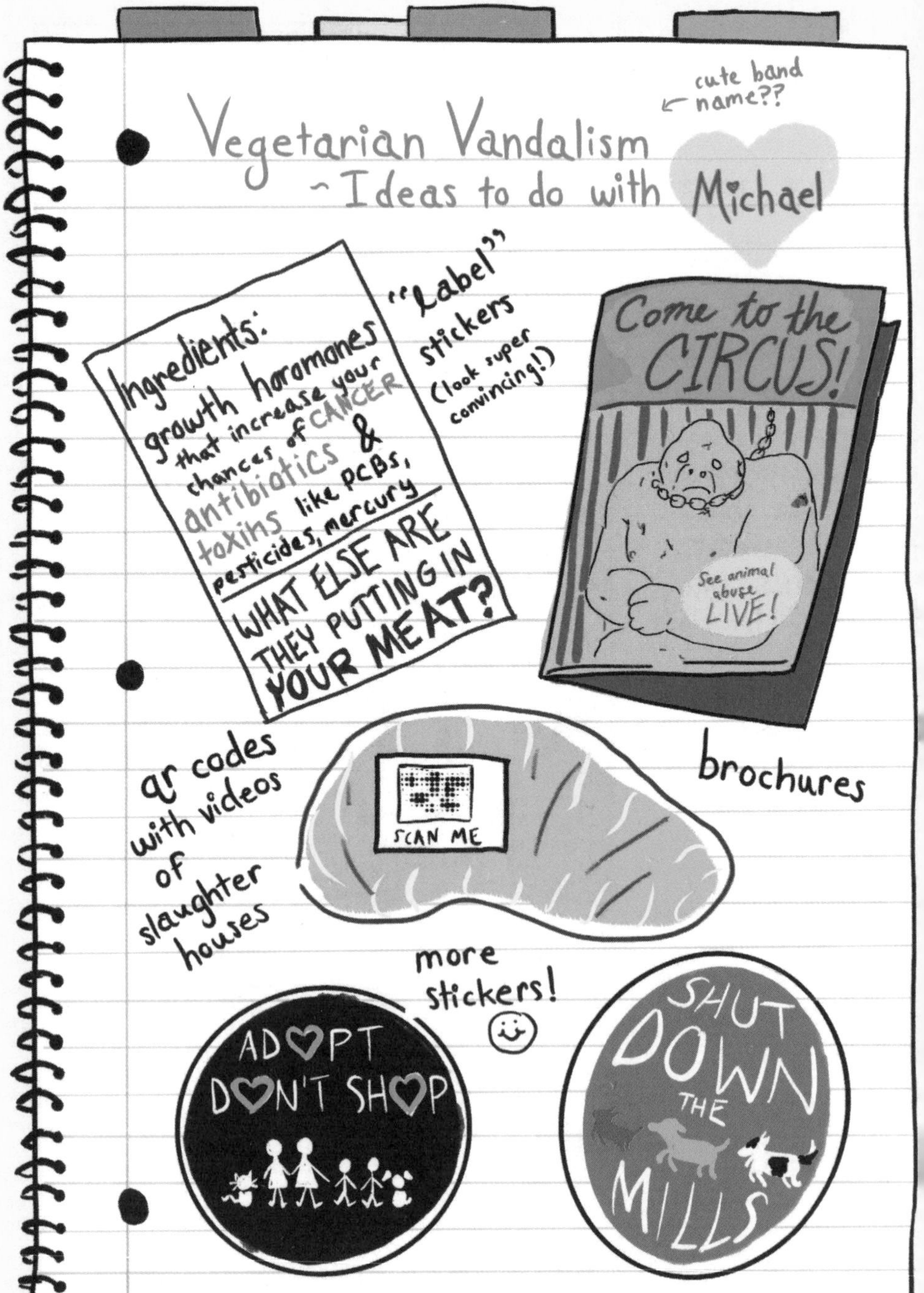

Vegetarian Vandalism
~Ideas to do with Michael
cute band name??
Ingredients:
growth horomones
that increase your chances of CANCER
& antibiotics
toxins like PCBs, pesticides, mercury
WHAT ELSE ARE THEY PUTTING IN YOUR MEAT?
"Label" stickers
(look super convincing!)
Come to the CIRCUS!
See animal abuse LIVE!
brochures
qr codes with videos of slaughter houses
SCAN ME
more stickers!
ADOPT DON'T SHOP
SHUT DOWN THE MILLS

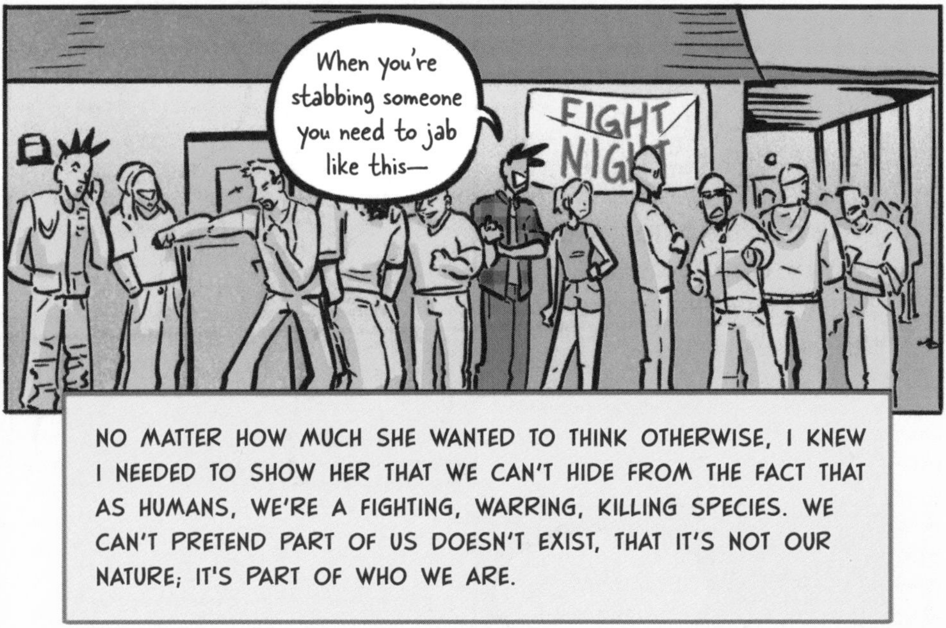

When you're stabbing someone you need to jab like this—
FIGHT NIGHT
NO MATTER HOW MUCH SHE WANTED TO THINK OTHERWISE, I KNEW I NEEDED TO SHOW HER THAT WE CAN'T HIDE FROM THE FACT THAT AS HUMANS, WE'RE A FIGHTING, WARRING, KILLING SPECIES. WE CAN'T PRETEND PART OF US DOESN'T EXIST, THAT IT'S NOT OUR NATURE; IT'S PART OF WHO WE ARE.

CHAPTER 9

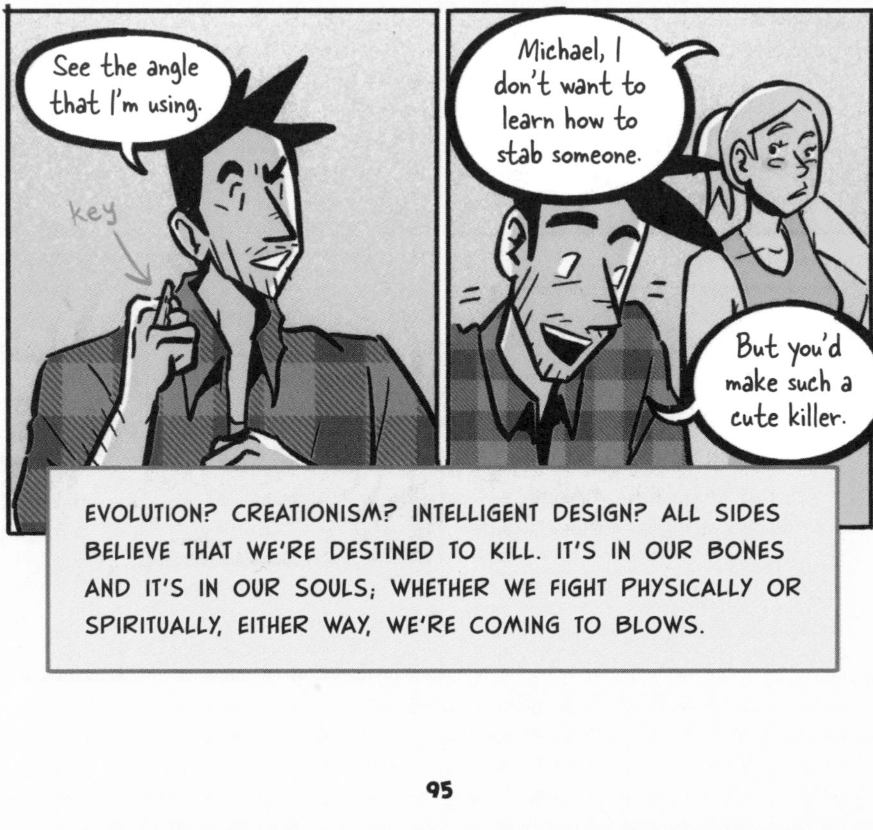

See the angle that I'm using.
key
Michael, I don't want to learn how to stab someone.
But you'd make such a cute killer.
EVOLUTION? CREATIONISM? INTELLIGENT DESIGN? ALL SIDES BELIEVE THAT WE'RE DESTINED TO KILL. IT'S IN OUR BONES AND IT'S IN OUR SOULS; WHETHER WE FIGHT PHYSICALLY OR SPIRITUALLY, EITHER WAY, WE'RE COMING TO BLOWS.

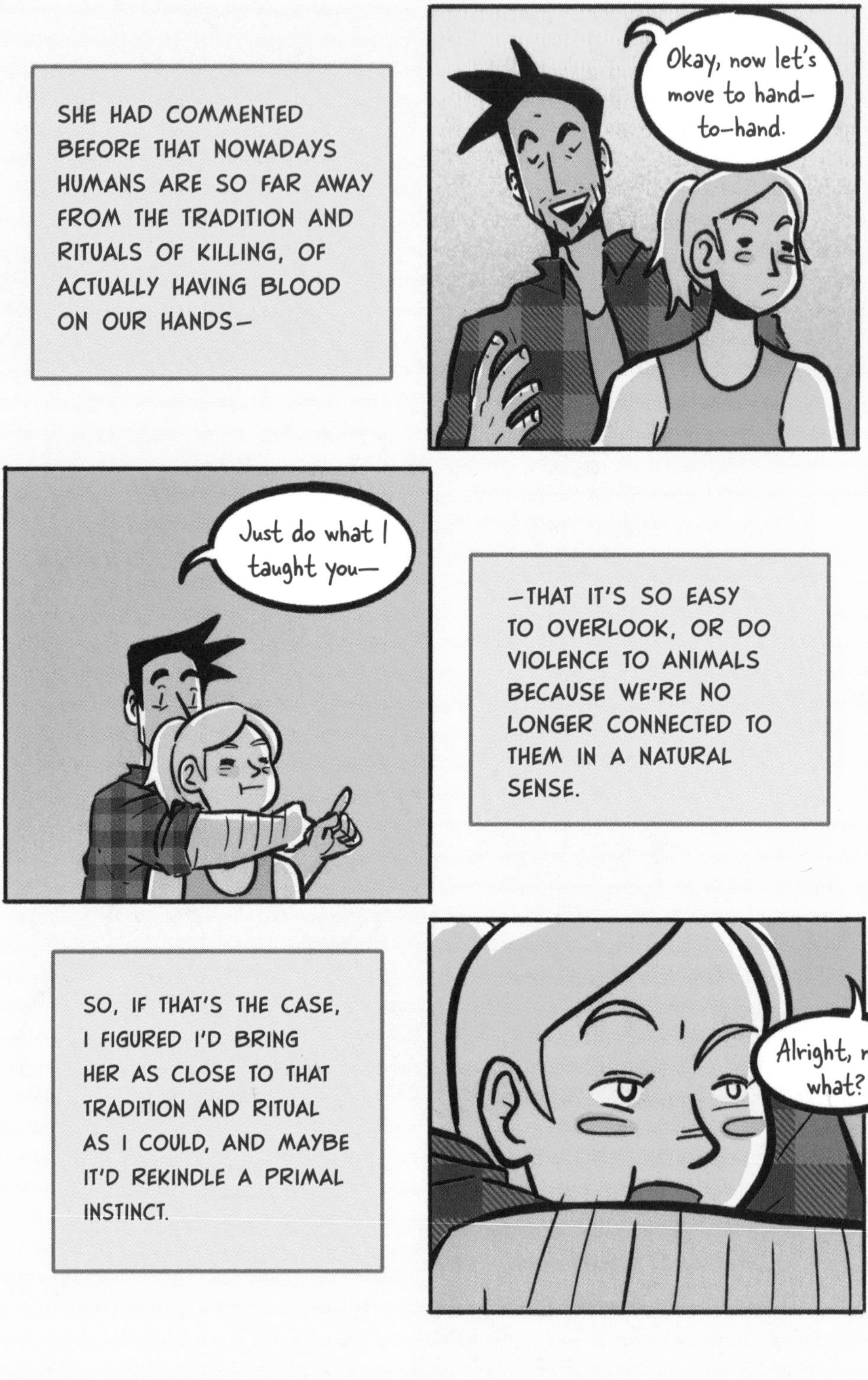
SHE HAD COMMENTED BEFORE THAT NOWADAYS HUMANS ARE SO FAR AWAY FROM THE TRADITION AND RITUALS OF KILLING, OF ACTUALLY HAVING BLOOD ON OUR HANDS—
Okay, now let's move to hand-to-hand.
Just do what I taught you—
—THAT IT'S SO EASY TO OVERLOOK, OR DO VIOLENCE TO ANIMALS BECAUSE WE'RE NO LONGER CONNECTED TO THEM IN A NATURAL SENSE.
SO, IF THAT'S THE CASE, I FIGURED I'D BRING HER AS CLOSE TO THAT TRADITION AND RITUAL AS I COULD, AND MAYBE IT'D REKINDLE A PRIMAL INSTINCT.
Alright, n what?

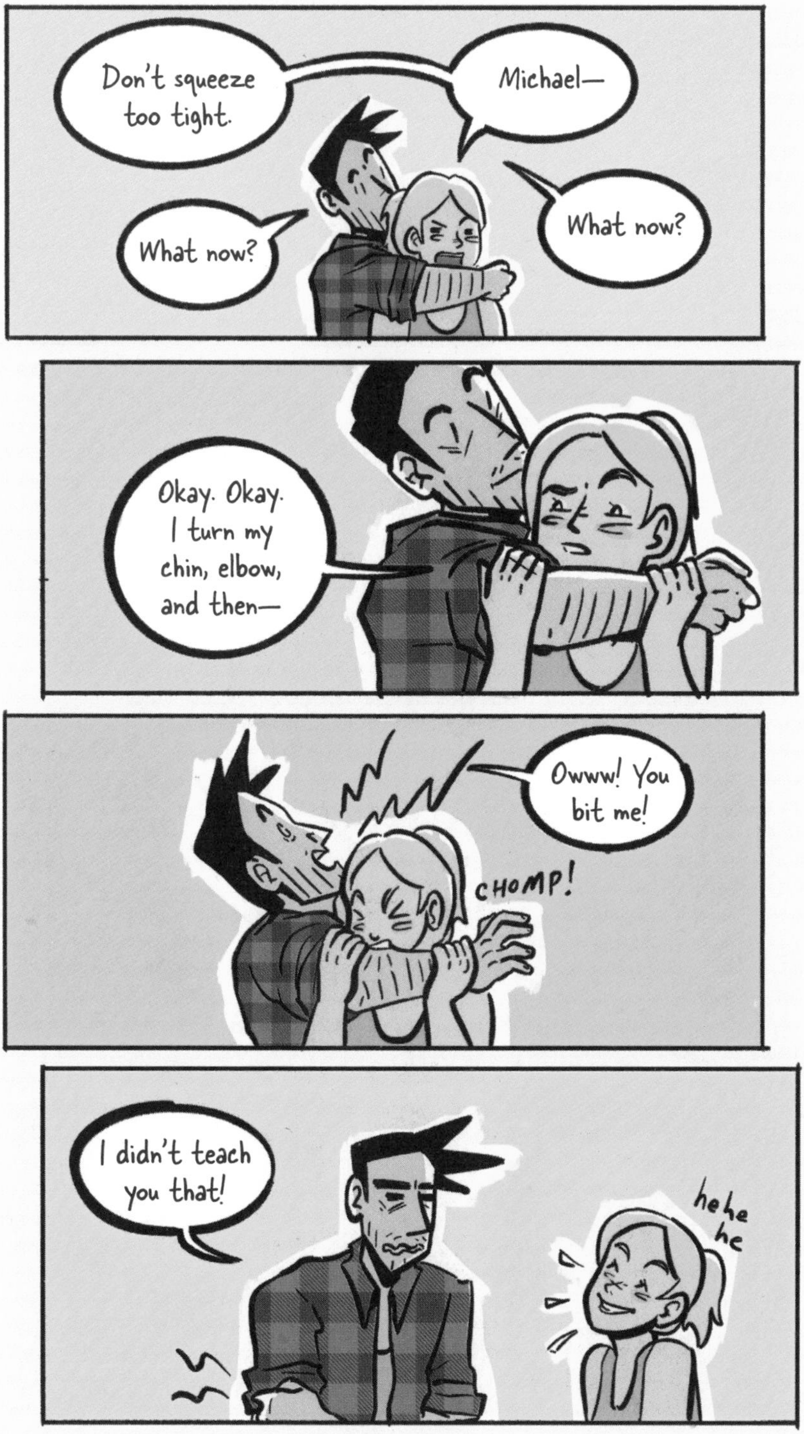
Don't squeeze too tight.
Michael—
What now?
What now?
Okay. Okay. I turn my chin, elbow, and then—
CHOMP!
Owww! You bit me!
I didn't teach you that!
hehe he

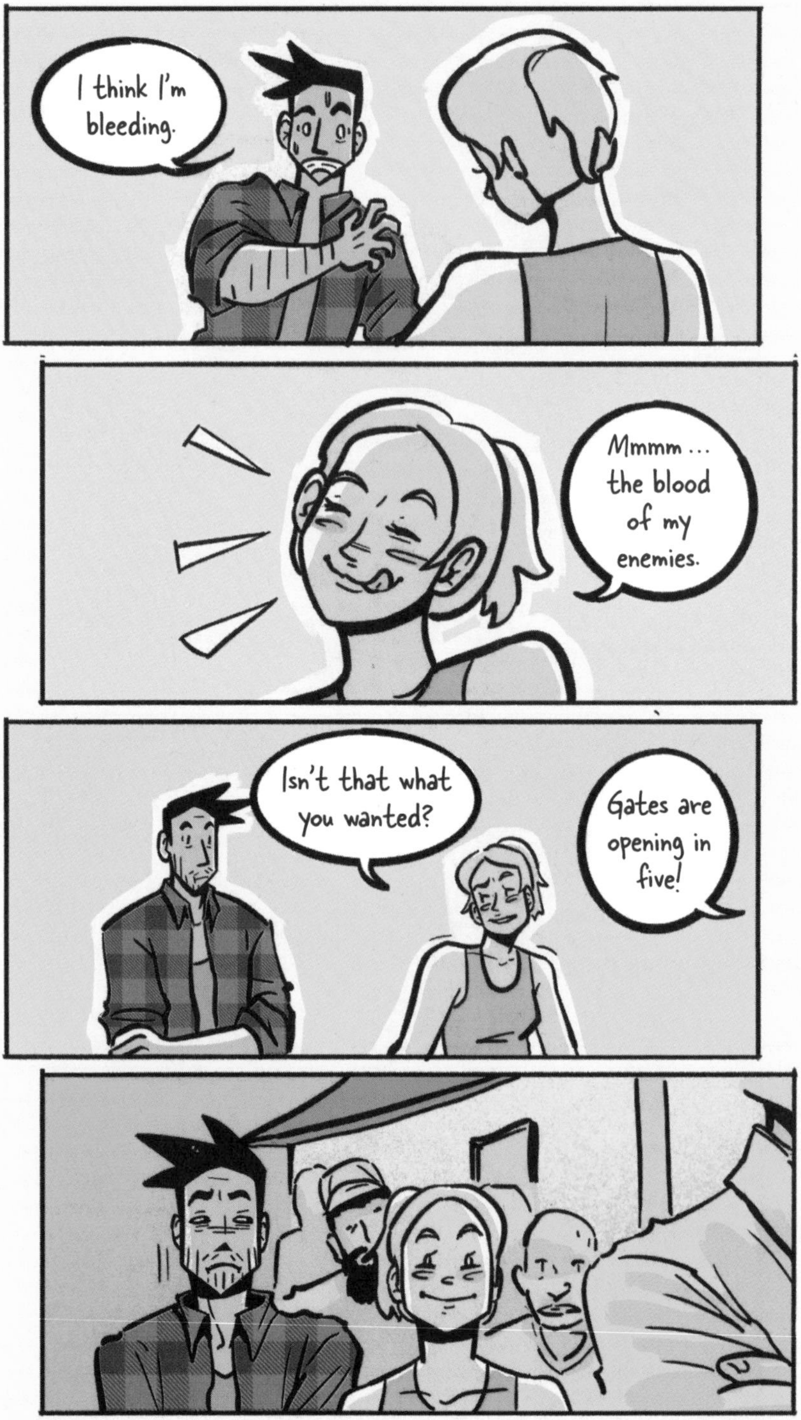
I think I'm bleeding.
Mmmm... the blood of my enemies.
Isn't that what you wanted?
Gates are opening in five!

NOW SERVING VEGGIE BURGERS
Hey, look at that!
I'll get us some burgers and drinks. Why don't you grab the seats—
?

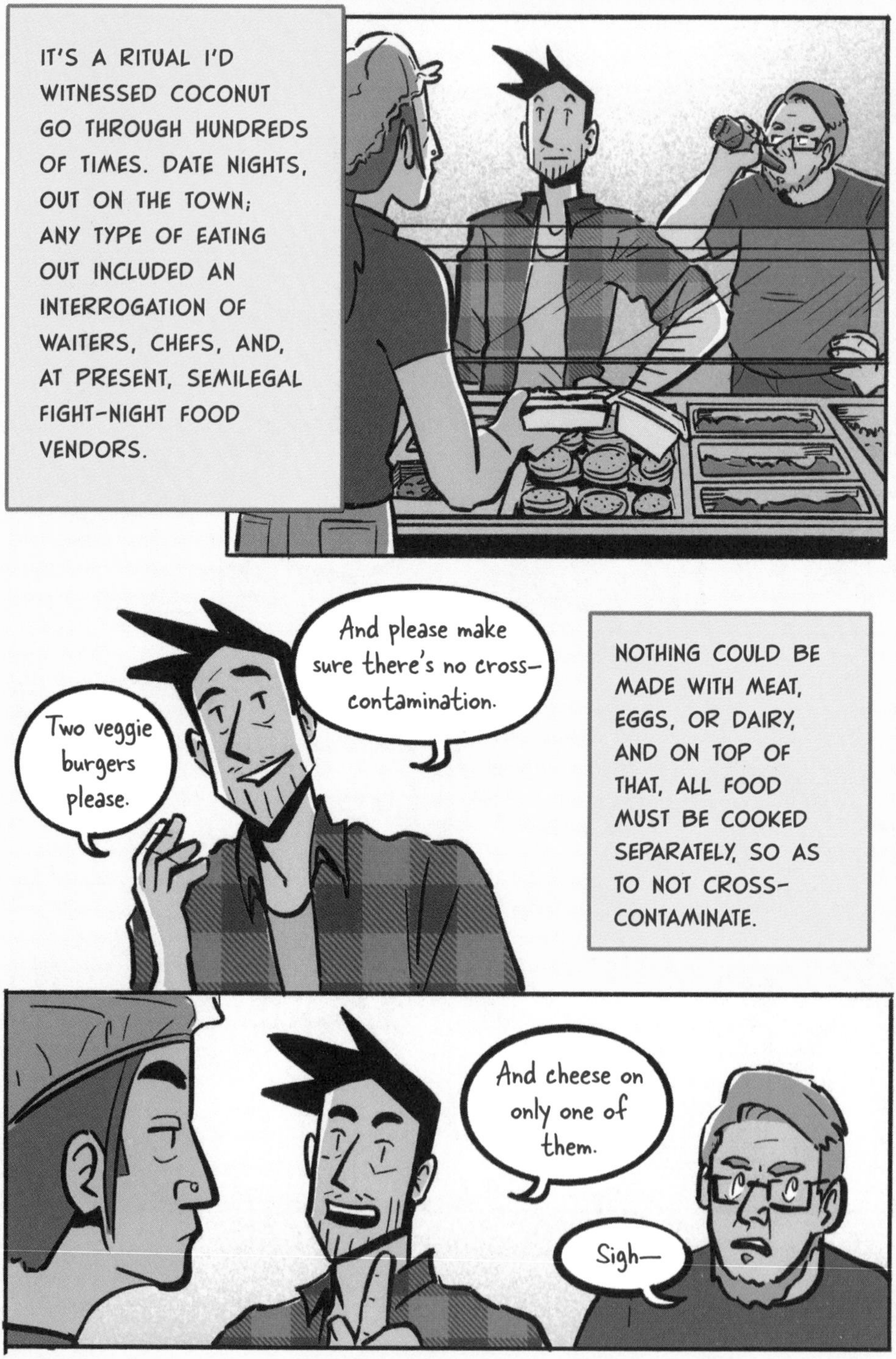
IT'S A RITUAL I'D WITNESSED COCONUT GO THROUGH HUNDREDS OF TIMES. DATE NIGHTS, OUT ON THE TOWN; ANY TYPE OF EATING OUT INCLUDED AN INTERROGATION OF WAITERS, CHEFS, AND, AT PRESENT, SEMILEGAL FIGHT-NIGHT FOOD VENDORS.
Two veggie burgers please.
And please make sure there's no cross-contamination.
NOTHING COULD BE MADE WITH MEAT, EGGS, OR DAIRY, AND ON TOP OF THAT, ALL FOOD MUST BE COOKED SEPARATELY, SO AS TO NOT CROSS-CONTAMINATE.
And cheese on only one of them.
Sigh—

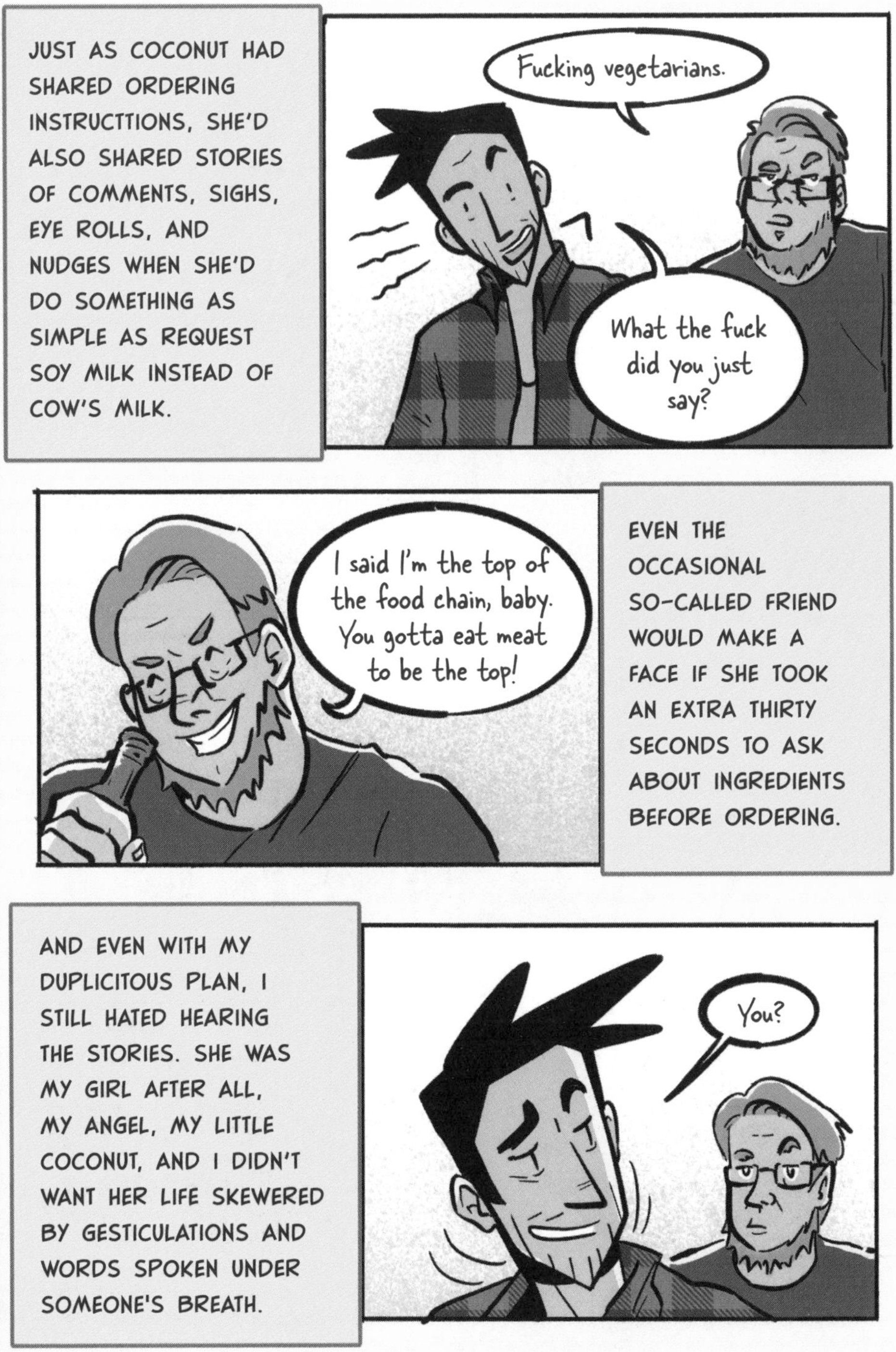
JUST AS COCONUT HAD SHARED ORDERING INSTRUCTTIONS, SHE'D ALSO SHARED STORIES OF COMMENTS, SIGHS, EYE ROLLS, AND NUDGES WHEN SHE'D DO SOMETHING AS SIMPLE AS REQUEST SOY MILK INSTEAD OF COW'S MILK.
Fucking vegetarians.
What the fuck did you just say?
I said I'm the top of the food chain, baby. You gotta eat meat to be the top!
EVEN THE OCCASIONAL SO-CALLED FRIEND WOULD MAKE A FACE IF SHE TOOK AN EXTRA THIRTY SECONDS TO ASK ABOUT INGREDIENTS BEFORE ORDERING.
AND EVEN WITH MY DUPLICITOUS PLAN, I STILL HATED HEARING THE STORIES. SHE WAS MY GIRL AFTER ALL, MY ANGEL, MY LITTLE COCONUT, AND I DIDN'T WANT HER LIFE SKEWERED BY GESTICULATIONS AND WORDS SPOKEN UNDER SOMEONE'S BREATH.
You?

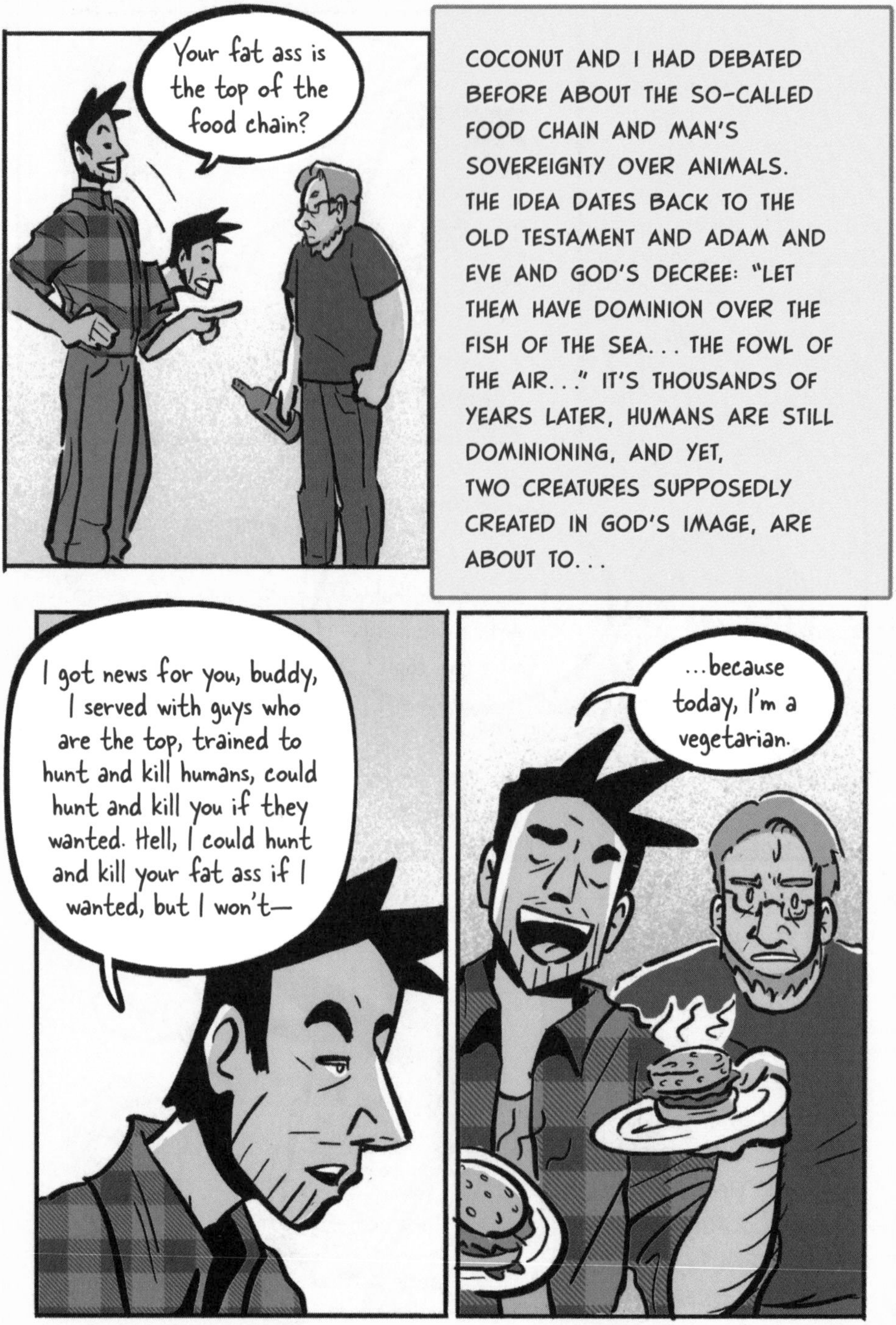
Your fat ass is the top of the food chain?
COCONUT AND I HAD DEBATED BEFORE ABOUT THE SO-CALLED FOOD CHAIN AND MAN'S SOVEREIGNTY OVER ANIMALS. THE IDEA DATES BACK TO THE OLD TESTAMENT AND ADAM AND EVE AND GOD'S DECREE: "LET THEM HAVE DOMINION OVER THE FISH OF THE SEA. . . THE FOWL OF THE AIR. . ." IT'S THOUSANDS OF YEARS LATER, HUMANS ARE STILL DOMINIONING, AND YET, TWO CREATURES SUPPOSEDLY CREATED IN GOD'S IMAGE, ARE ABOUT TO. . .
I got news for you, buddy, I served with guys who are the top, trained to hunt and kill humans, could hunt and kill you if they wanted. Hell, I could hunt and kill your fat ass if I wanted, but I won't—
...because today, I'm a vegetarian.

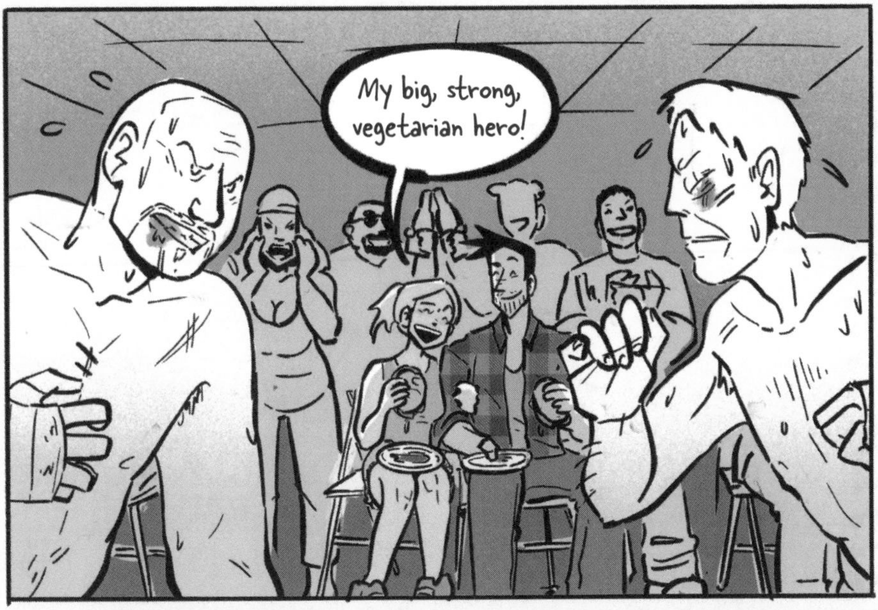
My big, strong, vegetarian hero!

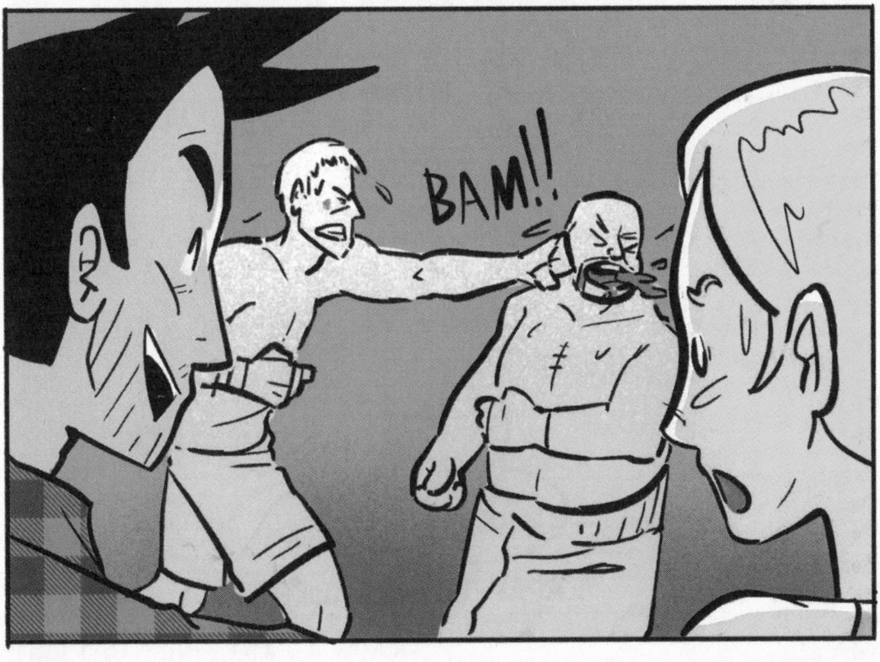
BAM!!

CLOSE QUARTERS COMBAT TO TEACH COCONUT

ELBOW AND KNEES INSTEAD OF FISTS AND KICKS - MORE LETHAL AT CLOSE RANGE

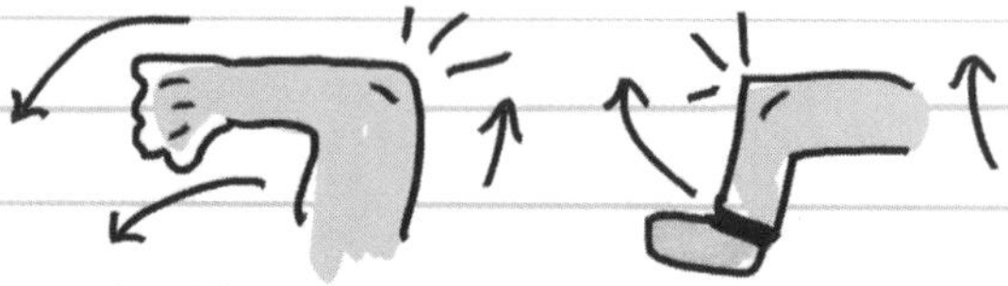

IF A GUY GRABS YOU FROM BEHIND? GRAB. TWIST. PULL! GRAB THE GUY'S JUNK AND PULL IT OFF HIS BODY.

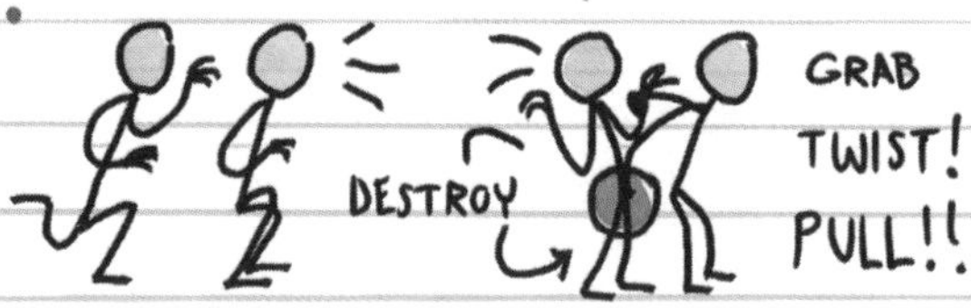
DESTROY
GRAB
TWIST!
PULL!!

COMPRESS CAROTID ARTERIES AND JUGULAR VEINS. STOP BLOOD FLOW TO THE BRAIN AND IN TEN SECONDS YOU'LL KNOCK SOMEONE OUT. THIRTY SECONDS YOU'LL KILL THEM.

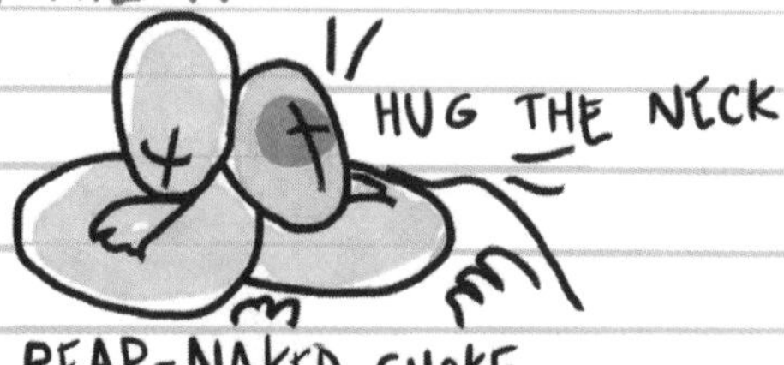
HUG THE NECK

REAR-NAKED CHOKE

TRAIN TO KILL. NOT TO FIGHT.

THE THING WAS, NOTHING WAS WORKING, NOT EVEN MY NUCLEAR OPTIONS, WHICH MEANT I HAD TO LOOK ELSEWHERE.

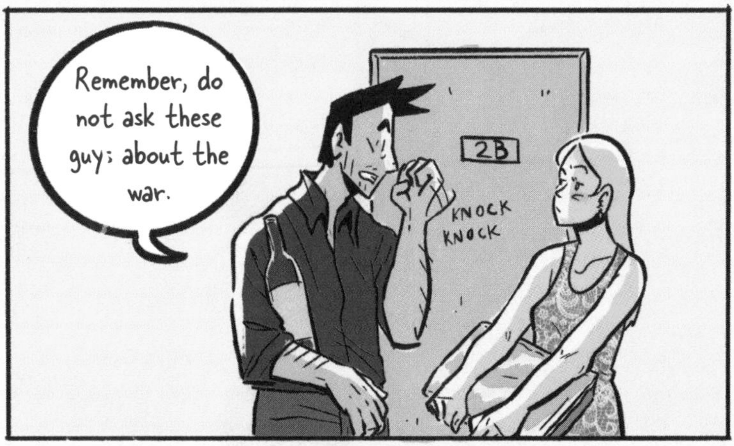
Remember, do not ask these guys about the war.
2B
KNOCK KNOCK

CHAPTER 10

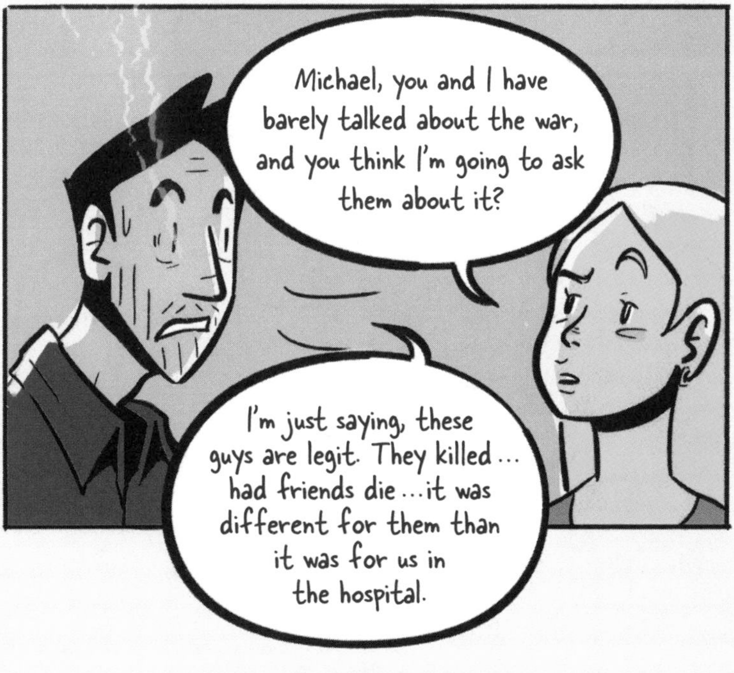
Michael, you and I have barely talked about the war, and you think I'm going to ask them about it?
I'm just saying, these guys are legit. They killed... had friends die... it was different for them than it was for us in the hospital.

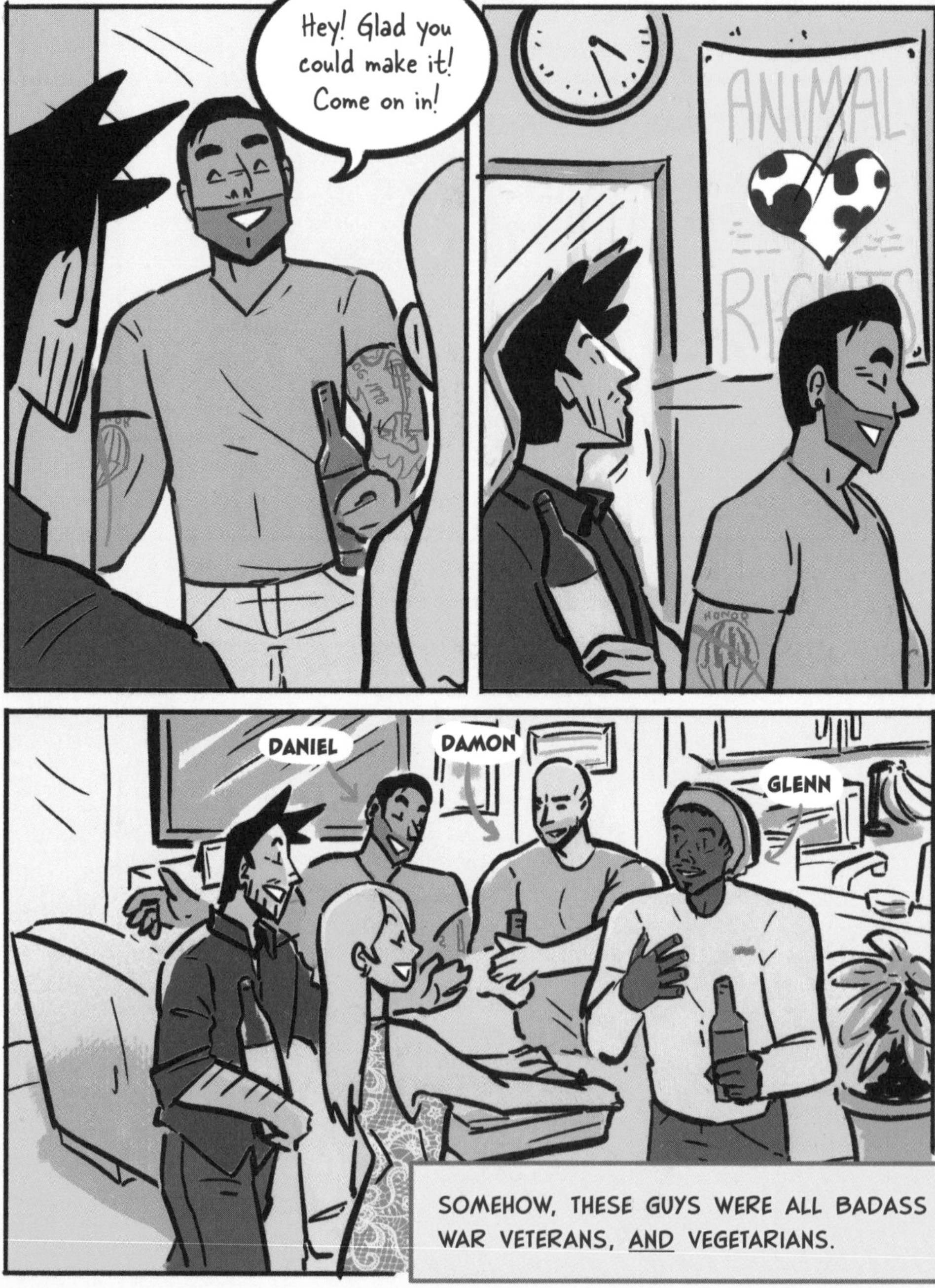
Hey! Glad you could make it! Come on in!
ANIMAL RIGHTS
DANIEL
DAMON
GLENN
SOMEHOW, THESE GUYS WERE ALL BADASS WAR VETERANS, AND VEGETARIANS.

I'D MET PLENTY OF SOLDIERS WHO CLAIMED TO BE VEGETARIAN OR EVEN VEGAN, BUT IN THOSE CASES, IT WAS OUT OF CONVENIENCE RATHER THAN CONVICTION. IN THE FIELD, ALL WE HAD TO EAT WERE MRE'S (MEALS READY TO EAT), WHICH CONSISTED OF PLASTIC-WRAPPED FOOD THAT CAN SIT ON A SHELF FOR YEARS AND STILL BE "EDIBLE." OFTEN YOU DON'T HAVE TIME TO COOK OR EVEN HEAT THE FOOD, AND YOU END UP EATING IT OUT OF THE SAME METAL CANISTER THAT YOU USED EARLIER THAT MORNING TO SHAVE.

THE ONLY DECENT MRE'S, WHICH COULD MAKE YOU FORGET FOR EVEN A MOMENT THAT YOU WERE EATING BOTTOM OF THE BARREL, WERE THE VEGETARIAN ONES, THE PASTAS AND LASAGNAS AND MACARONI AND CHEESES. IT WAS WHY EVERY NOW AND AGAIN YOU'D SEE SOME GUY CLAIMING TO NOT EAT MEAT FOR RELIGIOUS REASONS, JUST SO HE COULD GET A DECENT MEAL RATHER THAN ANOTHER BAG OF MEATLOAF AND MUSHROOMS. BUT THAT WASN'T THESE GUYS, THEY WERE THE REAL DEAL.

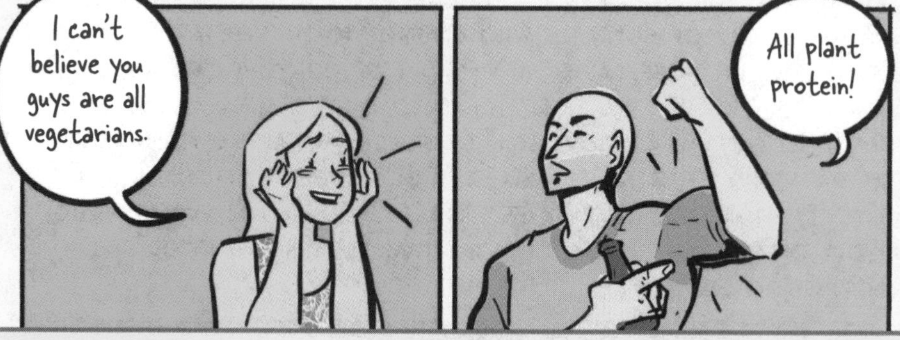
I can't believe you guys are all vegetarians.
All plant protein!

I WOULDN'T BELIEVE IT MYSELF IF THEY WEREN'T RIGHT IN FRONT OF ME. TOUGH GUYS. WAR VETS. GUYS WHO HAD TRAINED TO HUNT AND KILL PEOPLE. AND THEN . . . ACTUALLY KILLED THEM. THESE ULTIMATE HUNTERS OF PEOPLE WERE ABSTAINING FROM MEAT, TO AVOID KILLING ANYTHING ANYMORE, EVEN ANIMALS.

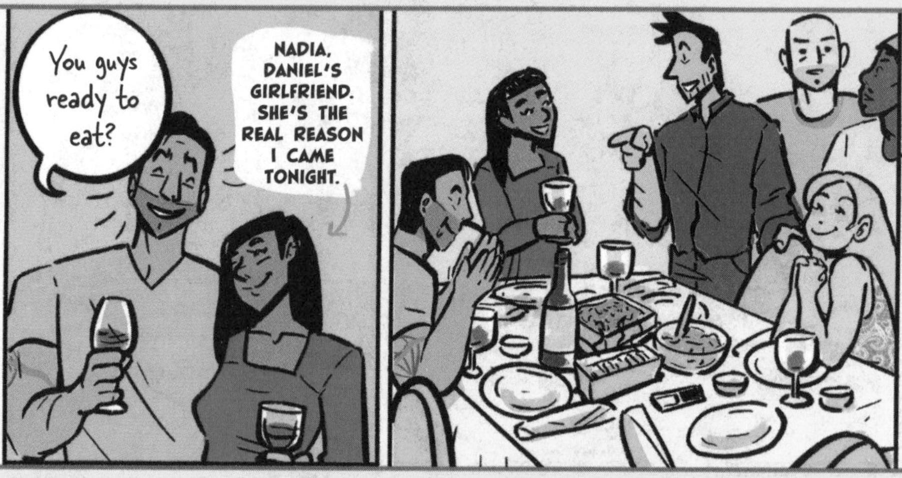
You guys ready to eat?
NADIA, DANIEL'S GIRLFRIEND. SHE'S THE REAL REASON I CAME TONIGHT.

DANIEL AND I HAD MET WEEKS EARLIER AT AN EVENT FOR HOMELESS VETERANS. WE'D HIT IT OFF BY BITCHING ABOUT THE BRASS IN THE MILITARY AND HOW AWFUL THEY WERE. AND WHEN I LEARNED THAT NOT ONLY WAS HE A VEGETARIAN, AND FRIENDS THAT HE SERVED WITH WERE TOO, BUT THAT HIS GIRLFRIEND WAS A MEAT EATER, AND THEY'D BEEN TOGETHER FOR FOUR YEARS WITH NO ISSUES, I KNEW I HAD TO SCOPE OUT HIS SCENE.

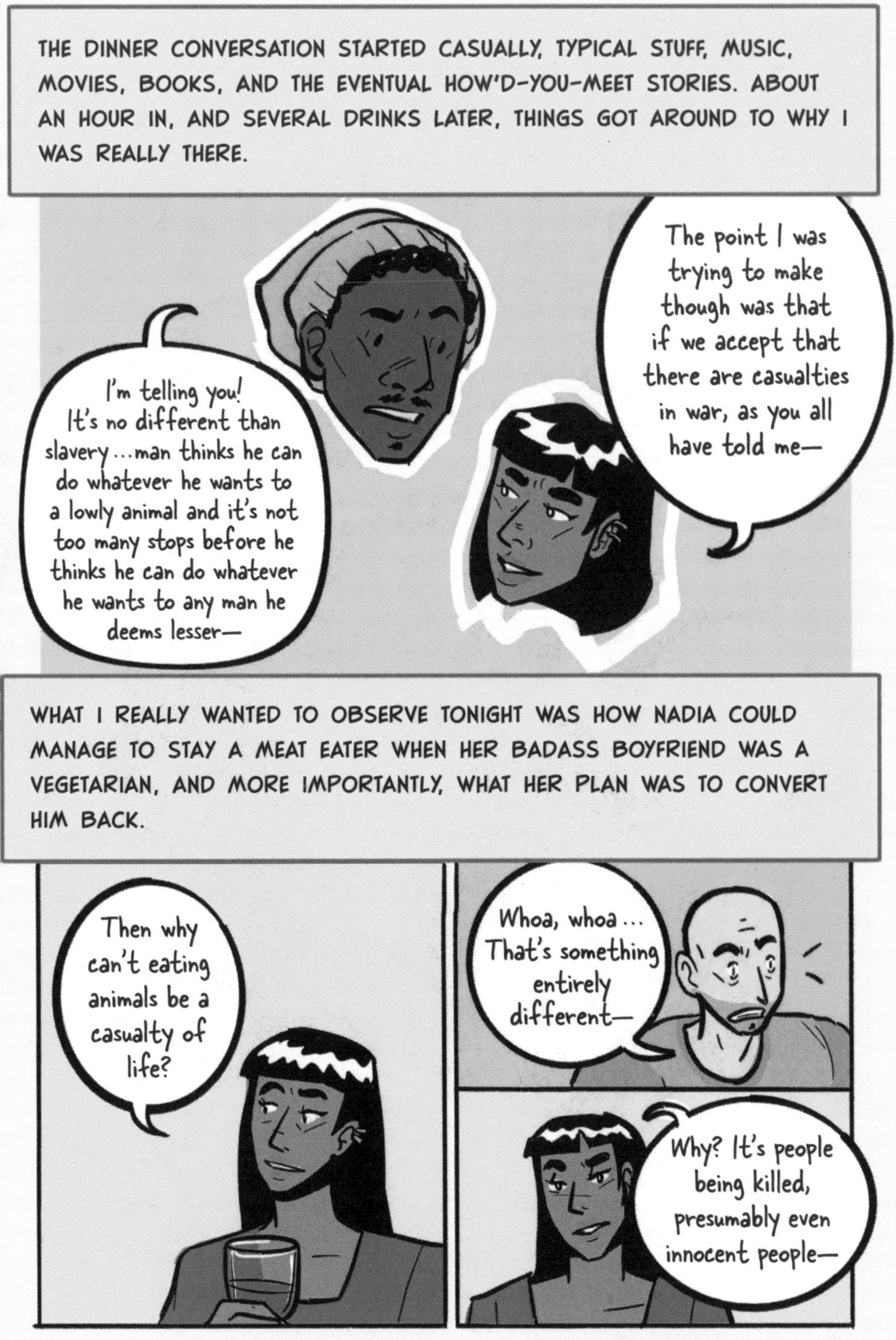
THE DINNER CONVERSATION STARTED CASUALLY, TYPICAL STUFF, MUSIC, MOVIES, BOOKS, AND THE EVENTUAL HOW'D-YOU-MEET STORIES. ABOUT AN HOUR IN, AND SEVERAL DRINKS LATER, THINGS GOT AROUND TO WHY I WAS REALLY THERE.
I'm telling you! It's no different than slavery...man thinks he can do whatever he wants to a lowly animal and it's not too many stops before he thinks he can do whatever he wants to any man he deems lesser—
The point I was trying to make though was that if we accept that there are casualties in war, as you all have told me—
WHAT I REALLY WANTED TO OBSERVE TONIGHT WAS HOW NADIA COULD MANAGE TO STAY A MEAT EATER WHEN HER BADASS BOYFRIEND WAS A VEGETARIAN, AND MORE IMPORTANTLY, WHAT HER PLAN WAS TO CONVERT HIM BACK.
Then why can't eating animals be a casualty of life?
Whoa, whoa... That's something entirely different—
Why? It's people being killed, presumably even innocent people—

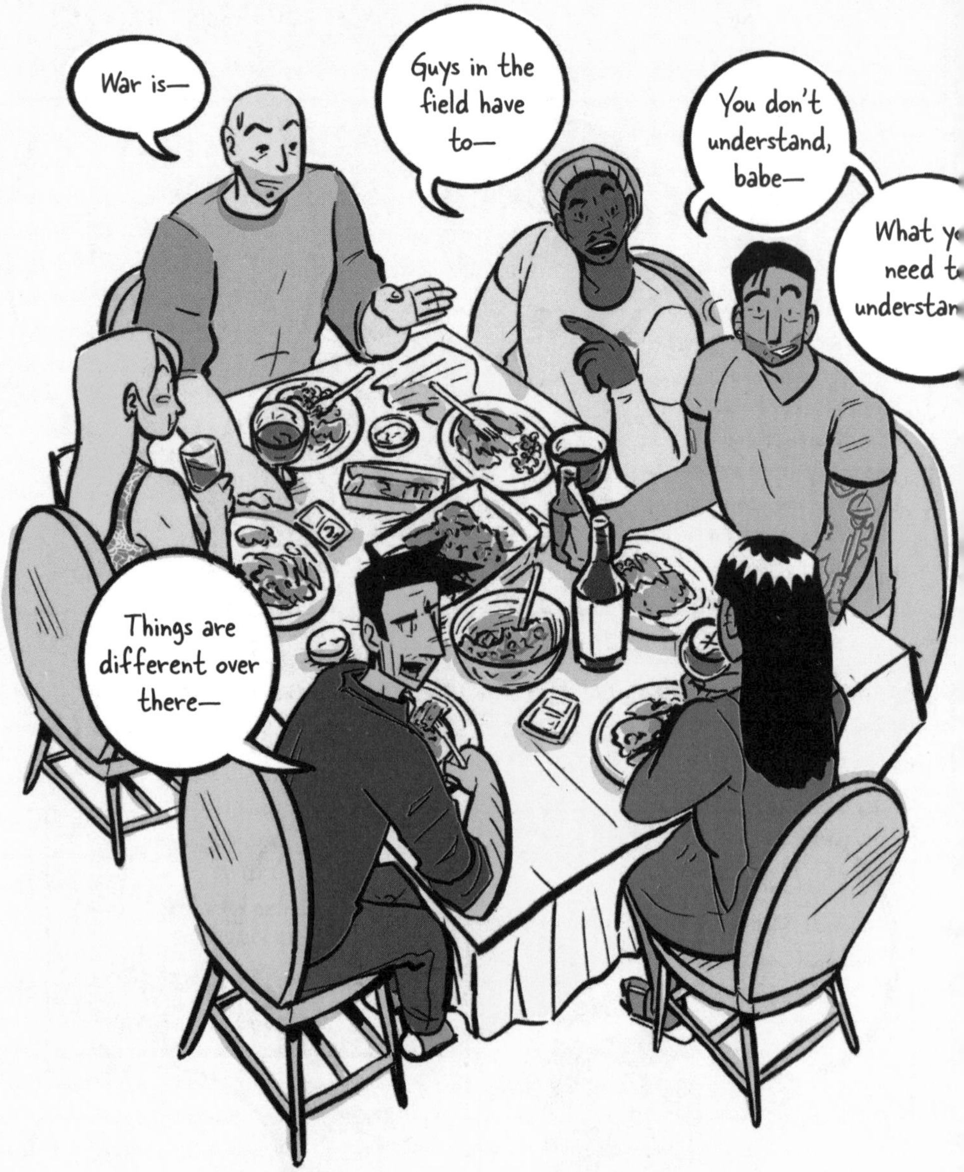
War is—
Guys in the field have to—
You don't understand, babe—
What y need t understan
Things are different over there—

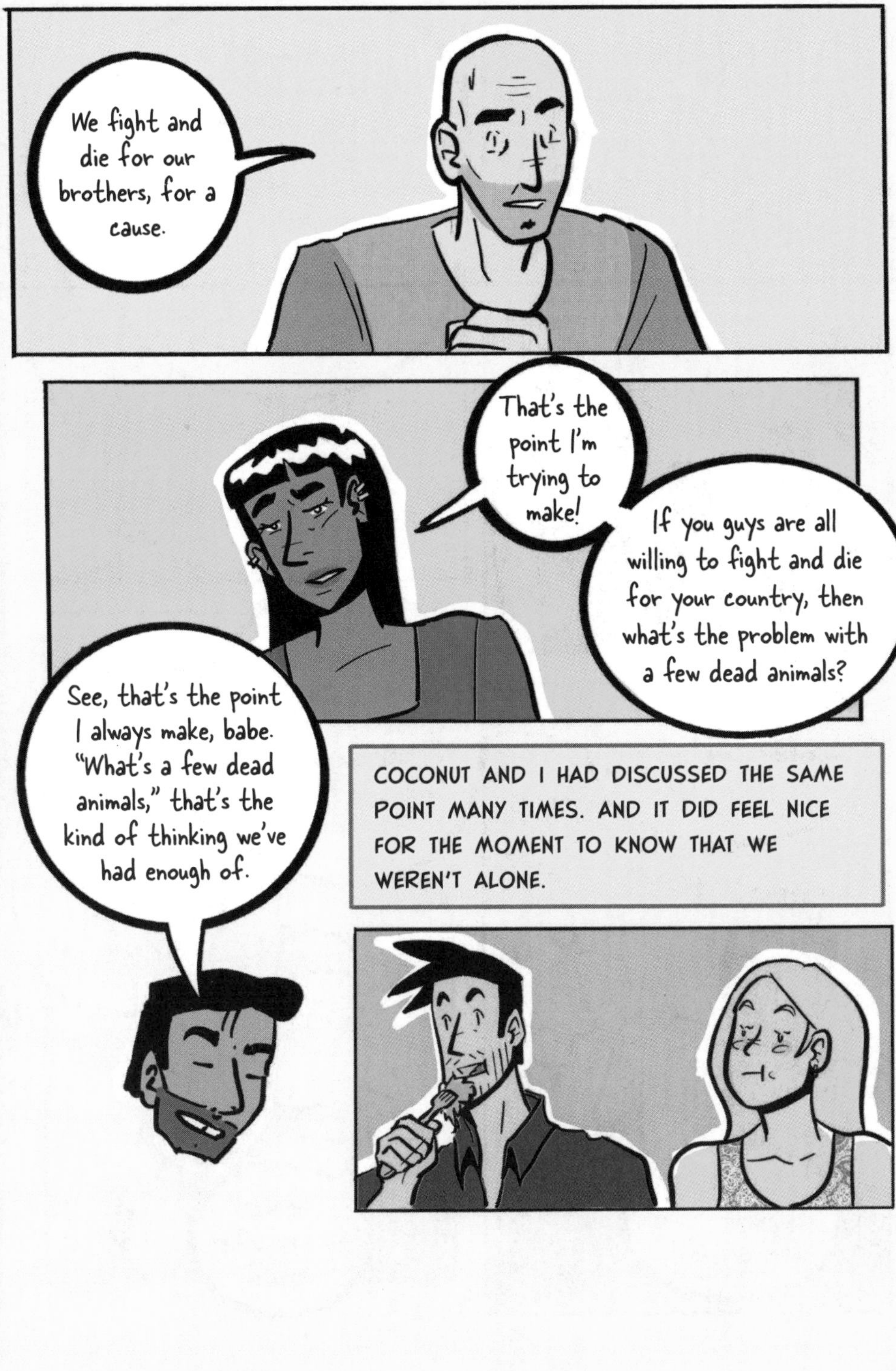

We fight and die for our brothers, for a cause.
That's the point I'm trying to make!
If you guys are all willing to fight and die for your country, then what's the problem with a few dead animals?
See, that's the point I always make, babe. "What's a few dead animals," that's the kind of thinking we've had enough of.
COCONUT AND I HAD DISCUSSED THE SAME POINT MANY TIMES. AND IT DID FEEL NICE FOR THE MOMENT TO KNOW THAT WE WEREN'T ALONE.

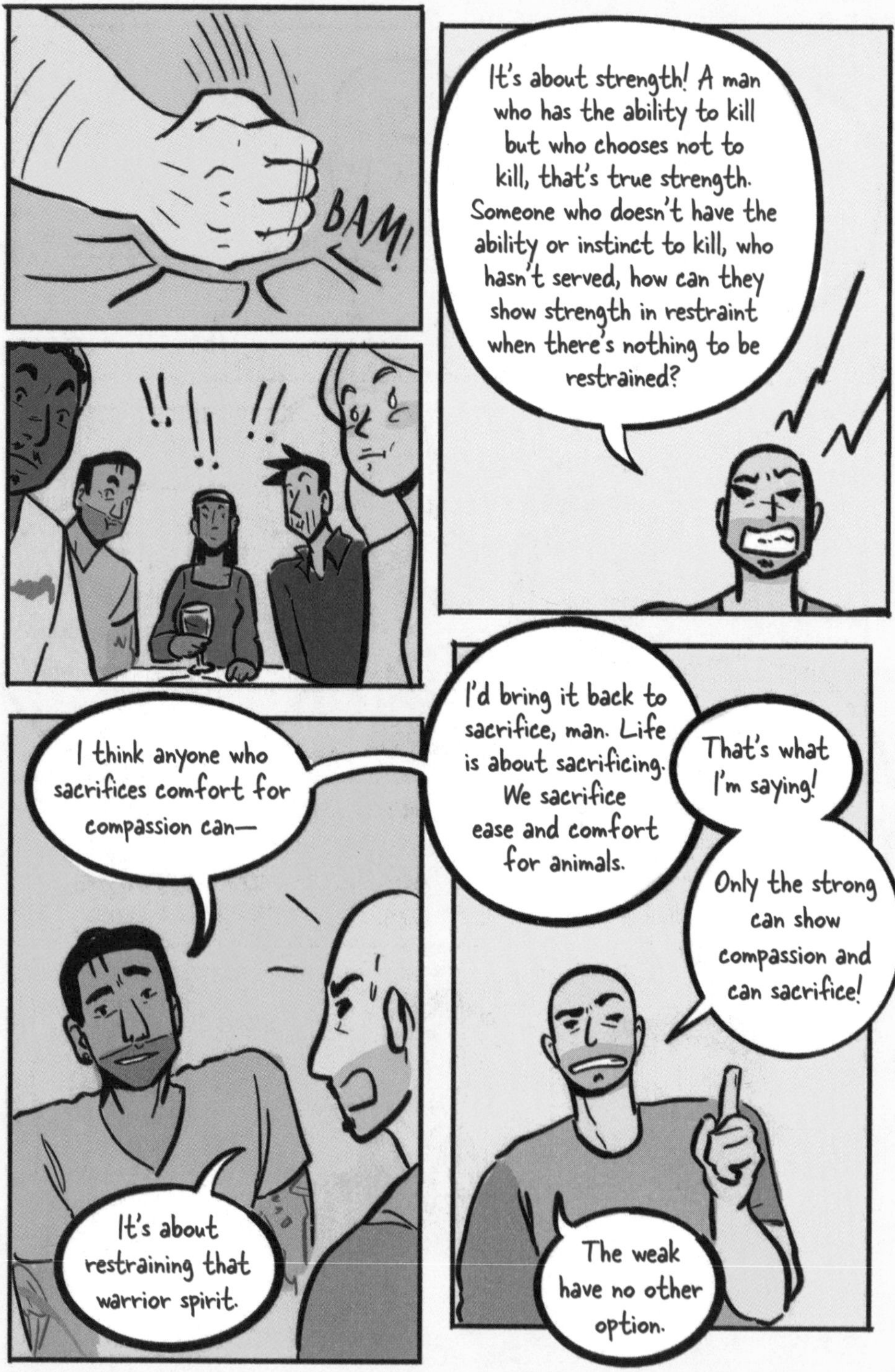
BAM!
!!
!!
!!
It's about strength! A man who has the ability to kill but who chooses not to kill, that's true strength. Someone who doesn't have the ability or instinct to kill, who hasn't served, how can they show strength in restraint when there's nothing to be restrained?
I think anyone who sacrifices comfort for compassion can—
It's about restraining that warrior spirit.
I'd bring it back to sacrifice, man. Life is about sacrificing. We sacrifice ease and comfort for animals.
That's what I'm saying!
Only the strong can show compassion and can sacrifice!
The weak have no other option.

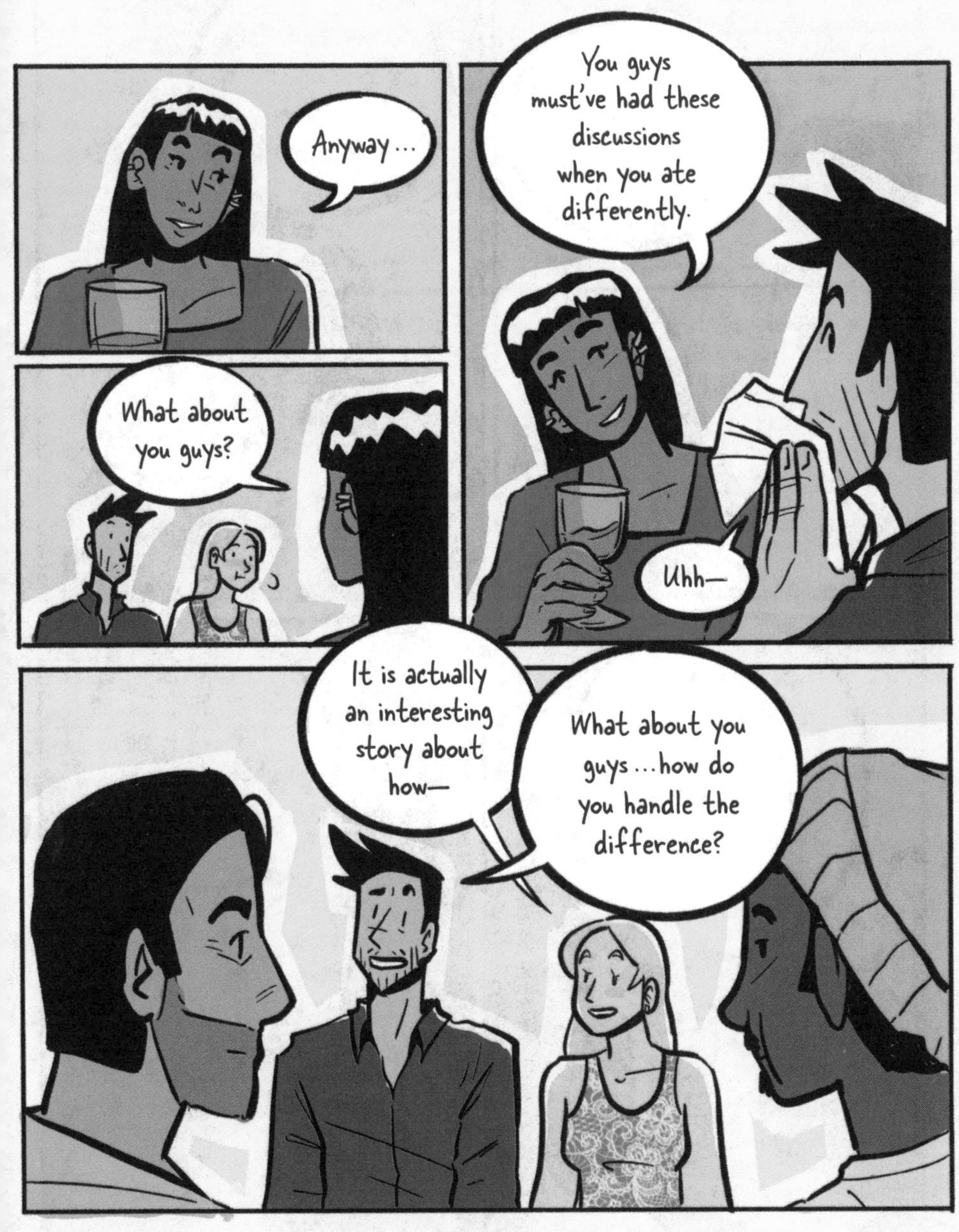
Anyway...
You guys must've had these discussions when you ate differently.
What about you guys?
Uhh—
It is actually an interesting story about how—
What about you guys...how do you handle the difference?

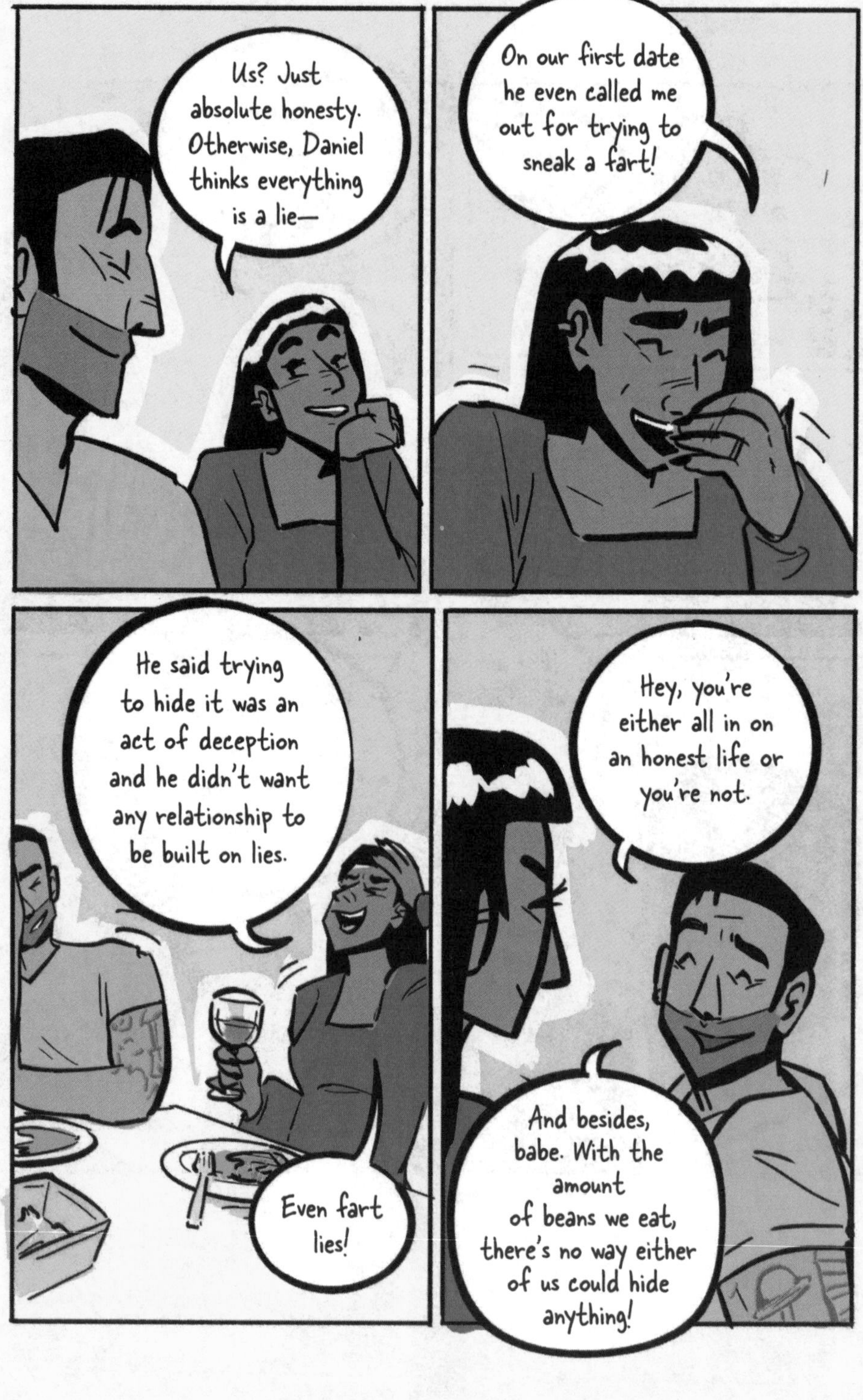
Us? Just absolute honesty. Otherwise, Daniel thinks everything is a lie—
On our first date he even called me out for trying to sneak a fart!
He said trying to hide it was an act of deception and he didn't want any relationship to be built on lies.
Even fart lies!
Hey, you're either all in on an honest life or you're not.
And besides, babe. With the amount of beans we eat, there's no way either of us could hide anything!

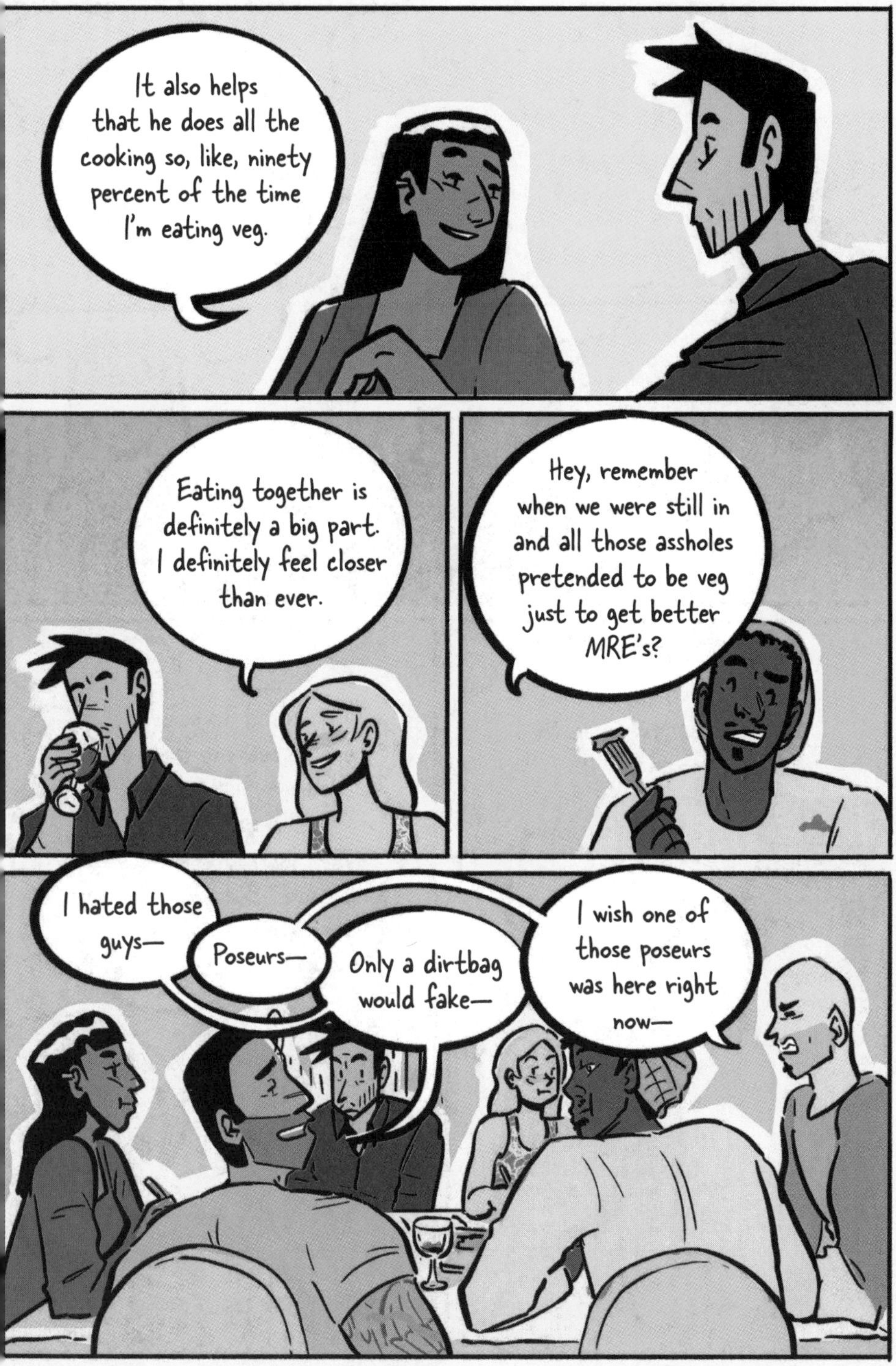
It also helps that he does all the cooking so, like, ninety percent of the time I'm eating veg.
Eating together is definitely a big part. I definitely feel closer than ever.
Hey, remember when we were still in and all those assholes pretended to be veg just to get better MRE's?
I hated those guys—
Poseurs—
Only a dirtbag would fake—
I wish one of those poseurs was here right now—

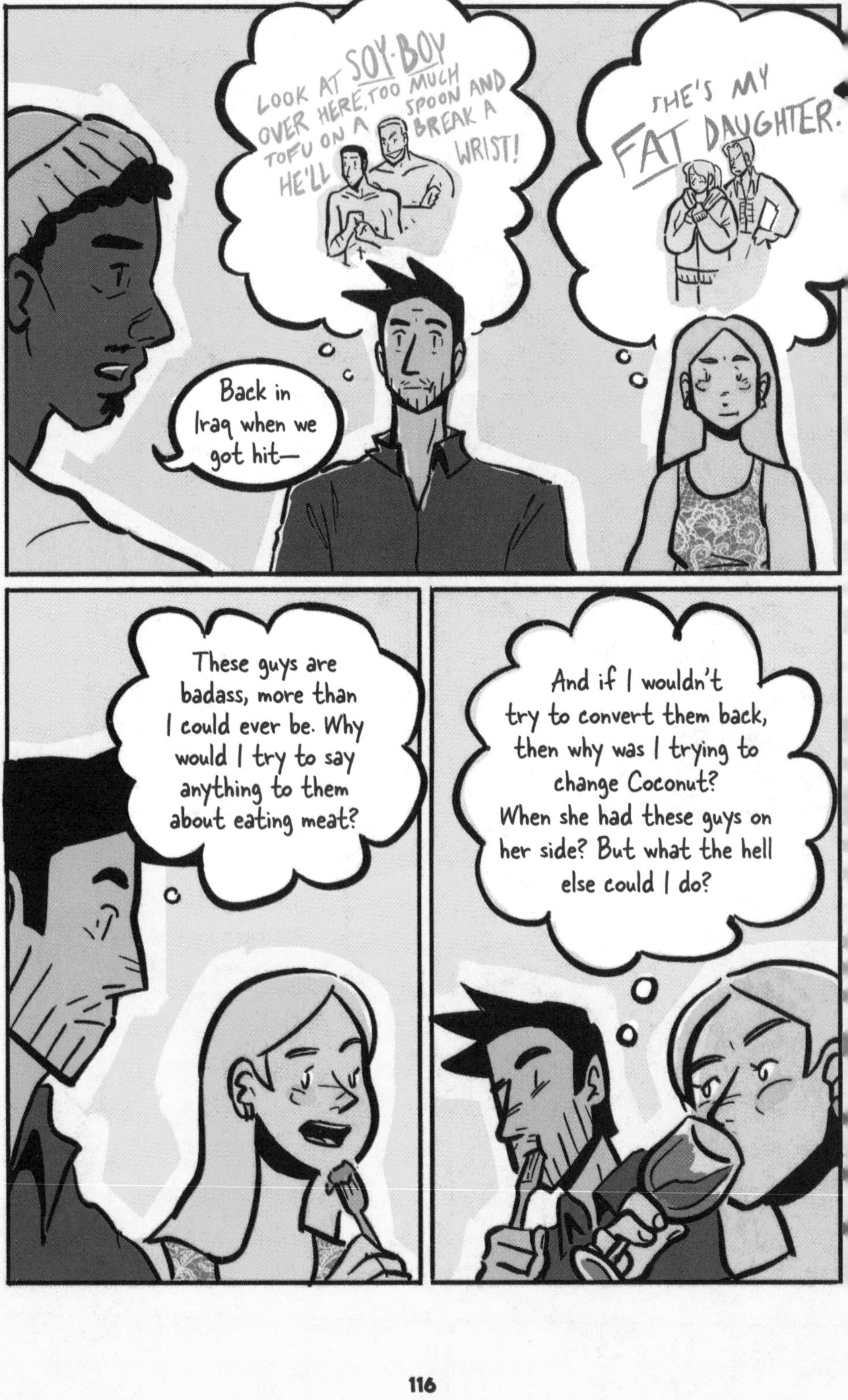
LOOK AT SOY-BOY OVER HERE, TOO MUCH TOFU ON A SPOON AND HE'LL BREAK A WRIST!
SHE'S MY FAT DAUGHTER.
Back in Iraq when we got hit—
These guys are badass, more than I could ever be. Why would I try to say anything to them about eating meat?
And if I wouldn't try to convert them back, then why was I trying to change Coconut? When she had these guys on her side? But what the hell else could I do?

Why People Become Vegetarians and Animal Rights Activists

Health – Diets with more vegetables/fruits and less meat are better for overall human health.

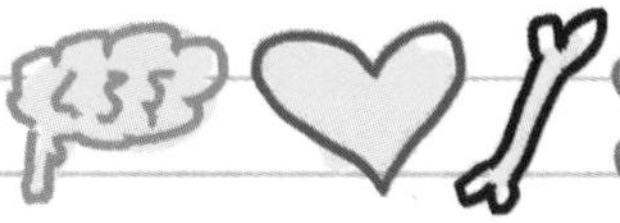

SKIN are all benefitted

Cruelty – The conditions that animals are forced into are abusive, exploitative, and inhumane.

Inhumane Meat Industry → Mistreatment of Animals → Decline of human health + environment

Environment – Eating mainly plants and fruits is better for the environment!

Cows fart Methane!!

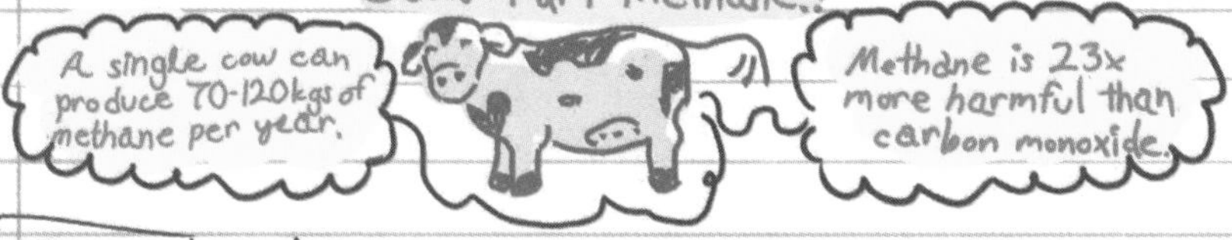
A single cow can produce 70-120kgs of methane per year.
Methane is 23x more harmful than carbon monoxide.

Ethics – We can survive without killing animals, therefore, we shouldn't kill them.

---

* Some people have seen enough killing and no longer want to be a part of the cycle.

DANIEL HAD LEFT ME WONDERING ABOUT THINGS.

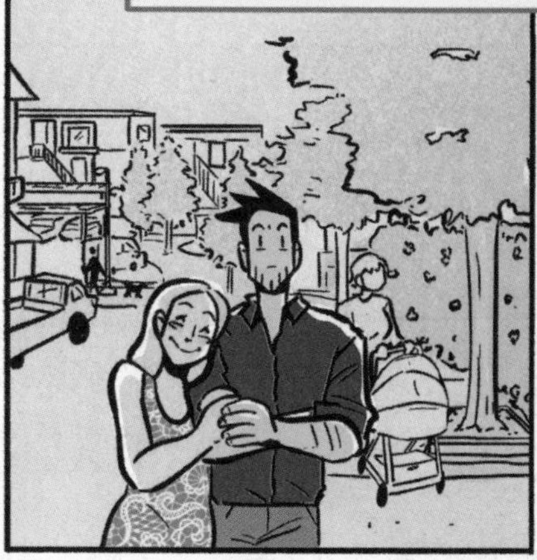

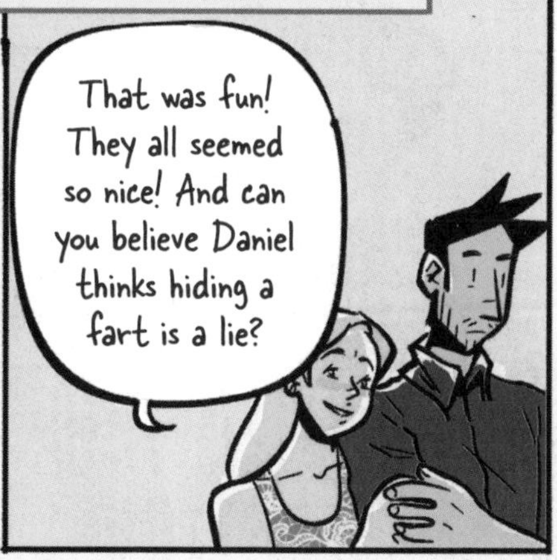
That was fun! They all seemed so nice! And can you believe Daniel thinks hiding a fart is a lie?

CHAPTER 11

LIKE, WHAT THE HELL WAS I DOING? HOW LONG WAS I GOING TO KEEP UP THE LIE? WOULD THE ENDS JUSTIFY THE MEANS? AND WHAT THE HELL EVEN WAS THE END? WHAT WERE MY OTHER OPTIONS THOUGH?

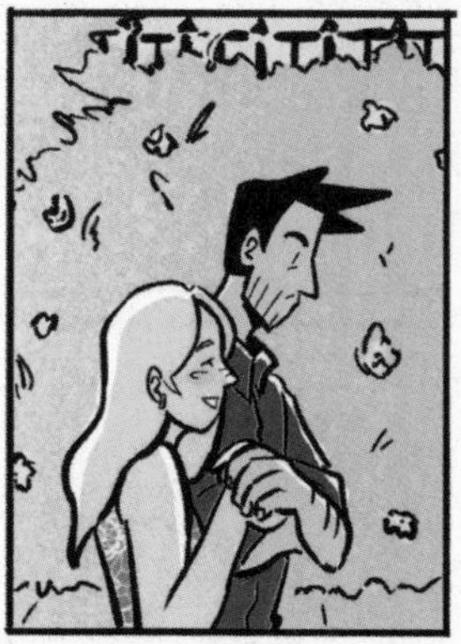

I WAS ACTUALLY FEELING GOOD WITH MY HEALTHIER LIFESTYLE. FEWER MORNING HEADACHES, AND NOT SO TIRED AFTER LUNCH. DID I WANT TO TAKE THAT AWAY FROM HER? OR EVEN FROM ME?

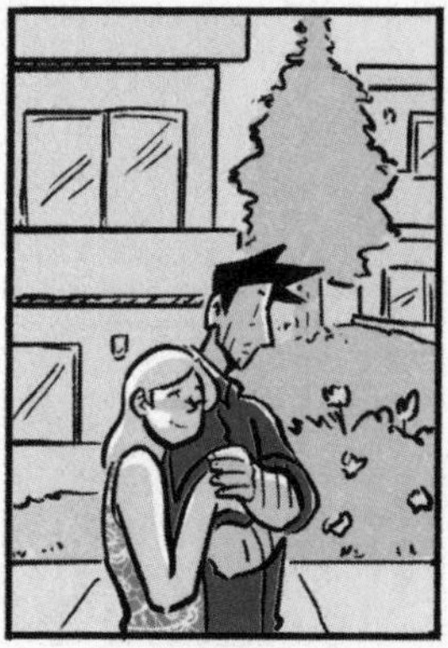

BUT I COULDN'T STAY VEGETARIAN FOREVER; I'D ALREADY LOST TWO POUNDS. AND SHE WAS JUST GOING FURTHER AND FURTHER DOWN THE ROAD OF ANIMAL RIGHTS, A ROAD I COULDN'T FOLLOW. WHAT ELSE COULD I DO?

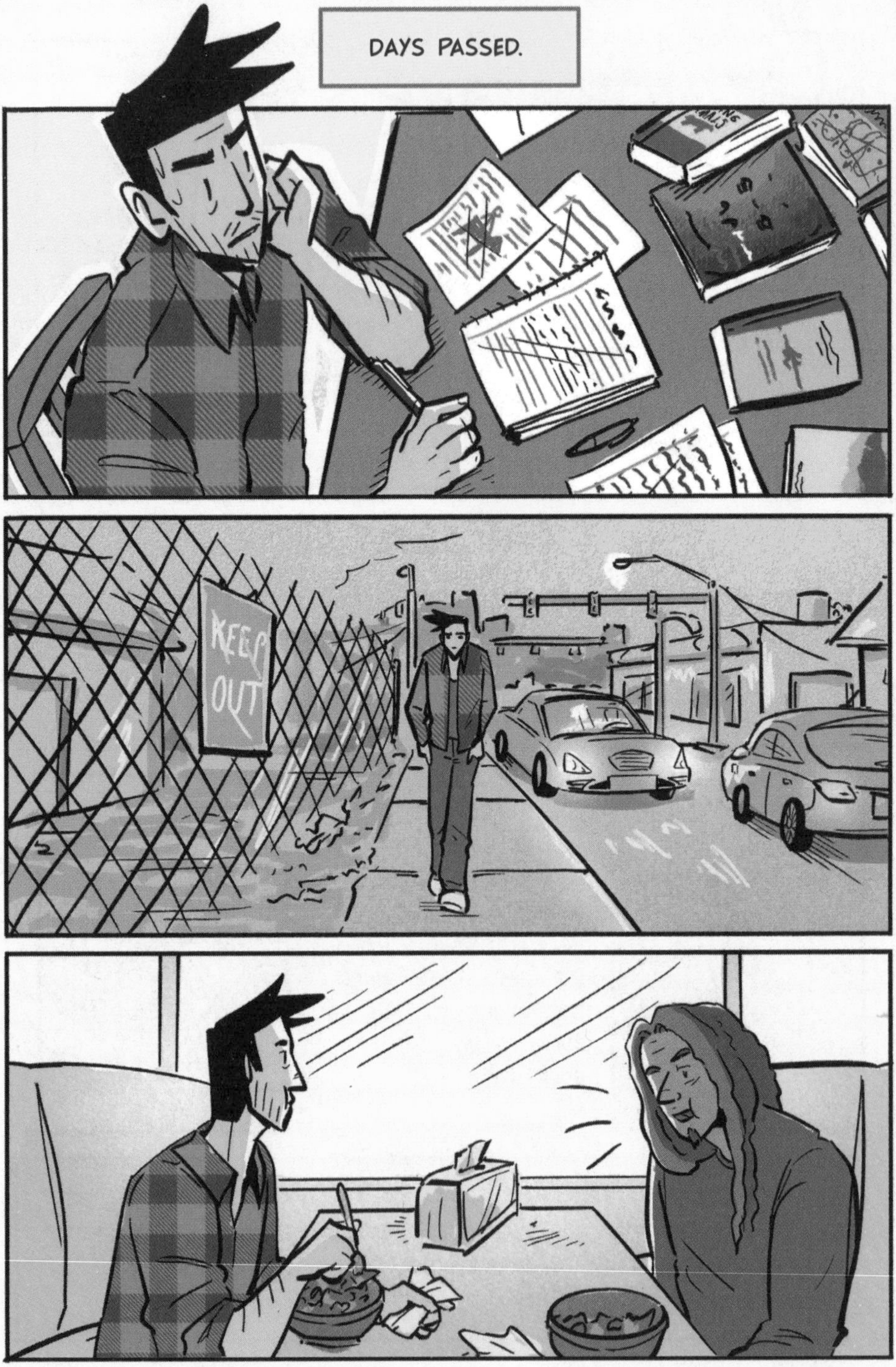
DAYS PASSED.
KEEP OUT

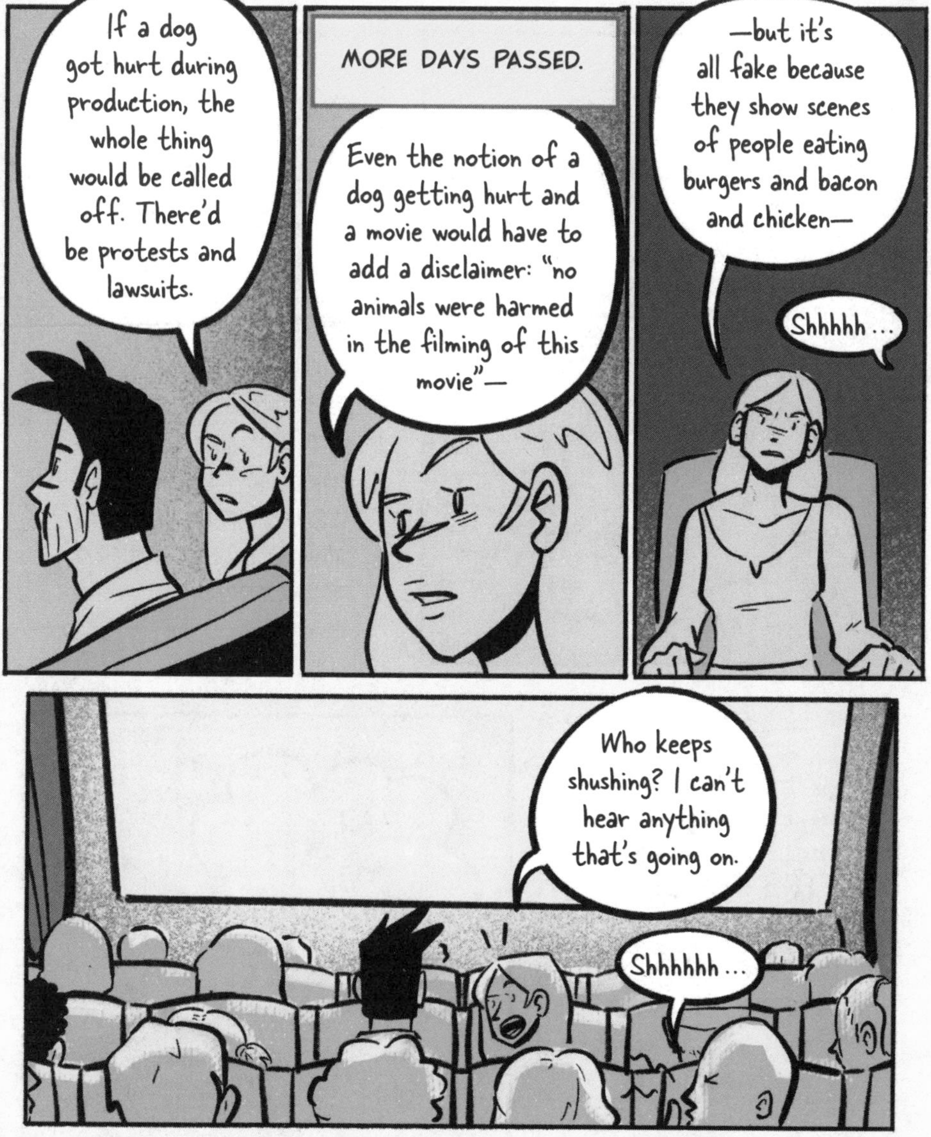
If a dog got hurt during production, the whole thing would be called off. There'd be protests and lawsuits.
MORE DAYS PASSED.
Even the notion of a dog getting hurt and a movie would have to add a disclaimer: "no animals were harmed in the filming of this movie"—
—but it's all fake because they show scenes of people eating burgers and bacon and chicken—
Shhhhh . . .
Who keeps shushing? I can't hear anything that's going on.
Shhhhhh . . .
I HAD NO IDEA HOW SOMETHING SO SMALL, FOOD, HAD GOTTEN THIS FAR BETWEEN US. THOUGH, IN COCONUT'S MIND, SHE'D SAY THAT THE "INHUMANE SLAUGHTER OF HUNDREDS OF MILLIONS OF ANIMALS" WASN'T SUCH A SMALL MATTER. BUT HOWEVER WE GOT HERE, I WAS NOW STUCK IN THIS FART OF DECEPTION, WITH A FAILING PLAN AND NO CLEAR WAY OUT.

NOTICE
DEAR JOHN,
"LOVE CONQUERS ALL." I'D HEARD THAT QUOTED BEFORE. BUT SINCE COMING BACK FROM THE WAR, I'D KNOWN DOZENS OF VETS WHO'D BEEN BROKEN UP WITH: DEAR JOHN LETTERS, ENGAGEMENTS CALLED OFF, DIVORCE PAPERS SERVED. LOVE COULDN'T CONQUER PTSD IT SEEMED. WHAT ELSE COULDN'T IT CONQUER? POLITICS?
IF ONE PERSON WAS A RIGHT-WING CONSERVATIVE AND THE OTHER A LEFT-WING PROGRESSIVE, COULD THEY STAY TOGETHER? OR SEX . . . IF ONE PERSON WAS INTO S&M OR POLYAMORY OR SOMETHING, AND THE OTHER WASN'T, COULD THEY LAST? HMM . . . MENTAL HEALTH. POLITICS. SEX. AND FOOD?
But is it really just a cheeseburger?

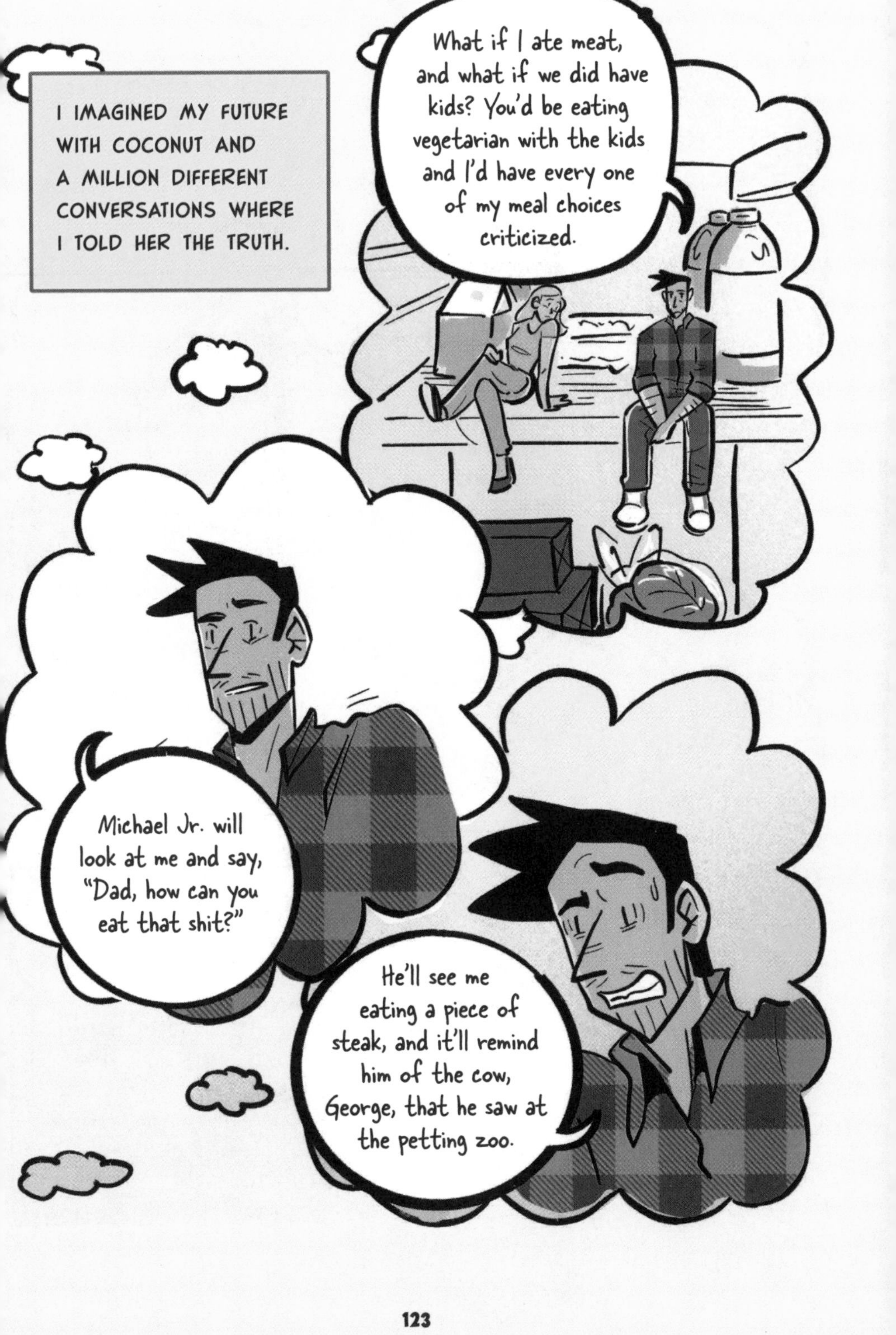
I IMAGINED MY FUTURE WITH COCONUT AND A MILLION DIFFERENT CONVERSATIONS WHERE I TOLD HER THE TRUTH.
What if I ate meat, and what if we did have kids? You'd be eating vegetarian with the kids and I'd have every one of my meal choices criticized.
Michael Jr. will look at me and say, "Dad, how can you eat that shit?"
He'll see me eating a piece of steak, and it'll remind him of the cow, George, that he saw at the petting zoo.

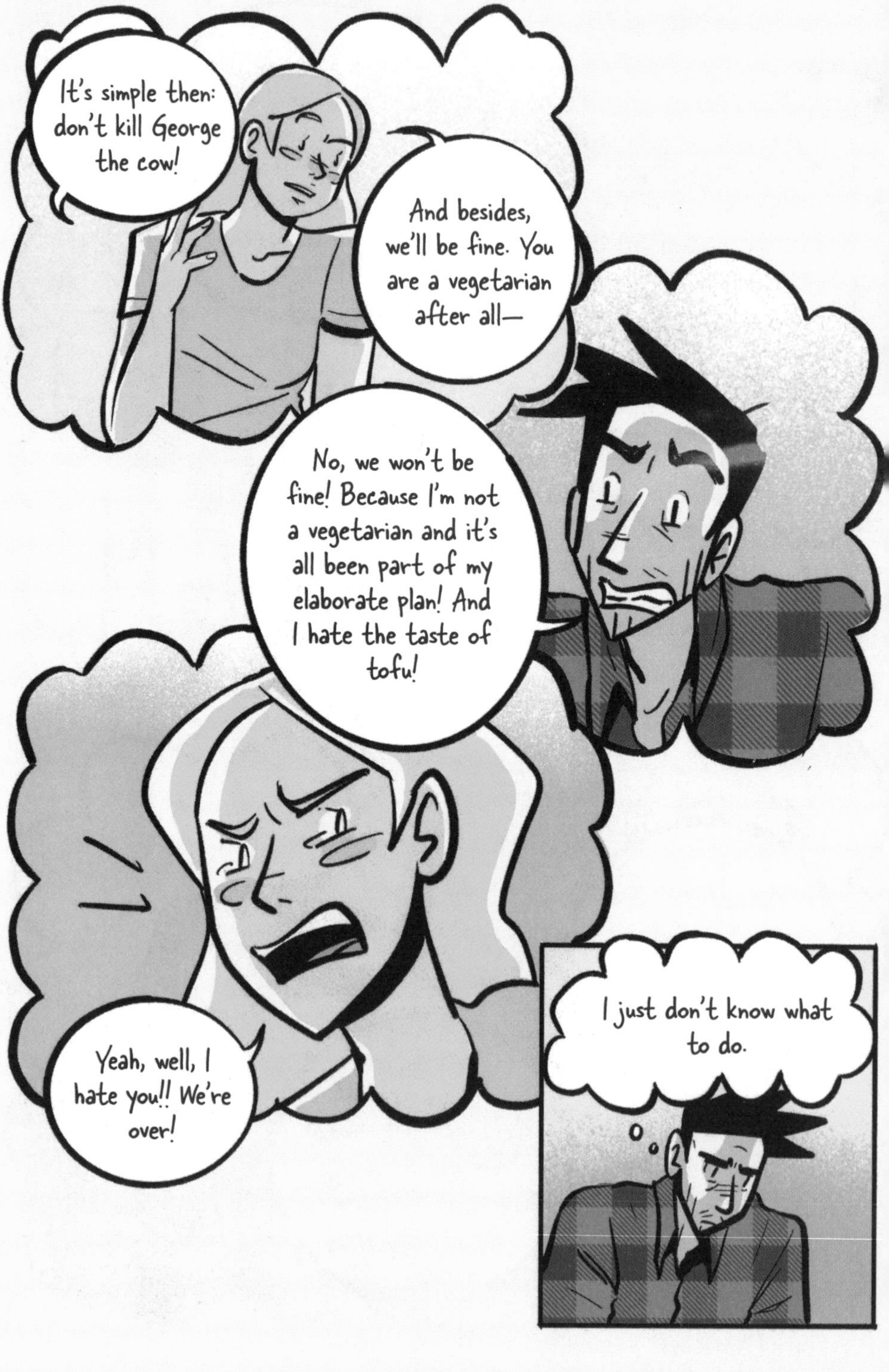
It's simple then: don't kill George the cow!
And besides, we'll be fine. You are a vegetarian after all—
No, we won't be fine! Because I'm not a vegetarian and it's all been part of my elaborate plan! And I hate the taste of tofu!
Yeah, well, I hate you!! We're over!
I just don't know what to do.

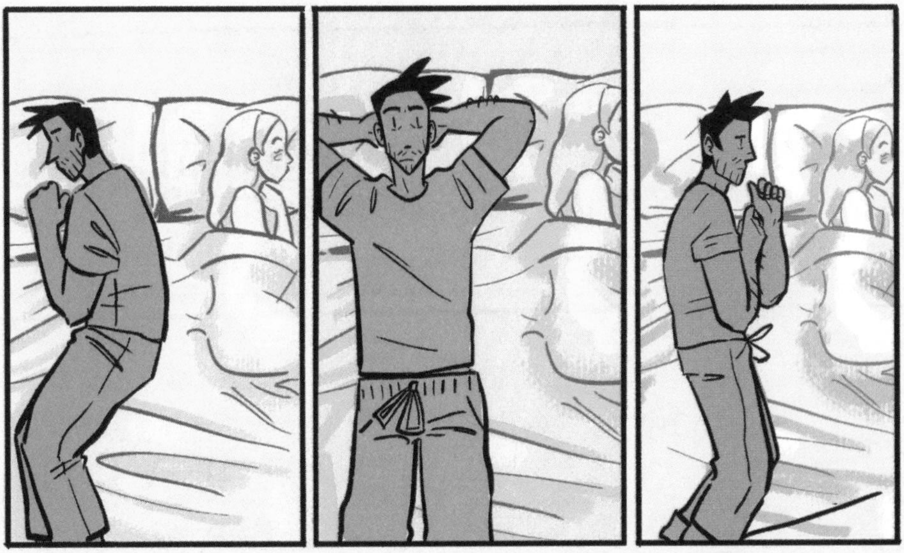

THE PHILOSOPHER ST. JOHN OF THE CROSS REFERRED TO SUCH MENTALLY AND EMOTIONALLY TORTUROUS TIMES IN OUR LIVES AS "THE DARK NIGHT OF THE SOUL." A PERSON TOSSES AND TURNS, WRINGS THEIR SOUL INSIDE OUT LOOKING FOR AN ANSWER, FOR THE RIGHT THING TO DO, AND THEN ULTIMATELY, FOR THE STRENGTH TO FOLLOW THROUGH.

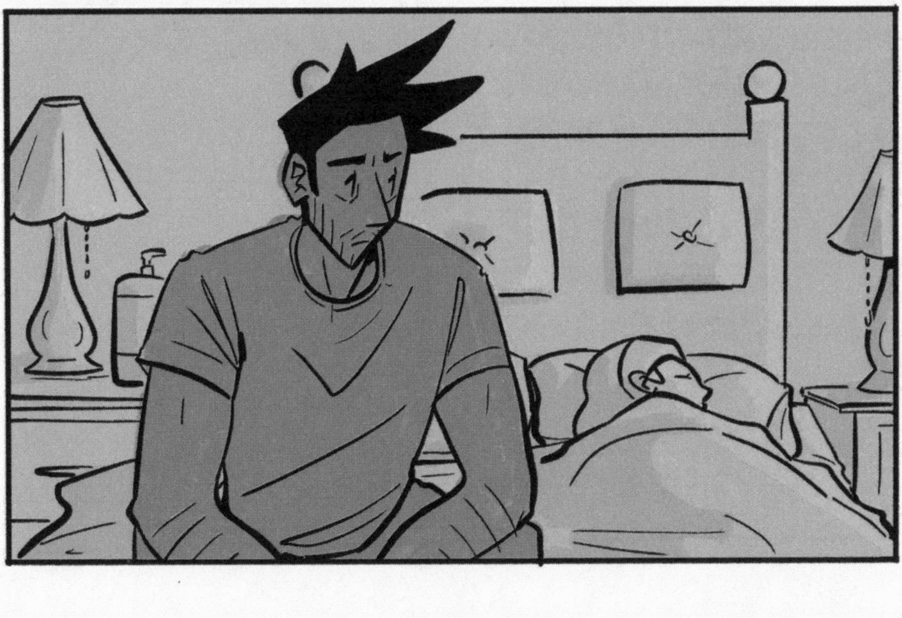

TO TELL HER	TO NOT TELL HER
MY PLAN'S NOT WORKING, I HAVE NO OTHER CHOICE	
THE TRUTH COULD STRENGTHEN OUR RELATIONSHIP	WHAT IF I LOSE HER?
ONCE I COME CLEAN, I WON'T HAVE TO BE VEGETARIAN ANY LONGER— BUT THEN WHAT?	~~MAYBE MY PLAN COULD STILL WORK AND I JUST NEED A LITTLE MORE TIME??~~
IT'LL ONLY GET WORSE THE LONGER I WAIT	

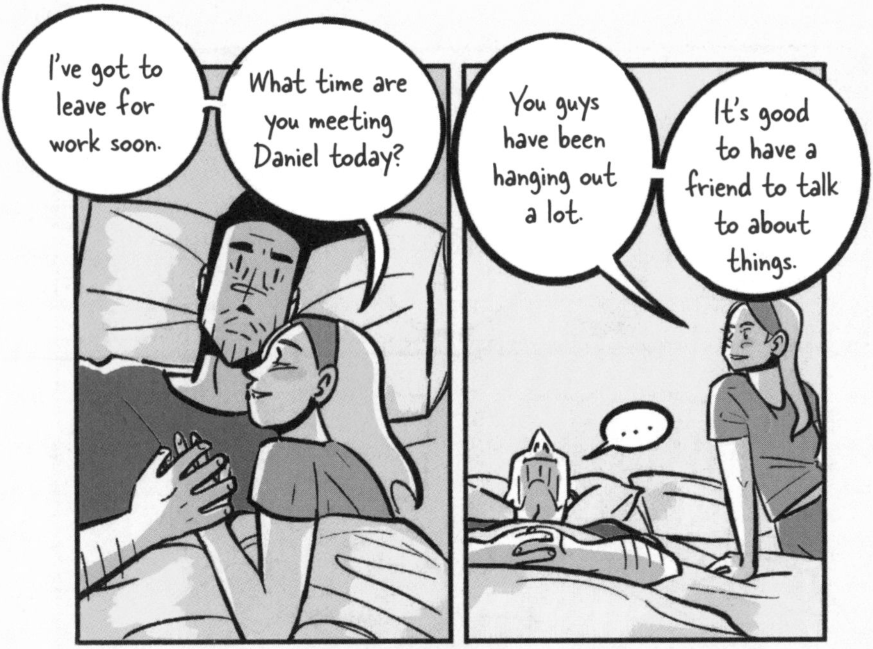
I've got to leave for work soon.
What time are you meeting Daniel today?
You guys have been hanging out a lot.
It's good to have a friend to talk to about things.
...

CHAPTER 12

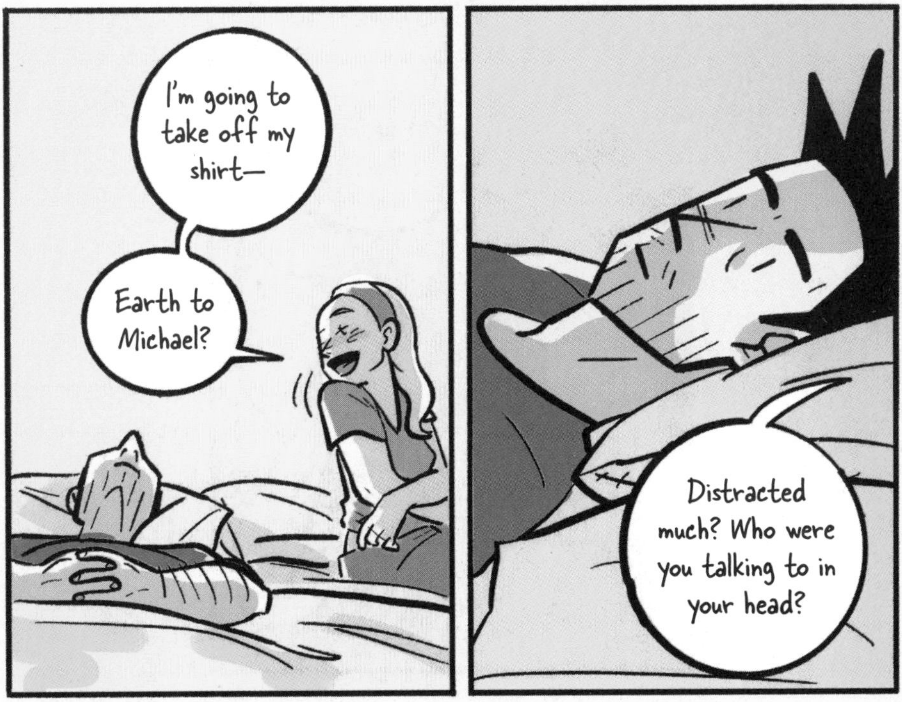
I'm going to take off my shirt—
Earth to Michael?
Distracted much? Who were you talking to in your head?

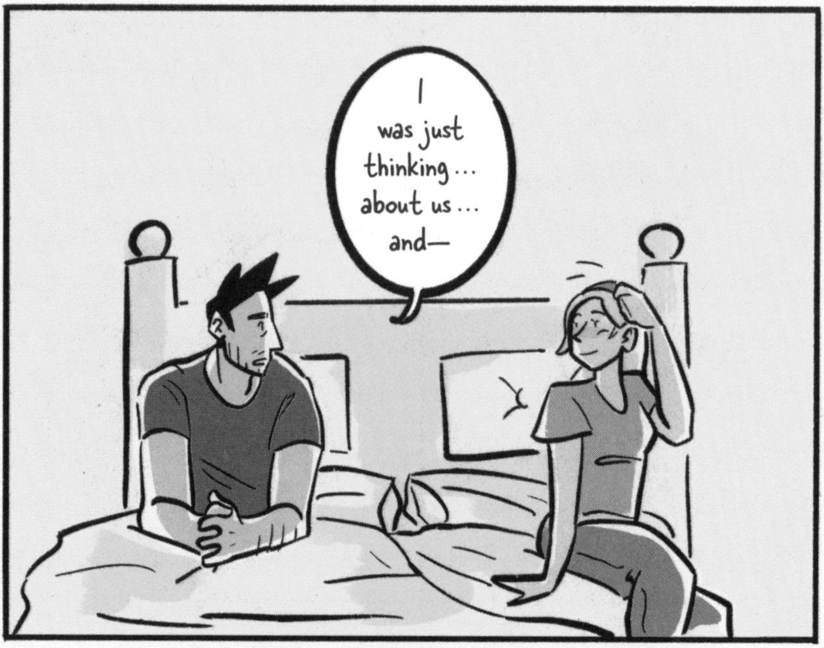
I was just thinking... about us... and—

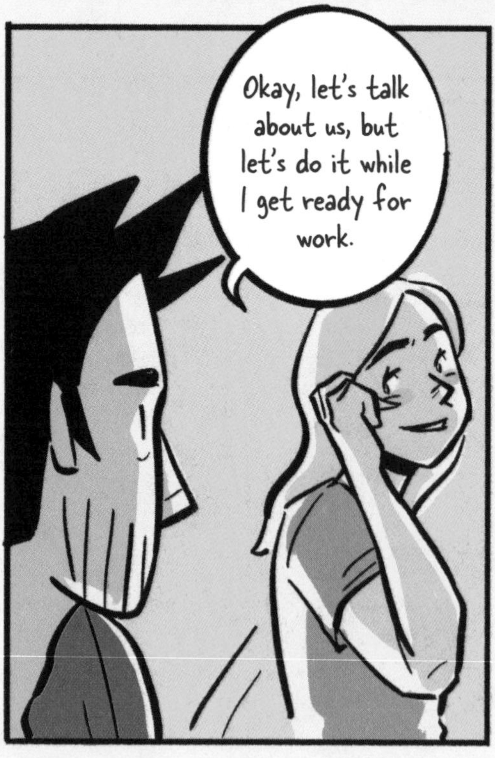
Okay, let's talk about us, but let's do it while I get ready for work.

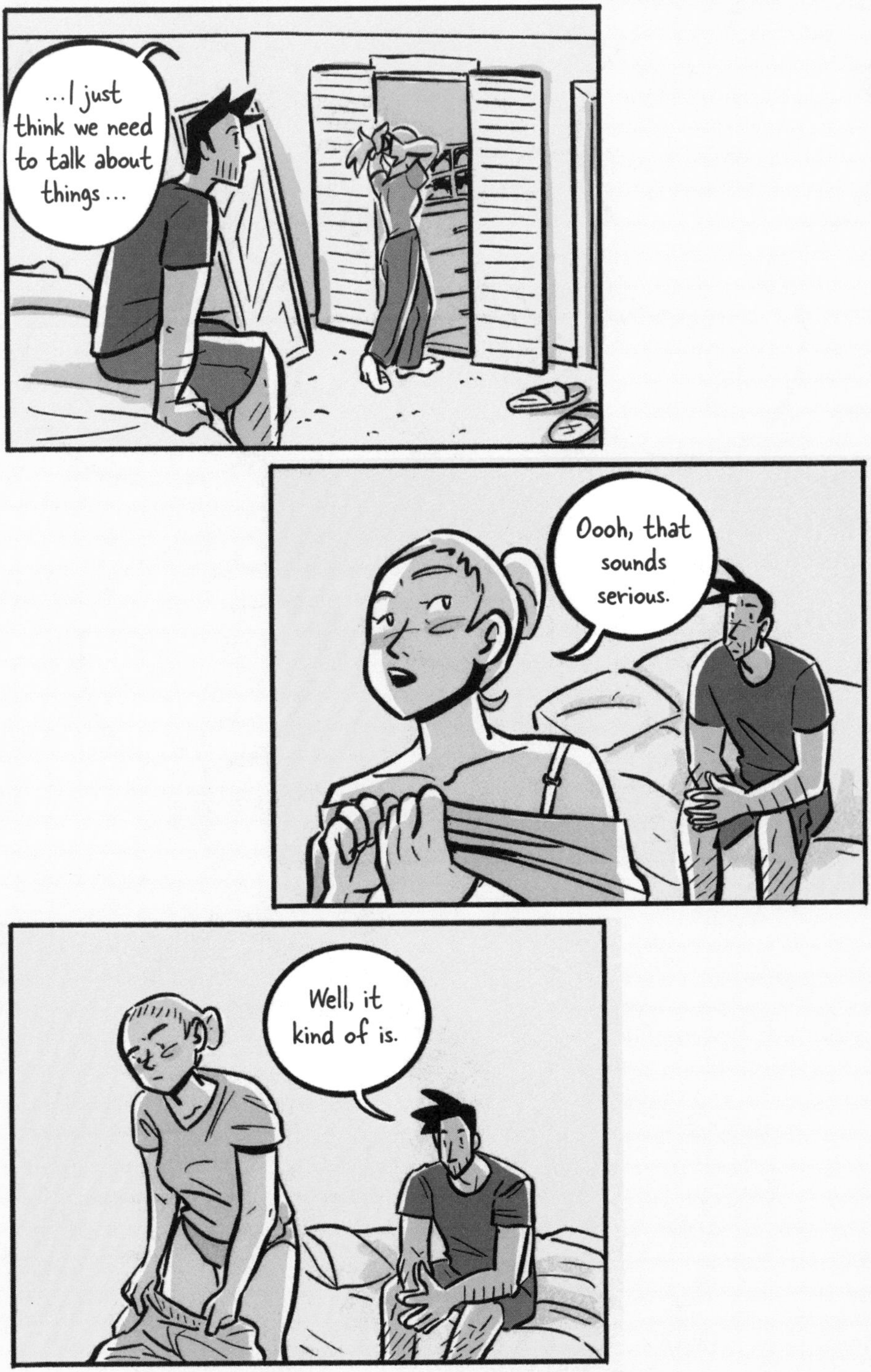
...I just think we need to talk about things...
Oooh, that sounds serious.
Well, it kind of is.

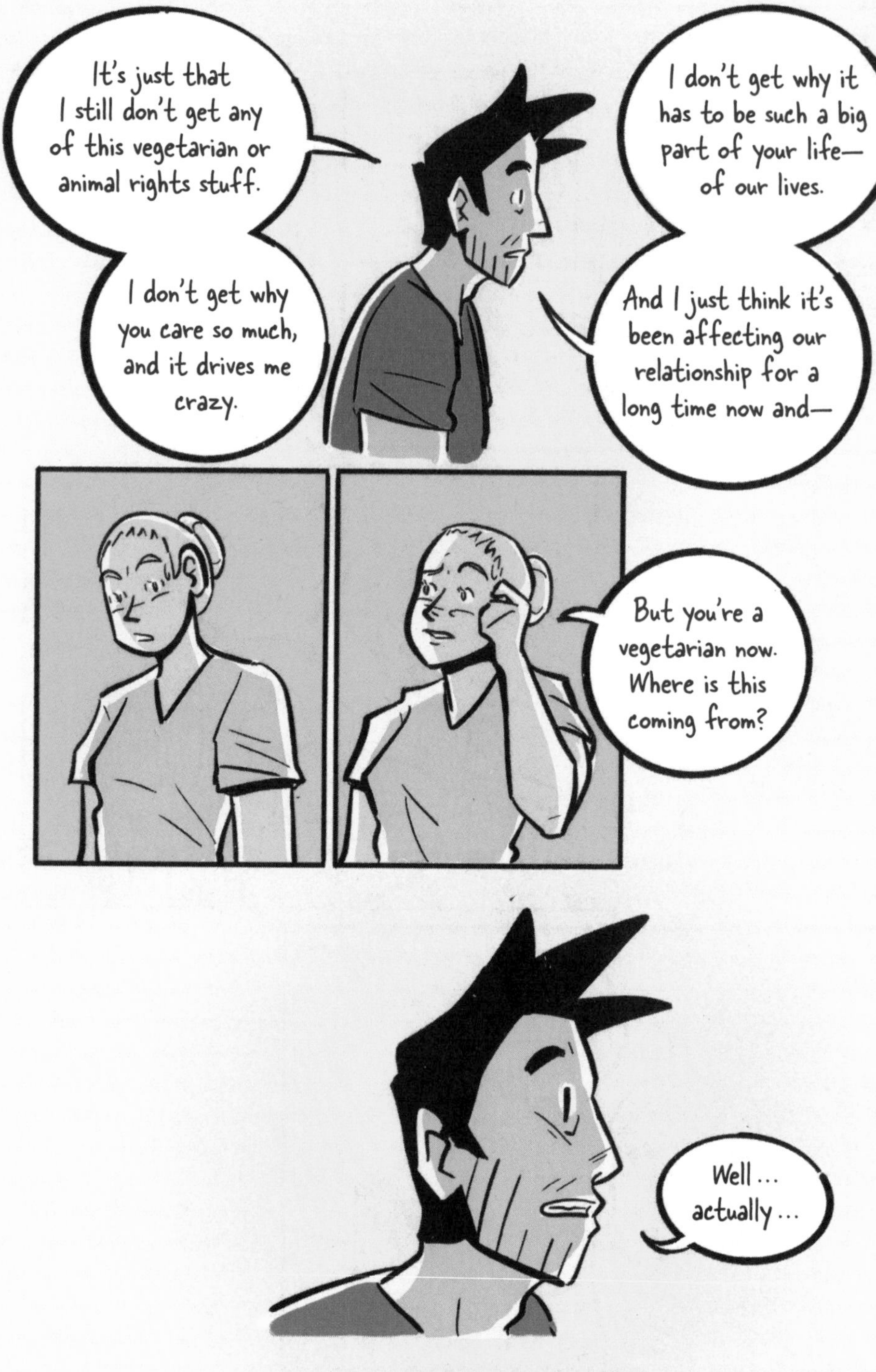
It's just that I still don't get any of this vegetarian or animal rights stuff.
I don't get why you care so much, and it drives me crazy.
I don't get why it has to be such a big part of your life—of our lives.
And I just think it's been affecting our relationship for a long time now and—
But you're a vegetarian now. Where is this coming from?
Well ... actually ...

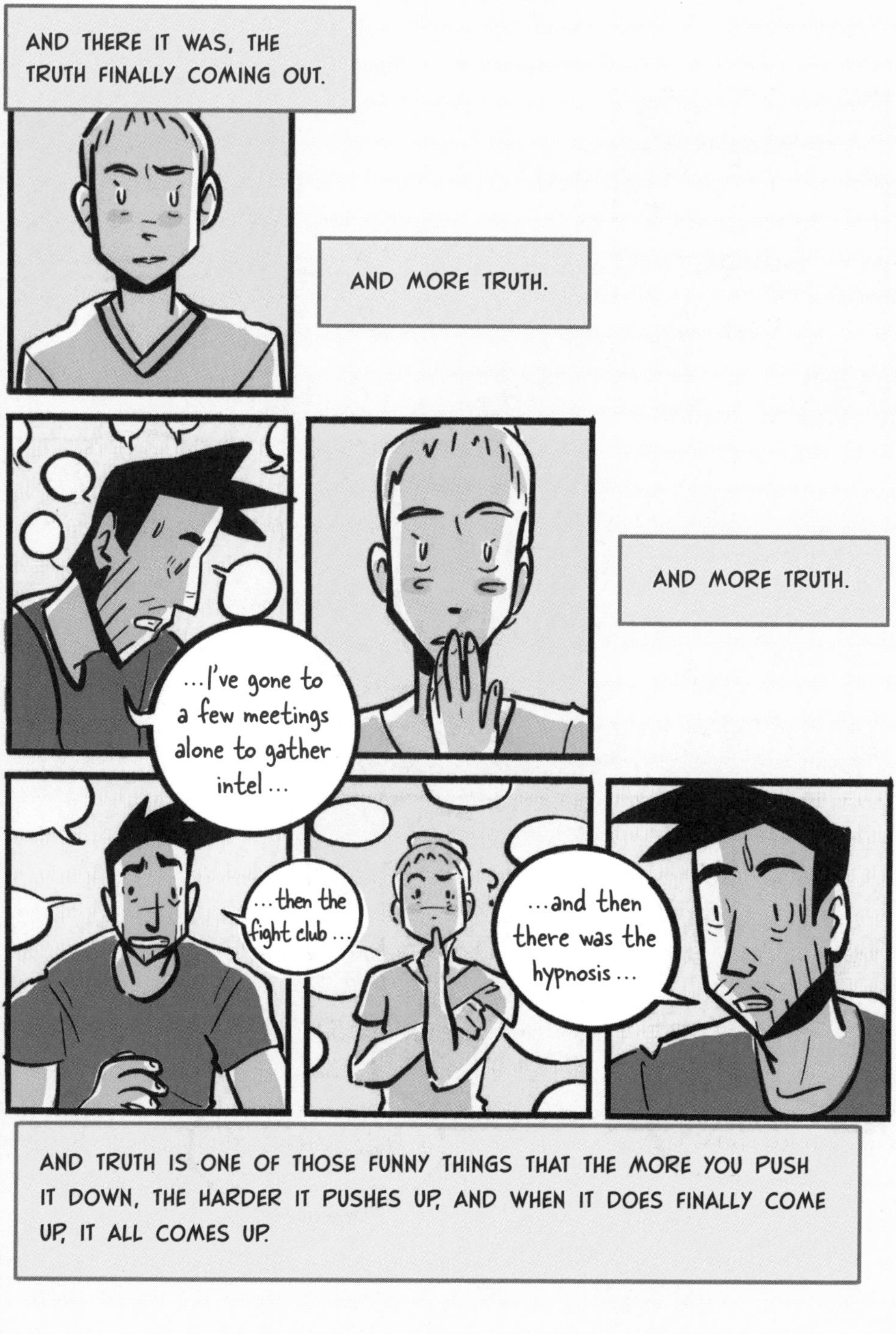
AND THERE IT WAS, THE TRUTH FINALLY COMING OUT.
AND MORE TRUTH.
AND MORE TRUTH.
...I've gone to a few meetings alone to gather intel...
...then the fight club...
...and then there was the hypnosis...
AND TRUTH IS ONE OF THOSE FUNNY THINGS THAT THE MORE YOU PUSH IT DOWN, THE HARDER IT PUSHES UP, AND WHEN IT DOES FINALLY COME UP, IT ALL COMES UP.

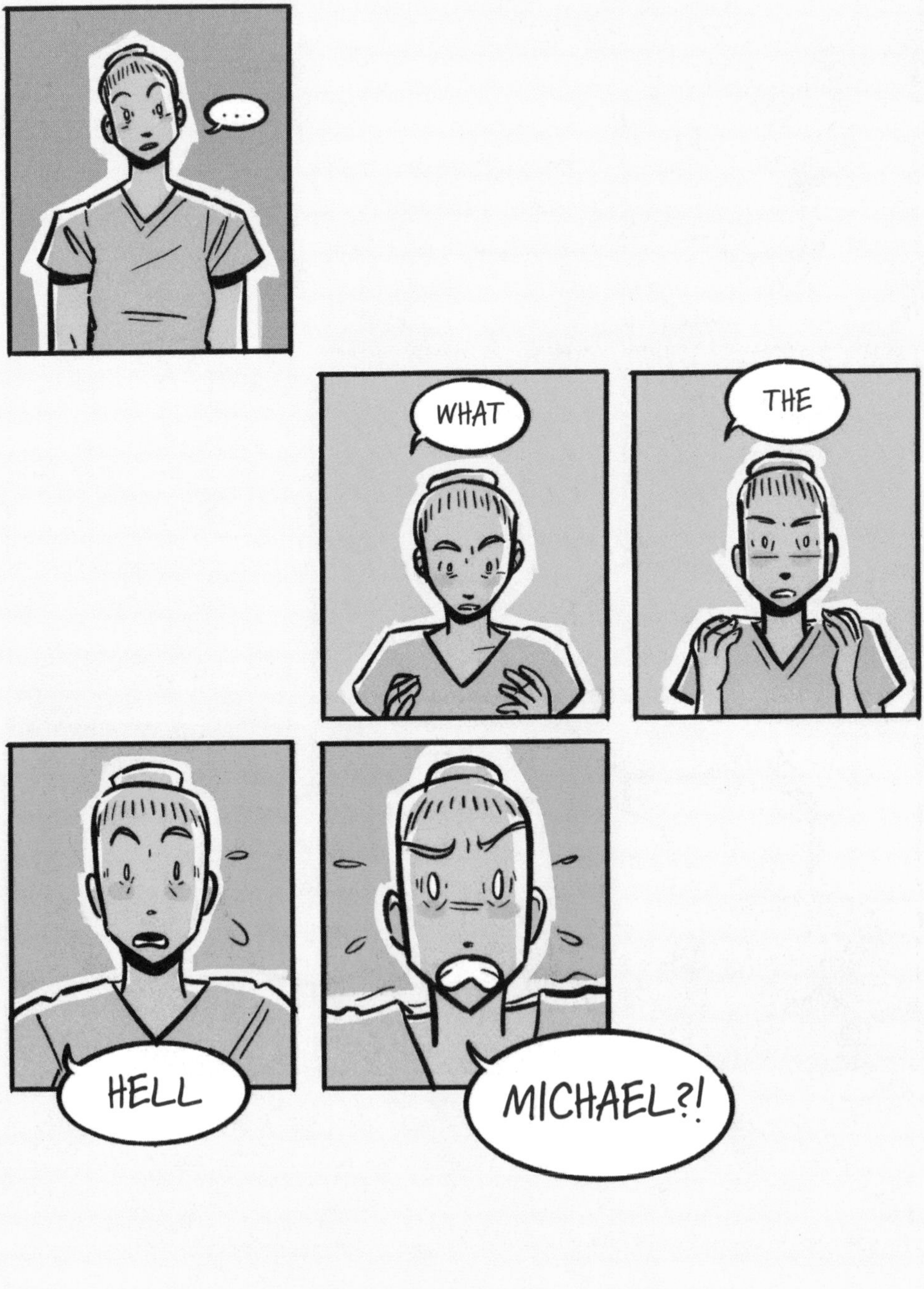
...
WHAT
THE
HELL
MICHAEL?!

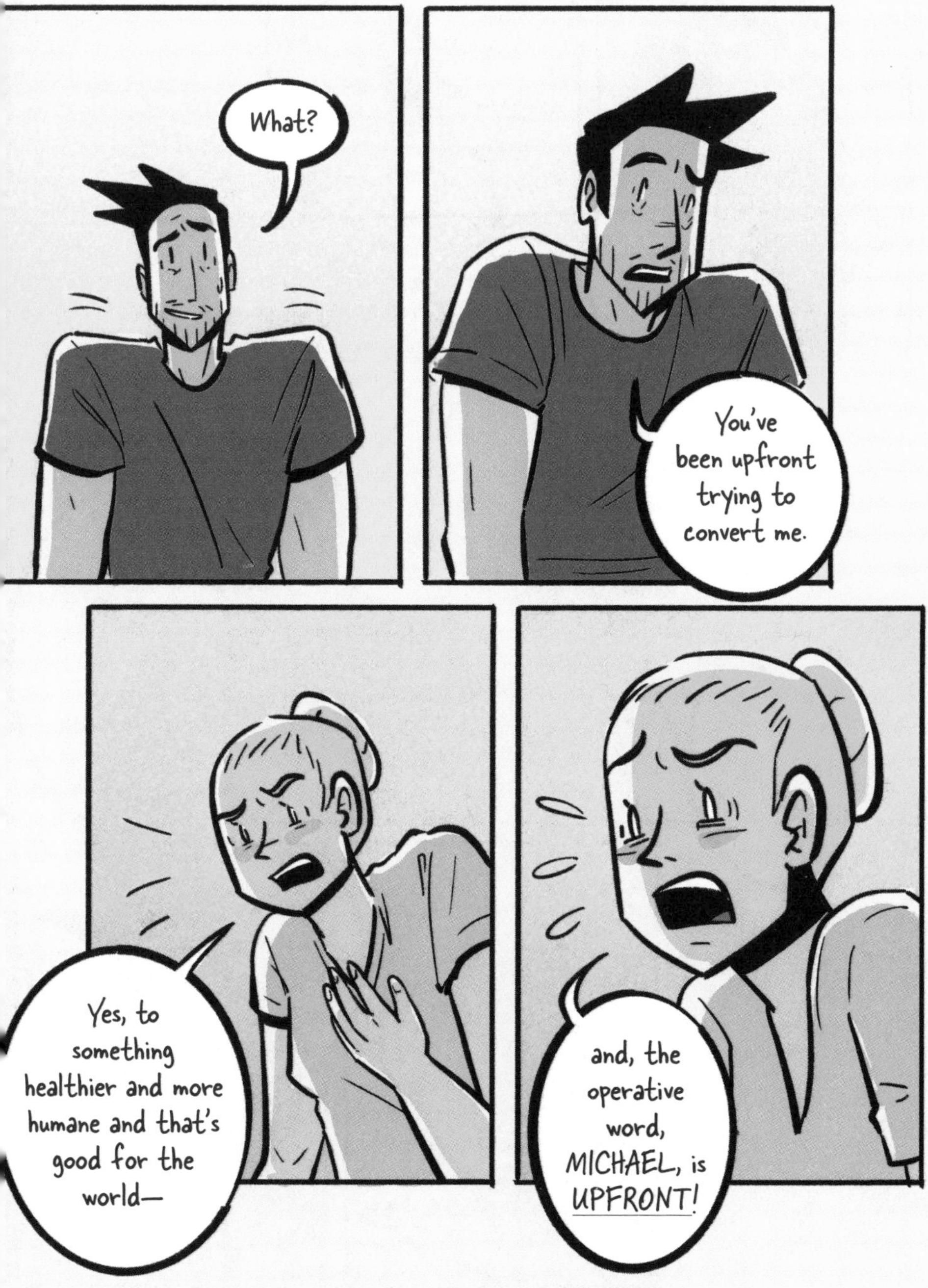
What?
You've been upfront trying to convert me.
Yes, to something healthier and more humane and that's good for the world—
and, the operative word, MICHAEL, is UPFRONT!

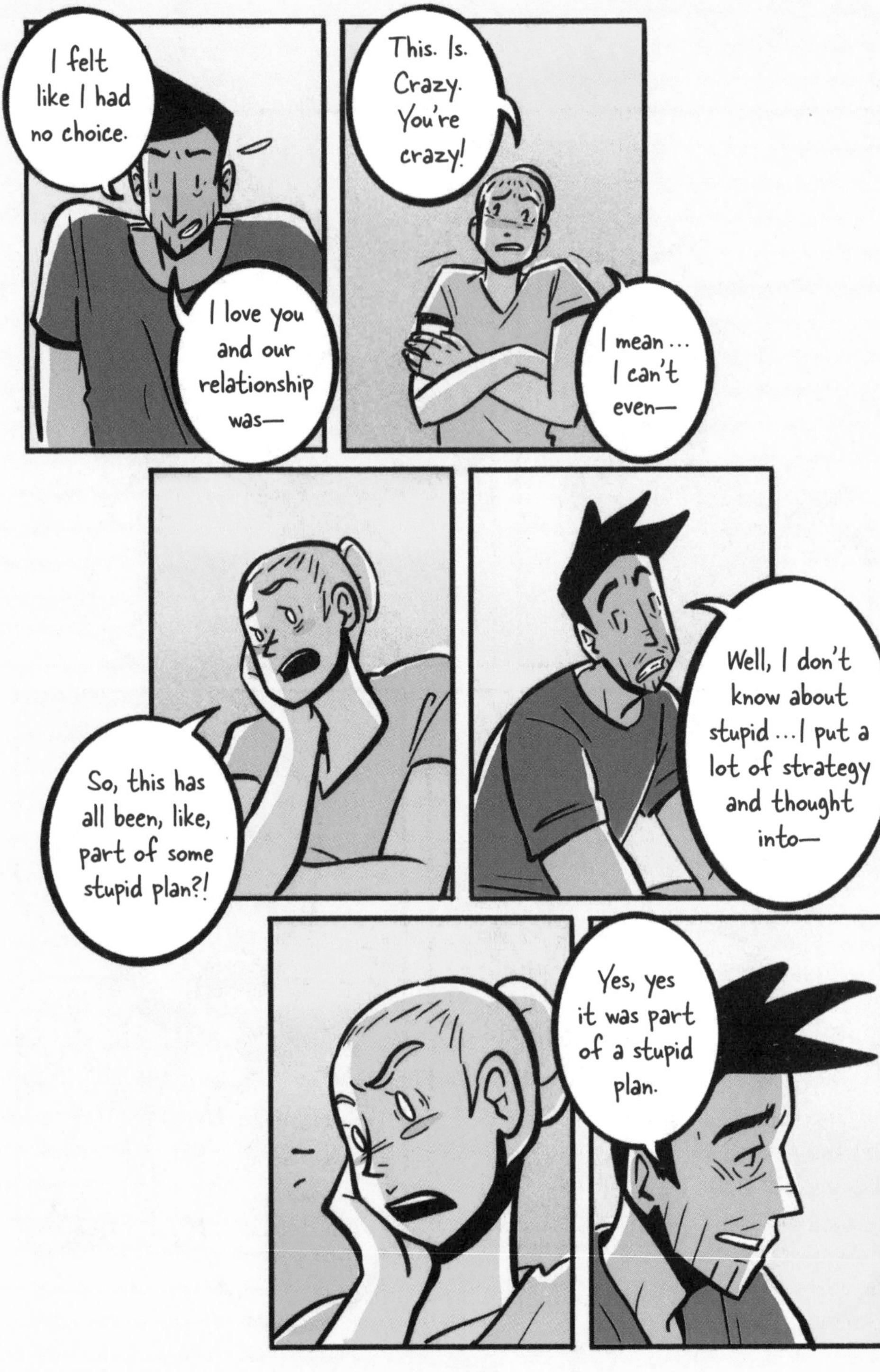
I felt like I had no choice.
I love you and our relationship was—
This. Is. Crazy. You're crazy!
I mean... I can't even—
So, this has all been, like, part of some stupid plan?!
Well, I don't know about stupid... I put a lot of strategy and thought into—
Yes, yes it was part of a stupid plan.

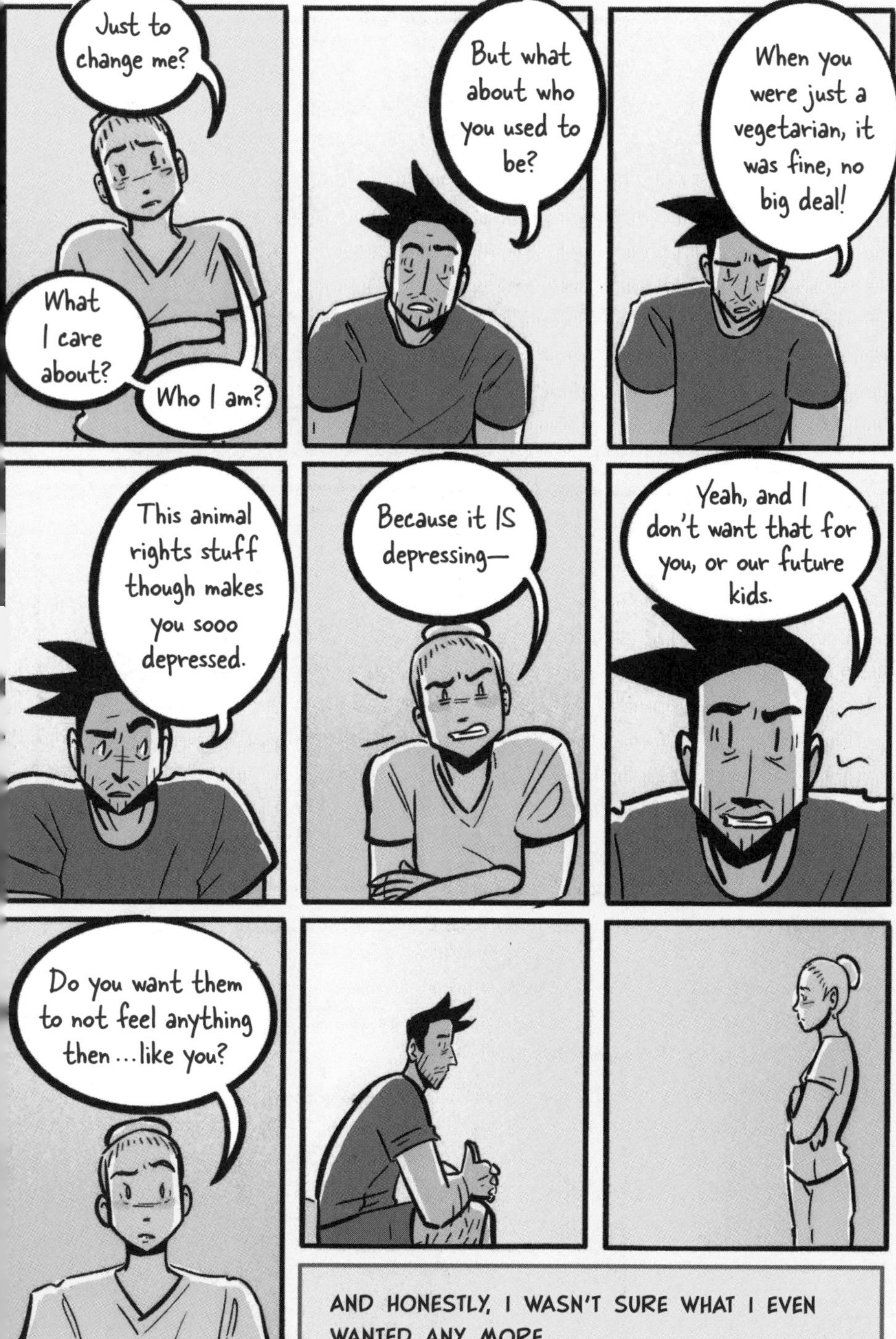
Just to change me?
What I care about?
Who I am?
But what about who you used to be?
When you were just a vegetarian, it was fine, no big deal!
This animal rights stuff though makes you sooo depressed.
Because it IS depressing—
Yeah, and I don't want that for you, or our future kids.
Do you want them to not feel anything then ... like you?
AND HONESTLY, I WASN'T SURE WHAT I EVEN WANTED ANY MORE.

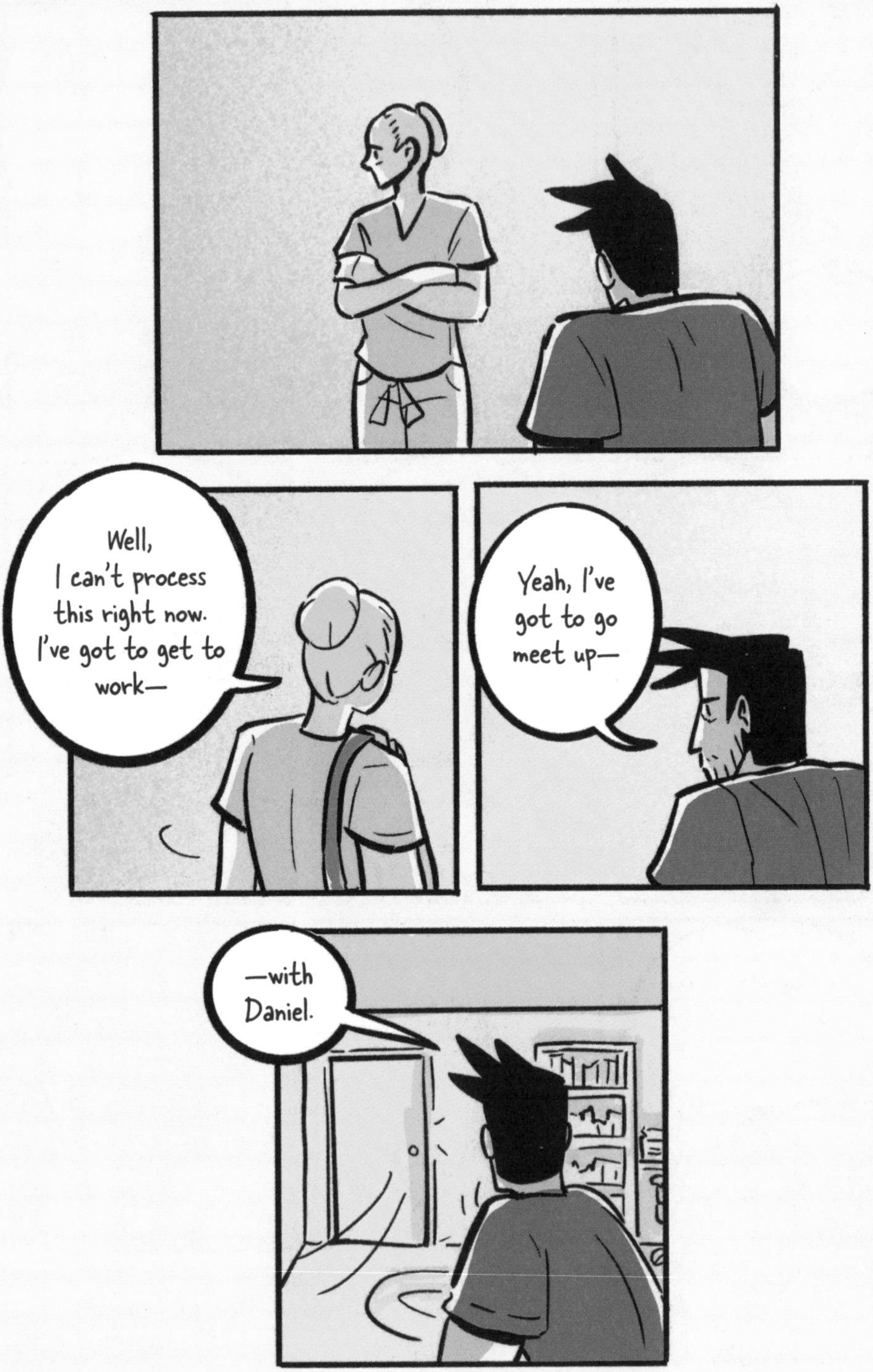
Well, I can't process this right now. I've got to get to work—
Yeah, I've got to go meet up—
—with Daniel.

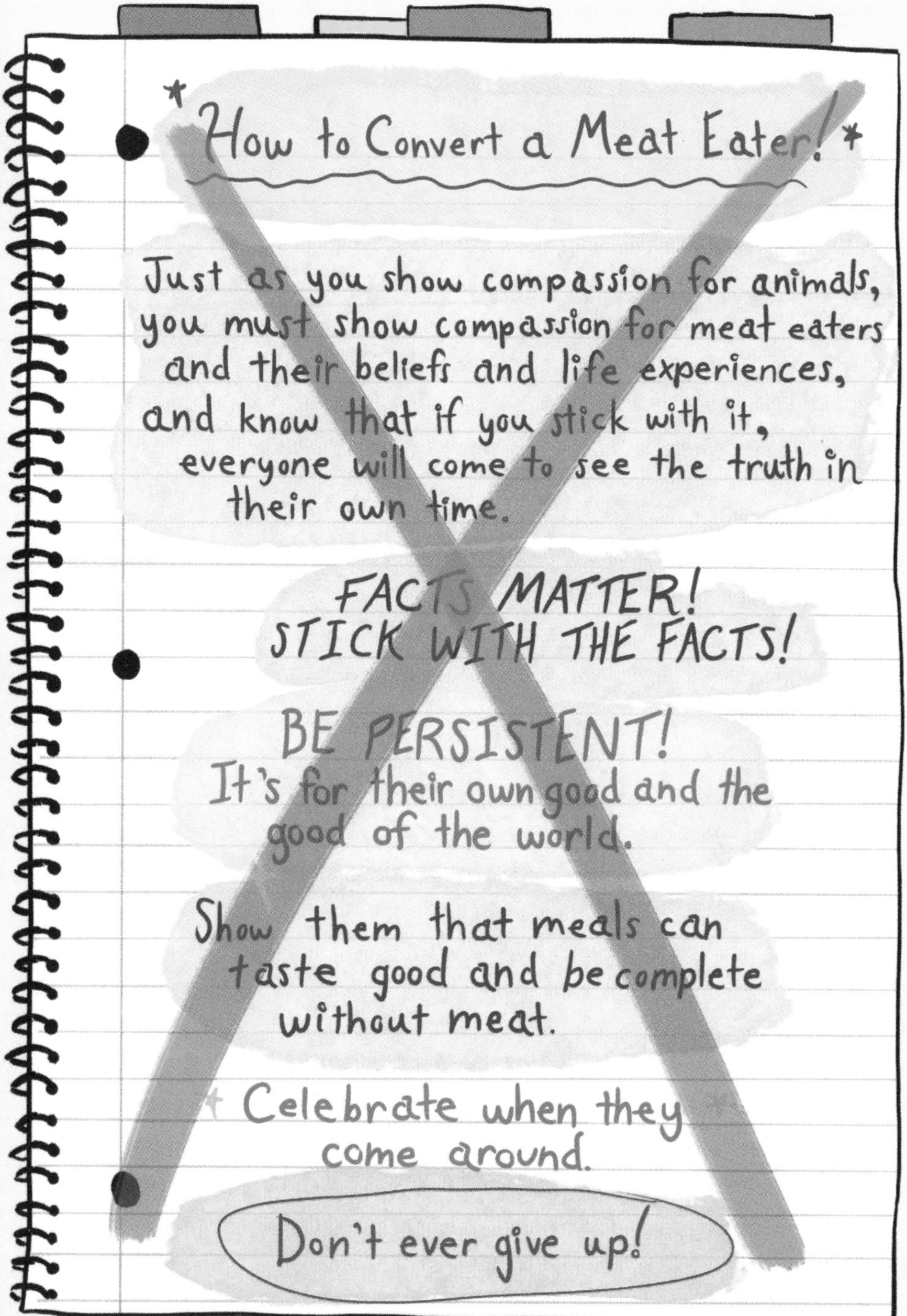
How to Convert a Meat Eater!
Just as you show compassion for animals, you must show compassion for meat eaters and their beliefs and life experiences, and know that if you stick with it, everyone will come to see the truth in their own time.
FACTS MATTER! STICK WITH THE FACTS!
BE PERSISTENT!
It's for their own good and the good of the world.
Show them that meals can taste good and be complete without meat.
Celebrate when they come around.
Don't ever give up!

IT'S IMPOSSIBLE TO FOCUS ON ANYTHING ELSE WHEN YOU HAVE A SIXTEEN-GAUGE NEEDLE IN YOUR ARM.

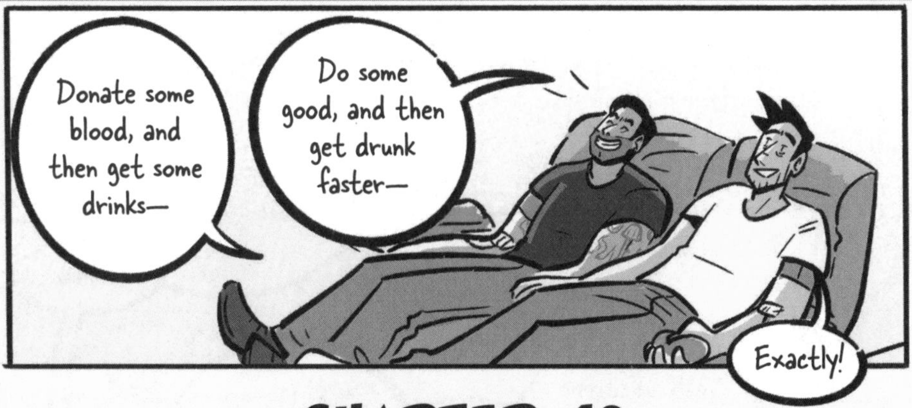

Donate some blood, and then get some drinks—
Do some good, and then get drunk faster—
Exactly!

CHAPTER 13

THE AVERAGE SOLDIER HAS ANYWHERE BETWEEN 150 TO 170 OUNCES OF BLOOD IN THEIR BODY (VARIANCE BASED ON HEIGHT AND WEIGHT), AND DEPENDING ON ANY WOUNDS THEY RECEIVE, A PERSON CAN BLEED OUT IN ANYWHERE FROM HOURS TO MINUTES TO EVEN SECONDS. USUALLY IT'S WHEN THEY'VE LOST AROUND 40% WHEN DEATH OCCURS.

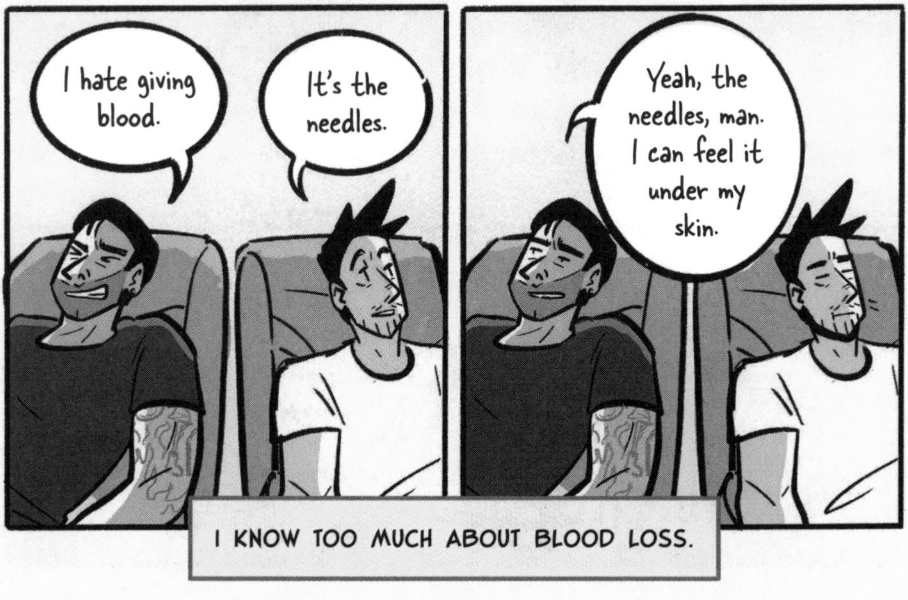

I hate giving blood.
It's the needles.
Yeah, the needles, man. I can feel it under my skin.

I KNOW TOO MUCH ABOUT BLOOD LOSS.

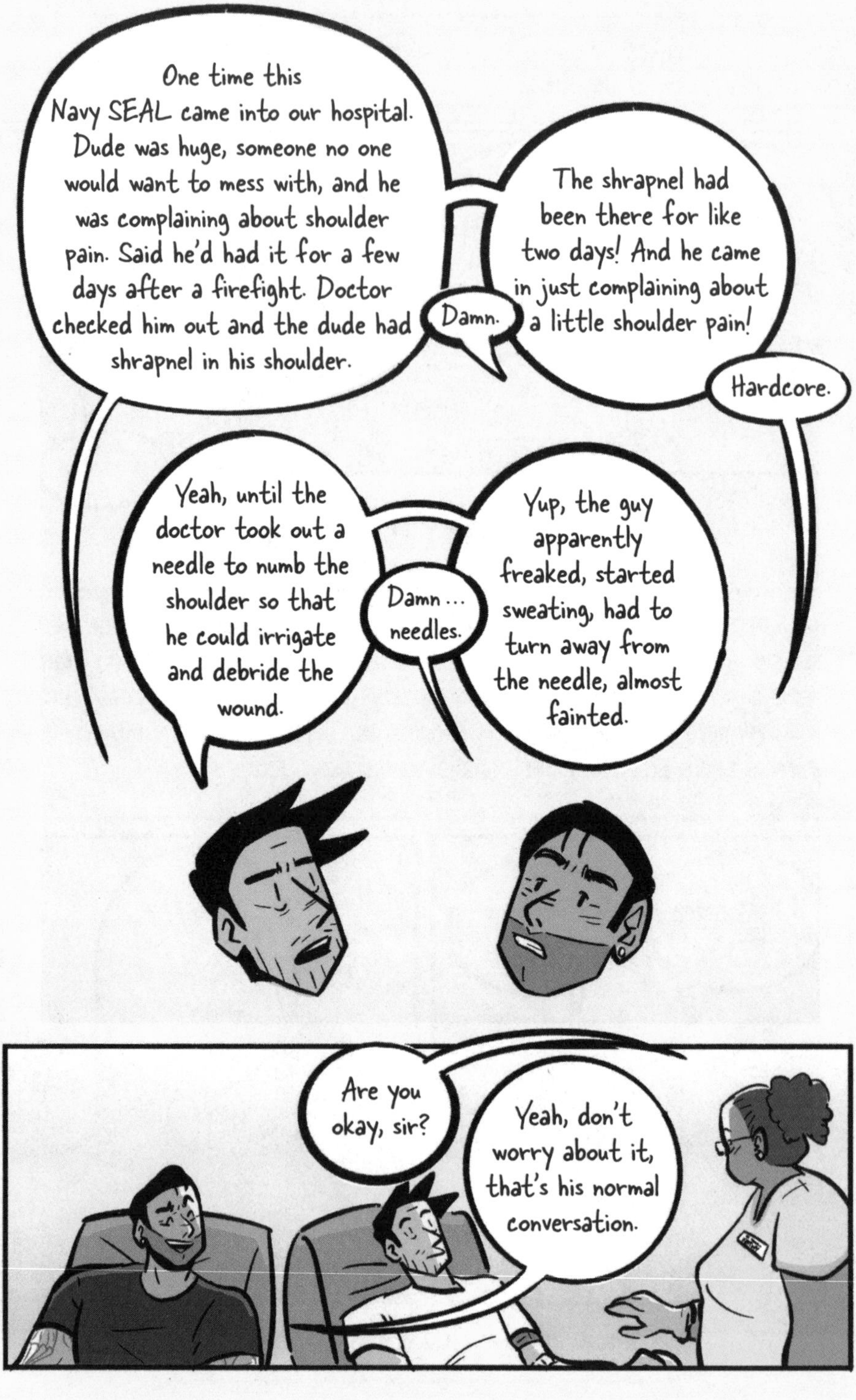
One time this Navy SEAL came into our hospital. Dude was huge, someone no one would want to mess with, and he was complaining about shoulder pain. Said he'd had it for a few days after a firefight. Doctor checked him out and the dude had shrapnel in his shoulder.
Damn.
The shrapnel had been there for like two days! And he came in just complaining about a little shoulder pain!
Hardcore.
Yeah, until the doctor took out a needle to numb the shoulder so that he could irrigate and debride the wound.
Damn... needles.
Yup, the guy apparently freaked, started sweating, had to turn away from the needle, almost fainted.
Are you okay, sir?
Yeah, don't worry about it, that's his normal conversation.

WITH NO FOOD IN OUR STOMACHS AND FEELING BLOOD-DONATION TIPSY, MARCHING TO OLD ARMY CADENCES SEEMED LIKE THE THING TO DO.

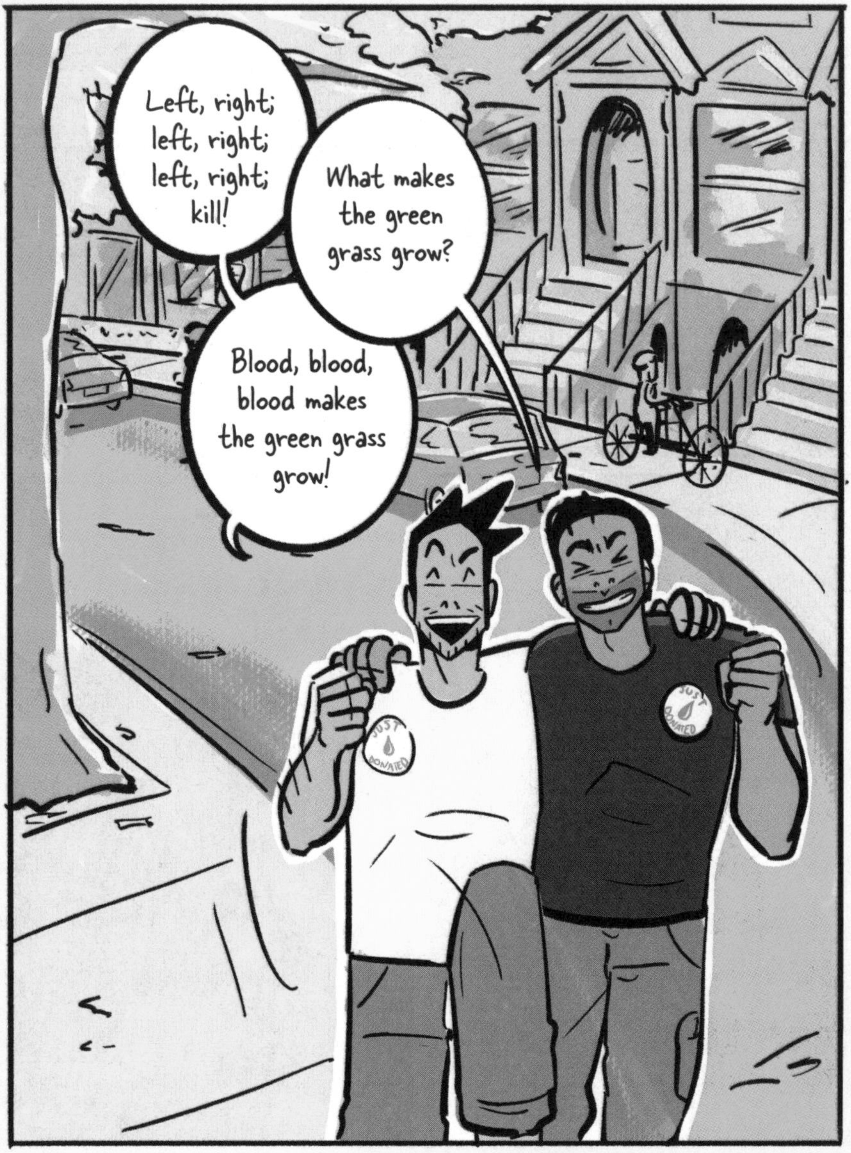
Left, right; left, right; left, right; kill!
What makes the green grass grow?
Blood, blood, blood makes the green grass grow!
JUST DONATED
JUST DONATED

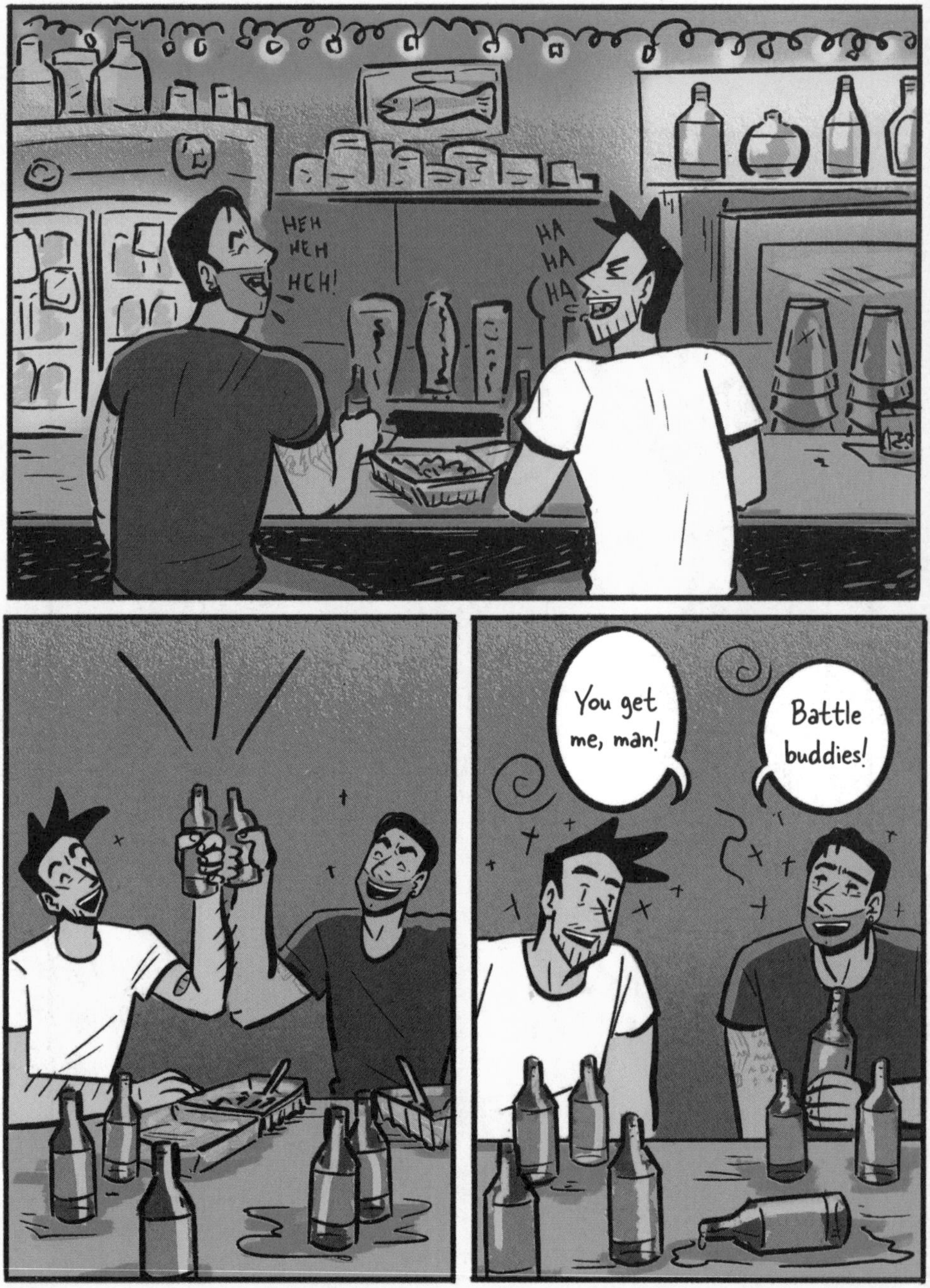
HEH HEH HEH!
HA HA HA
You get me, man!
Battle buddies!

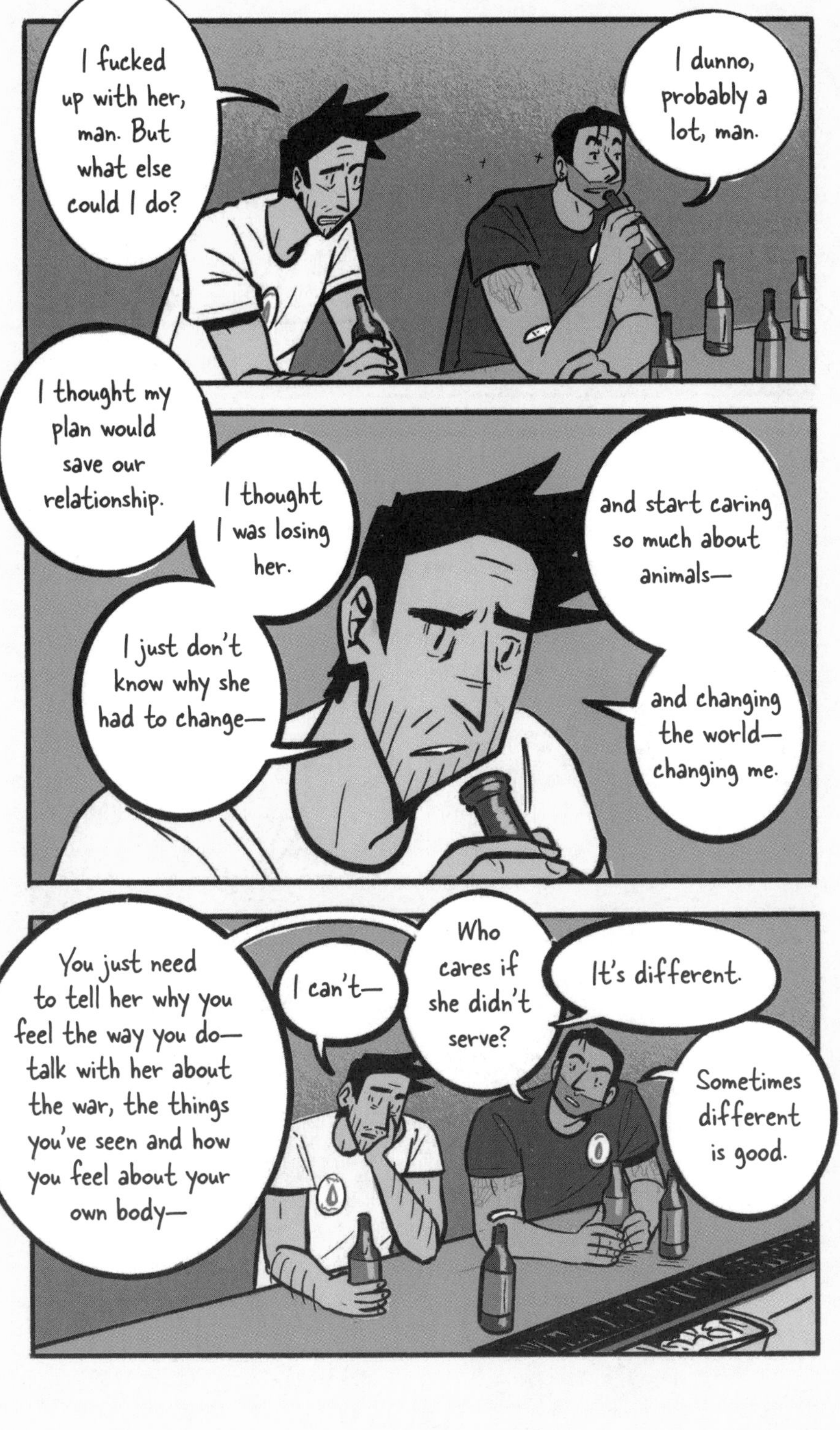
I fucked up with her, man. But what else could I do?
I dunno, probably a lot, man.
I thought my plan would save our relationship.
I thought I was losing her.
I just don't know why she had to change—
and start caring so much about animals—
and changing the world—changing me.
You just need to tell her why you feel the way you do—talk with her about the war, the things you've seen and how you feel about your own body—
I can't—
Who cares if she didn't serve?
It's different.
Sometimes different is good.

You just gotta understand where she's coming from. And you gotta respect the animal rights stuff.
Respect it? It ruined my relationship.
Nah, man. Don't think of it like that. A person needs something to live for, a battle to keep them going. Your girl found her battle. You thought it was against you and your relationship, but it wasn't. You just didn't read the terrain right.
Huh?

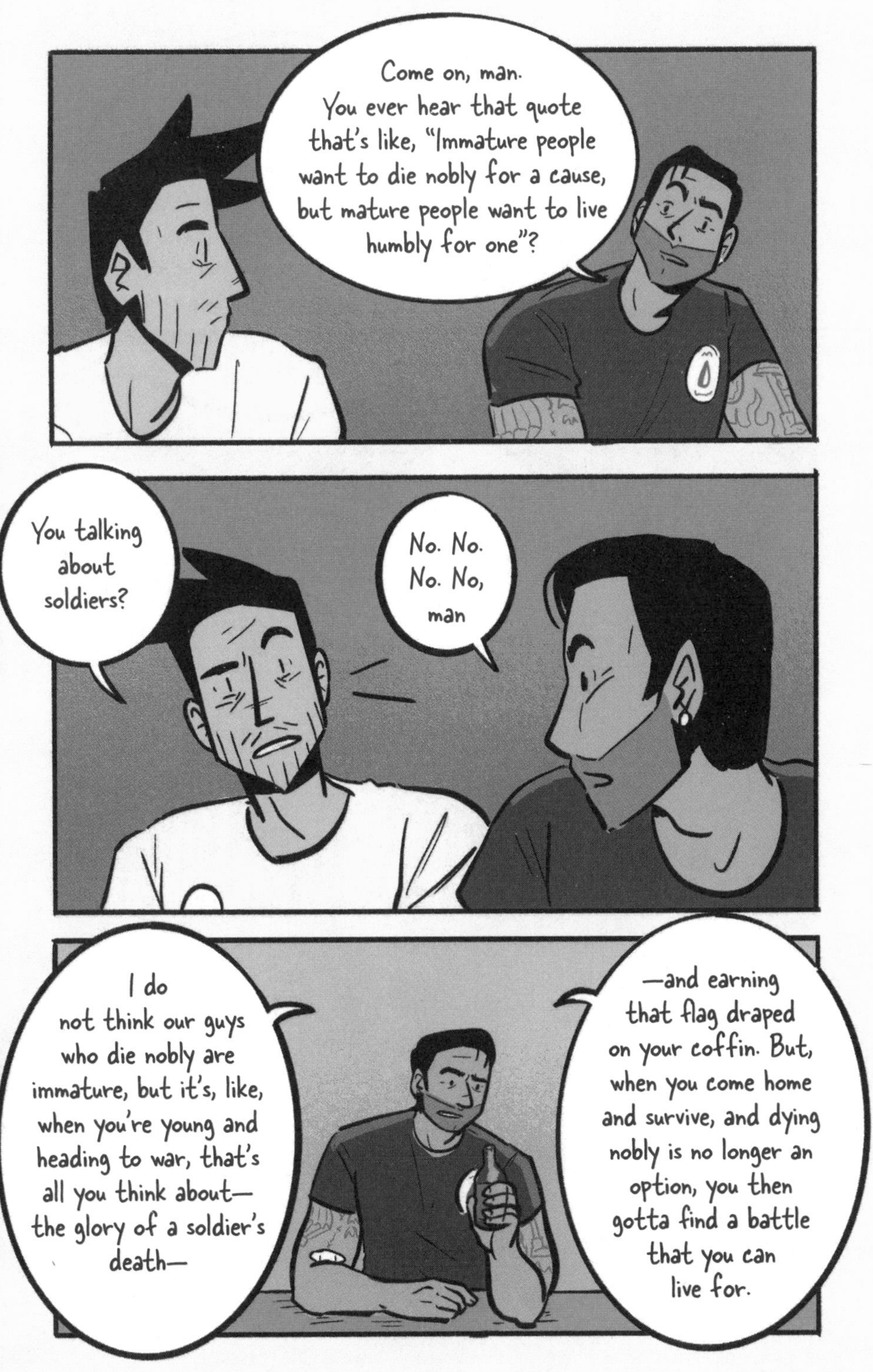
Come on, man. You ever hear that quote that's like, "Immature people want to die nobly for a cause, but mature people want to live humbly for one"?
You talking about soldiers?
No. No. No. No, man
I do not think our guys who die nobly are immature, but it's, like, when you're young and heading to war, that's all you think about— the glory of a soldier's death—
—and earning that flag draped on your coffin. But, when you come home and survive, and dying nobly is no longer an option, you then gotta find a battle that you can live for.

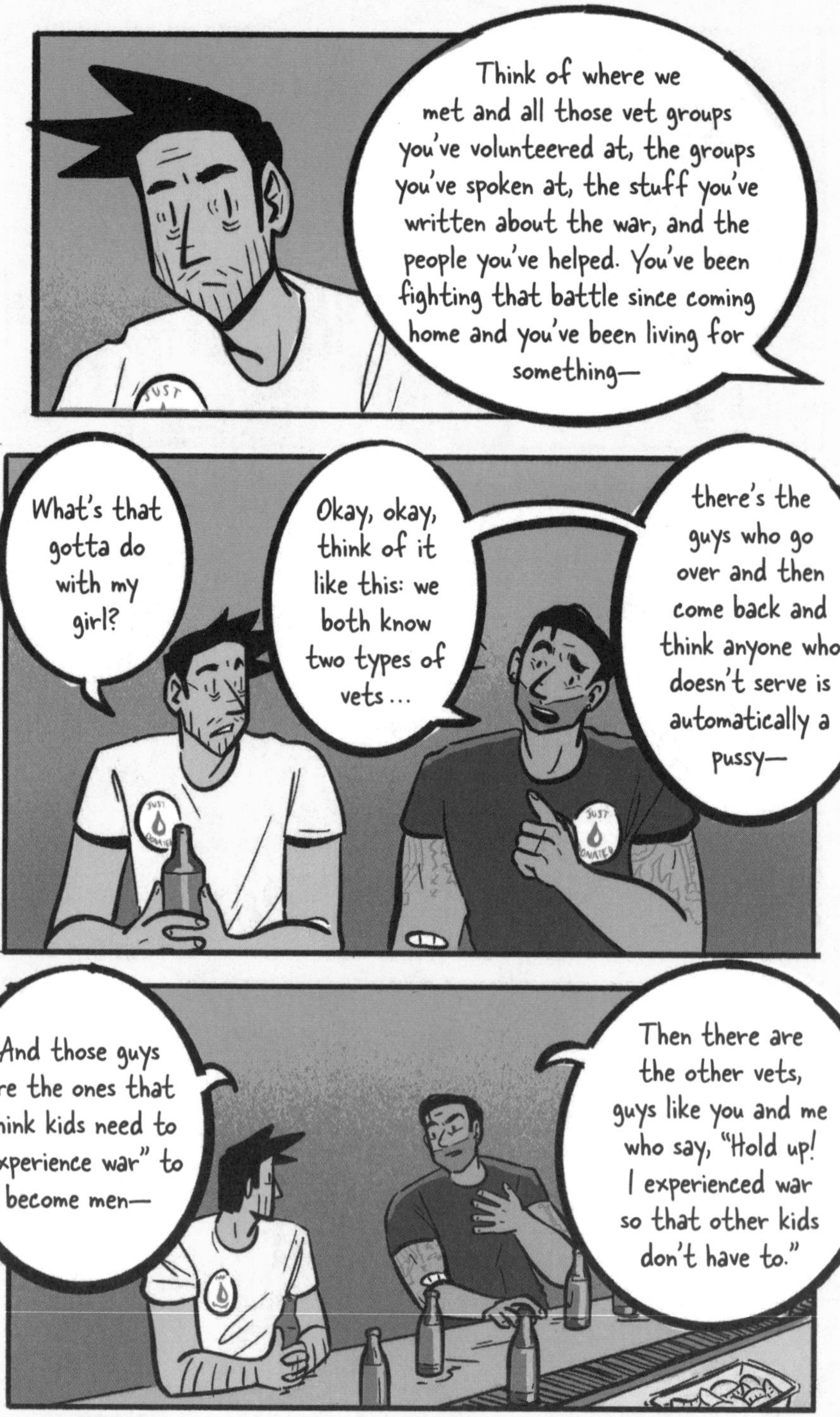
Think of where we met and all those vet groups you've volunteered at, the groups you've spoken at, the stuff you've written about the war, and the people you've helped. You've been fighting that battle since coming home and you've been living for something—
What's that gotta do with my girl?
Okay, okay, think of it like this: we both know two types of vets...
there's the guys who go over and then come back and think anyone who doesn't serve is automatically a pussy—
JUST DONATED
And those guys are the ones that think kids need to "experience war" to become men—
Then there are the other vets, guys like you and me who say, "Hold up! I experienced war so that other kids don't have to."

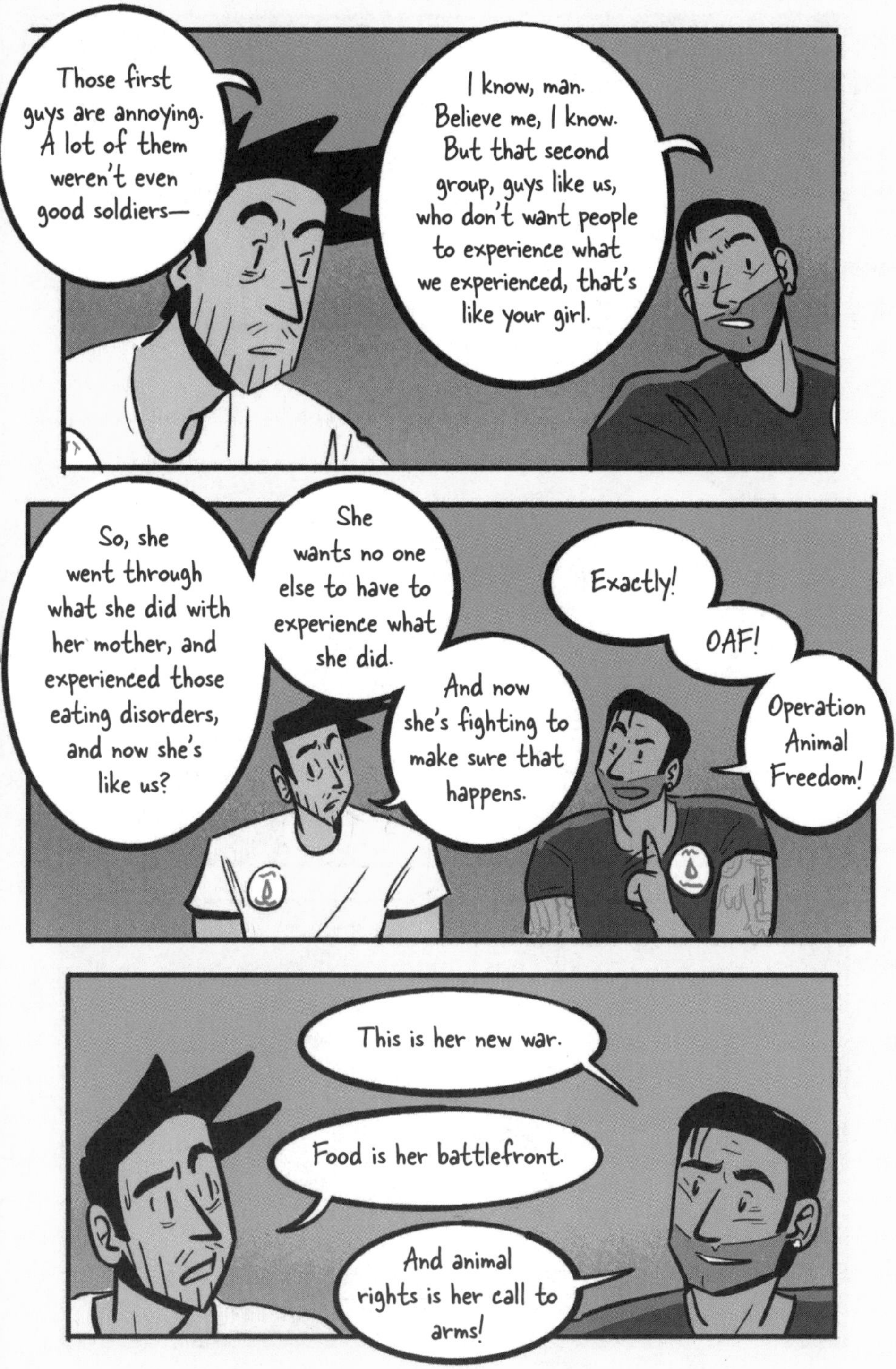

Those first guys are annoying. A lot of them weren't even good soldiers—
I know, man. Believe me, I know. But that second group, guys like us, who don't want people to experience what we experienced, that's like your girl.
So, she went through what she did with her mother, and experienced those eating disorders, and now she's like us?
She wants no one else to have to experience what she did.
And now she's fighting to make sure that happens.
Exactly!
OAF!
Operation Animal Freedom!
This is her new war.
Food is her battlefront.
And animal rights is her call to arms!

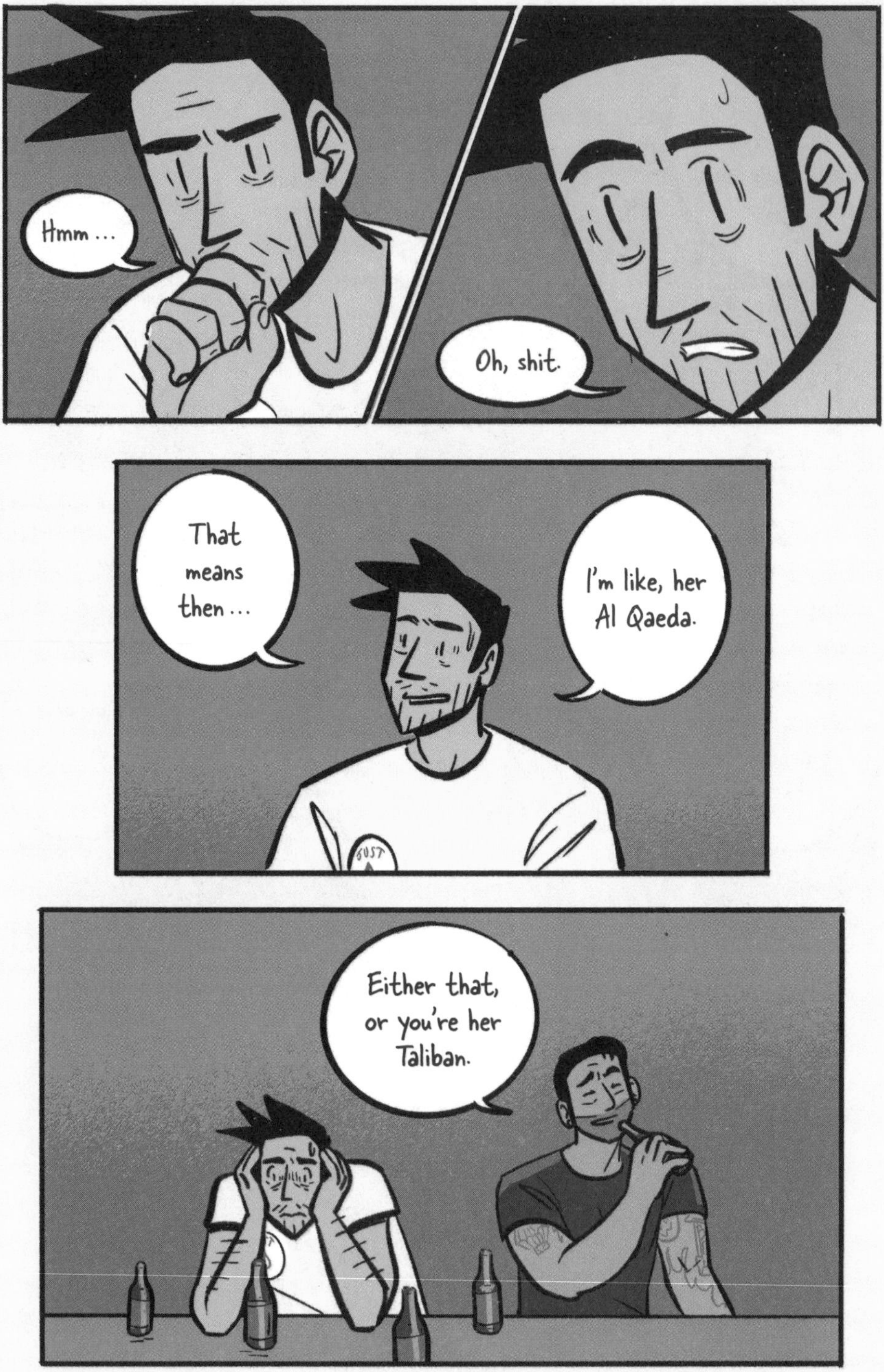
Hmm ...
Oh, shit.
That means then ...
I'm like, her Al Qaeda.
Either that, or you're her Taliban.

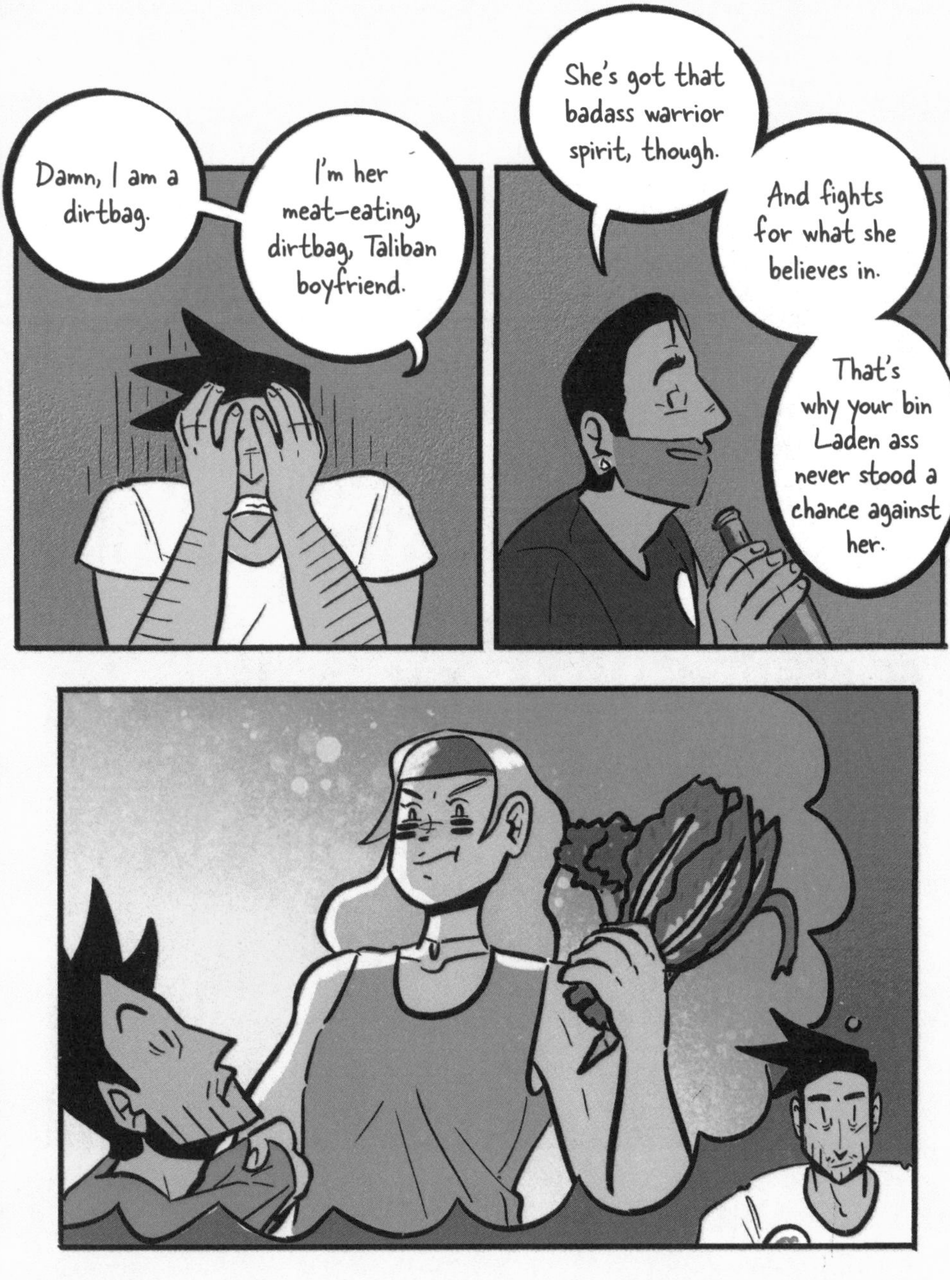
Damn, I am a dirtbag.
I'm her meat-eating, dirtbag, Taliban boyfriend.
She's got that badass warrior spirit, though.
And fights for what she believes in.
That's why your bin Laden ass never stood a chance against her.

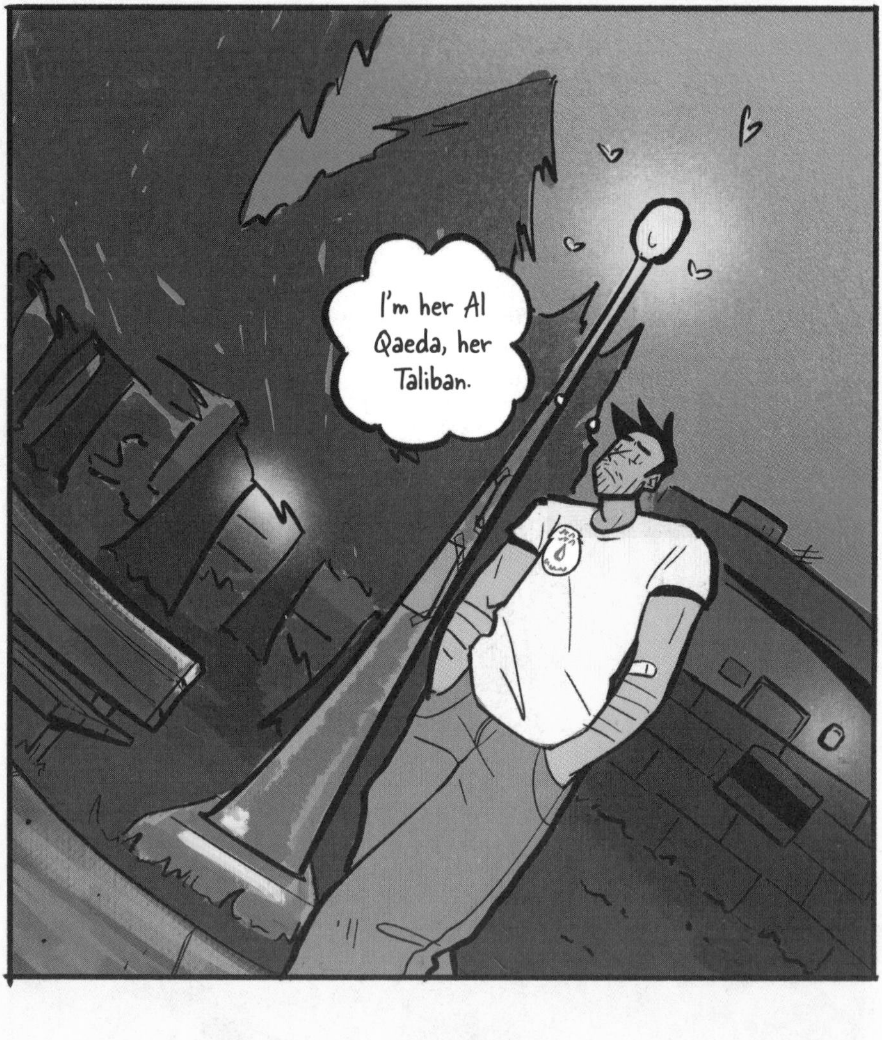
I'm her Al Qaeda, her Taliban.

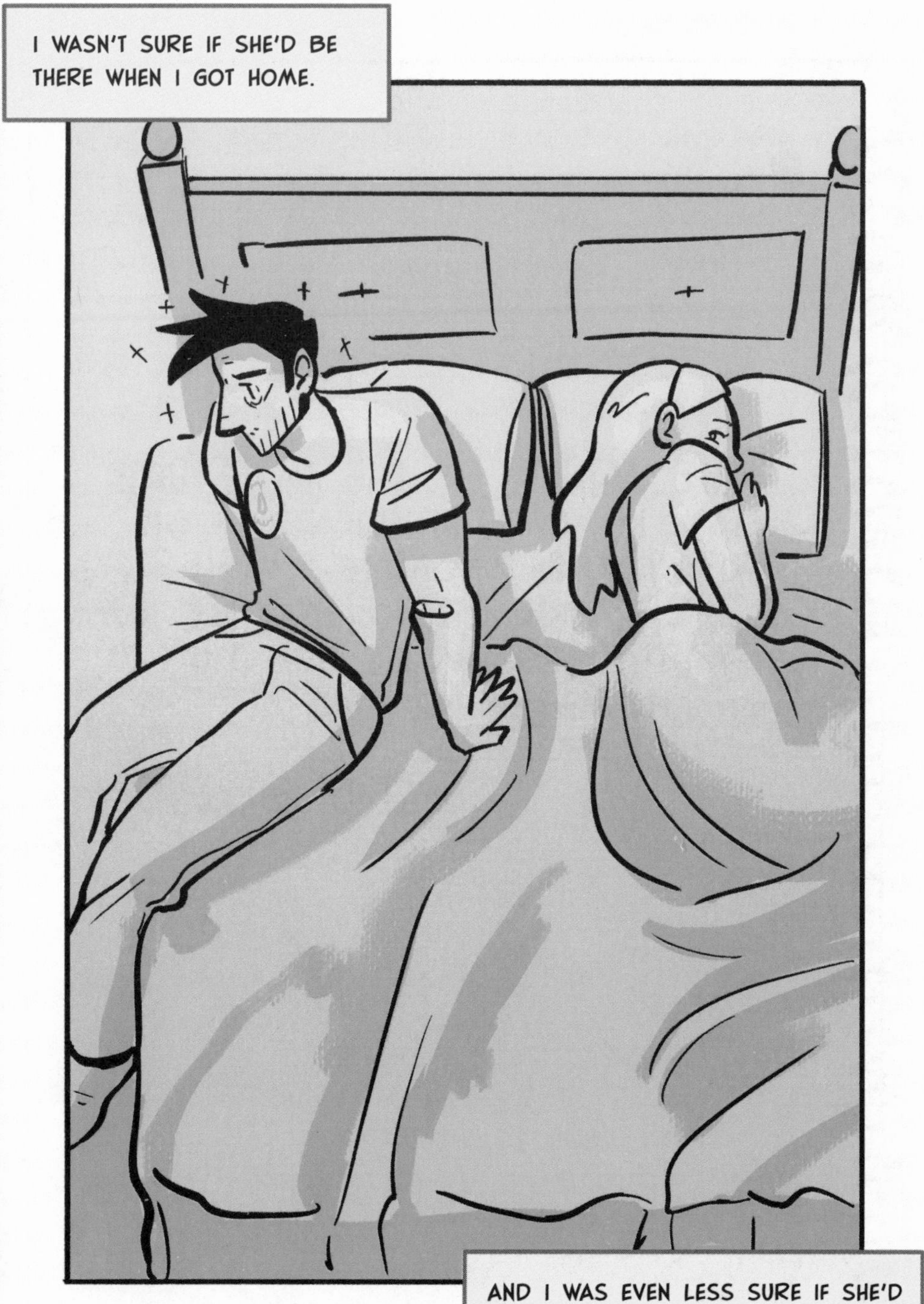
I WASN'T SURE IF SHE'D BE THERE WHEN I GOT HOME.
AND I WAS EVEN LESS SURE IF SHE'D BE THERE WHEN I WOKE UP.

"THE MARK OF THE IMMATURE MAN IS THAT HE WANTS TO DIE NOBLY FOR A CAUSE, WHILE THE MARK OF THE MATURE MAN IS THAT HE WANTS TO LIVE HUMBLY FOR ONE."

—J.D. SALINGER

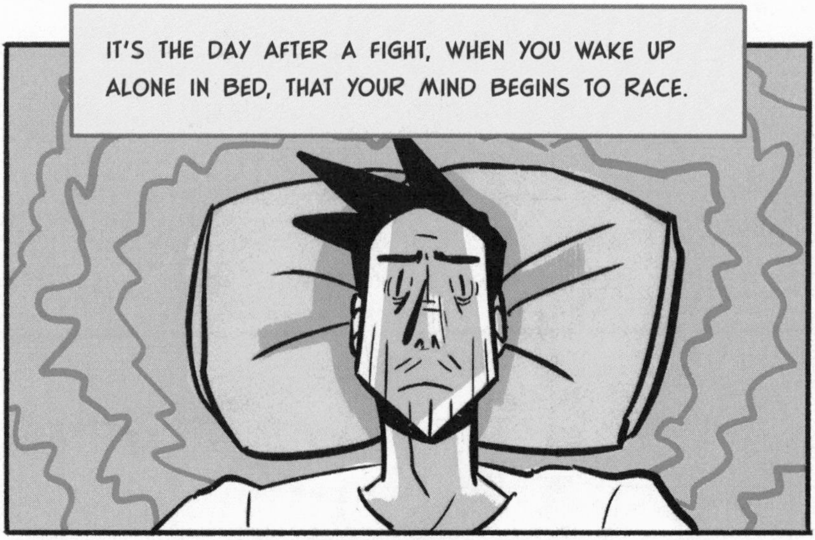
IT'S THE DAY AFTER A FIGHT, WHEN YOU WAKE UP ALONE IN BED, THAT YOUR MIND BEGINS TO RACE.

CHAPTER 14

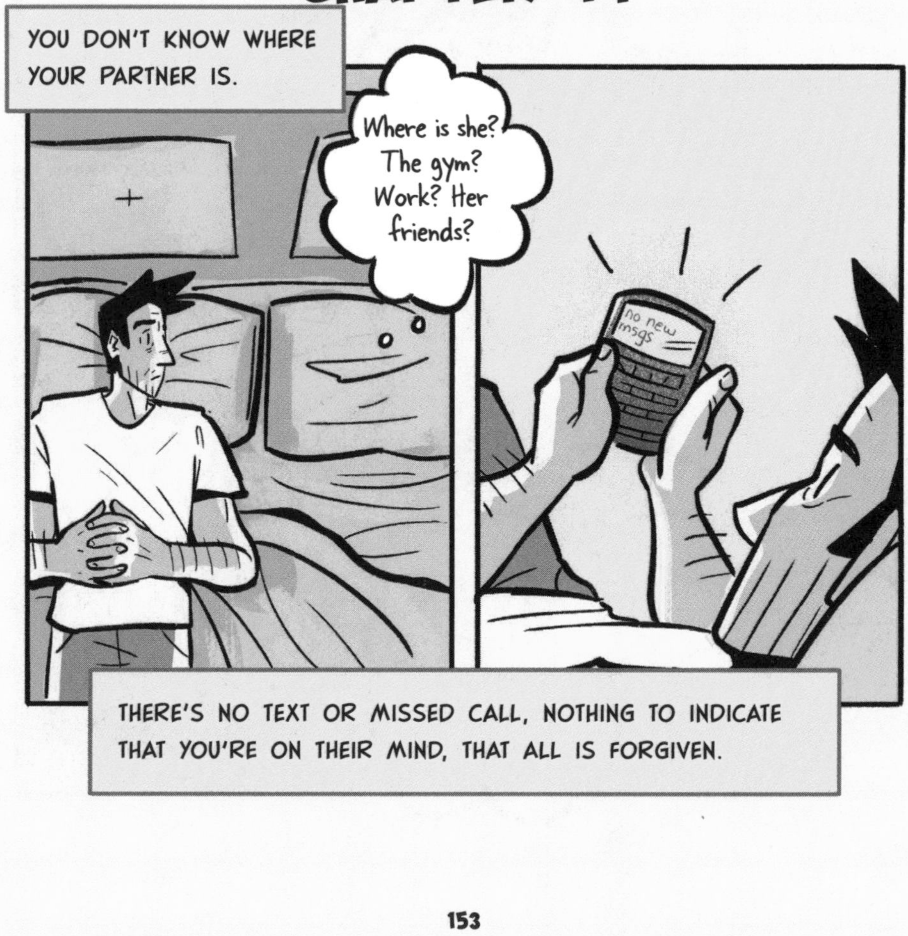
YOU DON'T KNOW WHERE YOUR PARTNER IS.
Where is she? The gym? Work? Her friends?
no new msgs
THERE'S NO TEXT OR MISSED CALL, NOTHING TO INDICATE THAT YOU'RE ON THEIR MIND, THAT ALL IS FORGIVEN.

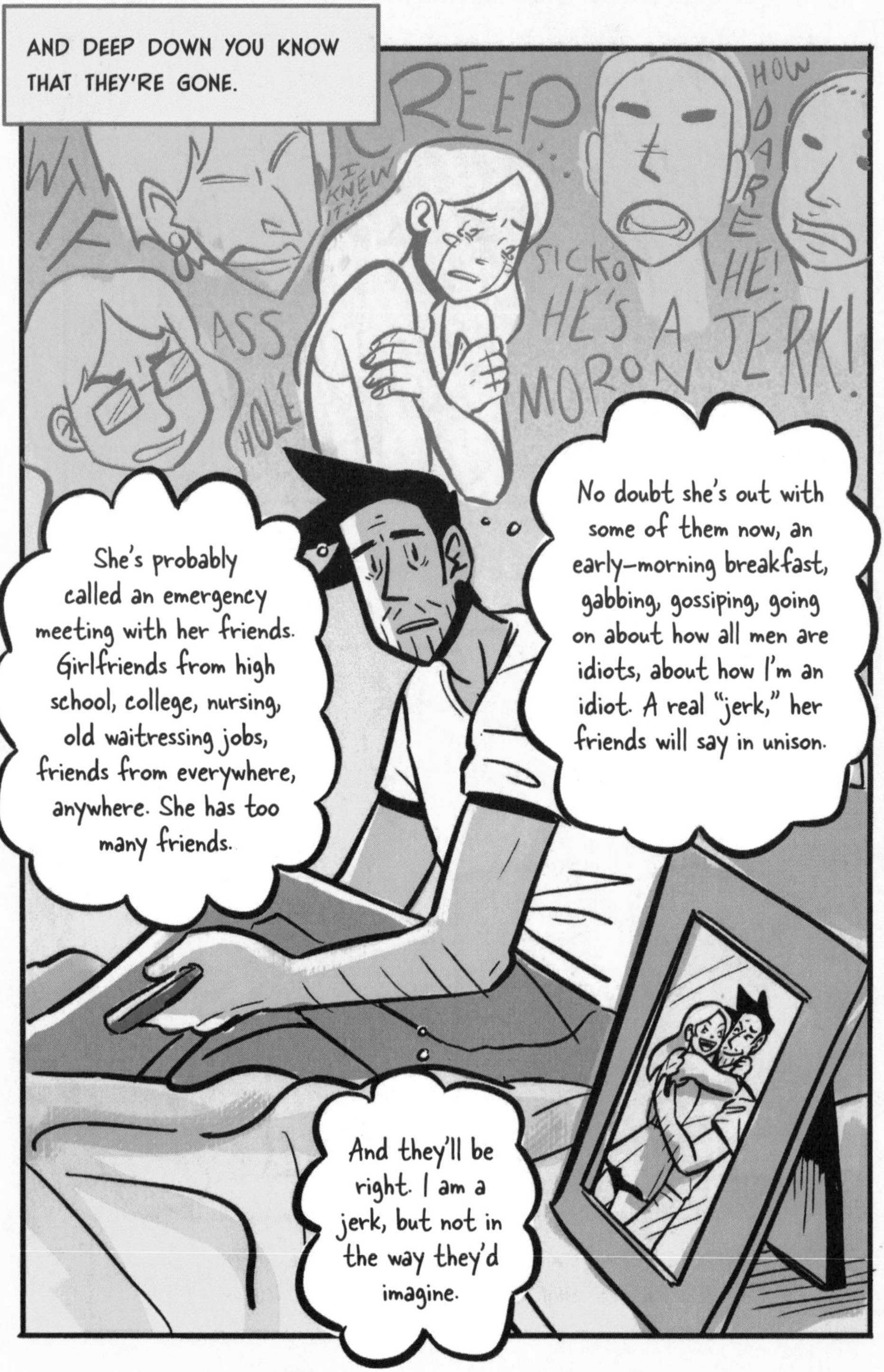
AND DEEP DOWN YOU KNOW THAT THEY'RE GONE.
CREEP...
HOW DARE HE!
I KNEW IT!!
WTF
SICKO
HE'S A JERK!
MORON
ASS HOLE
She's probably called an emergency meeting with her friends. Girlfriends from high school, college, nursing, old waitressing jobs, friends from everywhere, anywhere. She has too many friends.
No doubt she's out with some of them now, an early-morning breakfast, gabbing, gossiping, going on about how all men are idiots, about how I'm an idiot. A real "jerk," her friends will say in unison.
And they'll be right. I am a jerk, but not in the way they'd imagine.

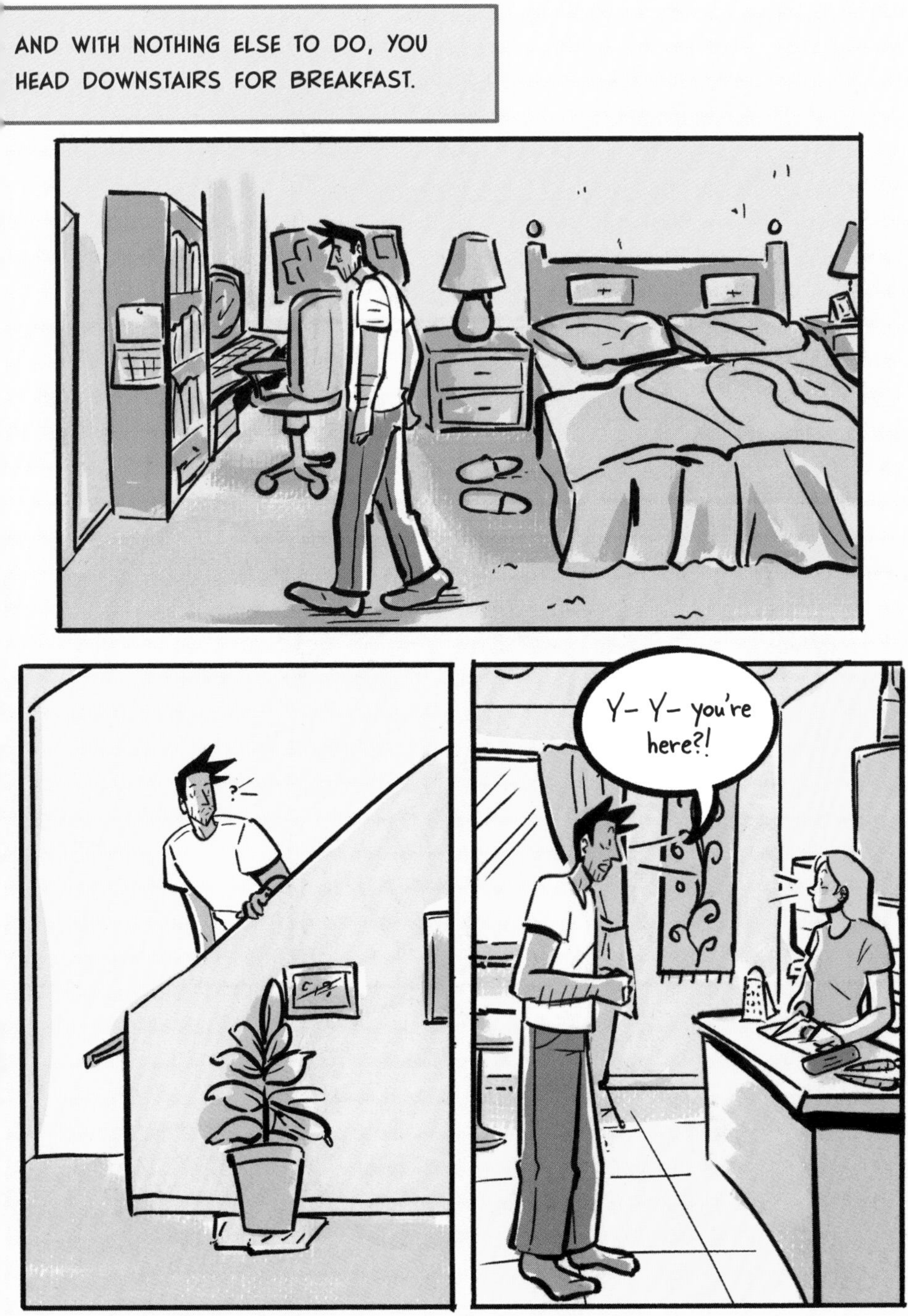
AND WITH NOTHING ELSE TO DO, YOU HEAD DOWNSTAIRS FOR BREAKFAST.
Y- Y- you're here?!

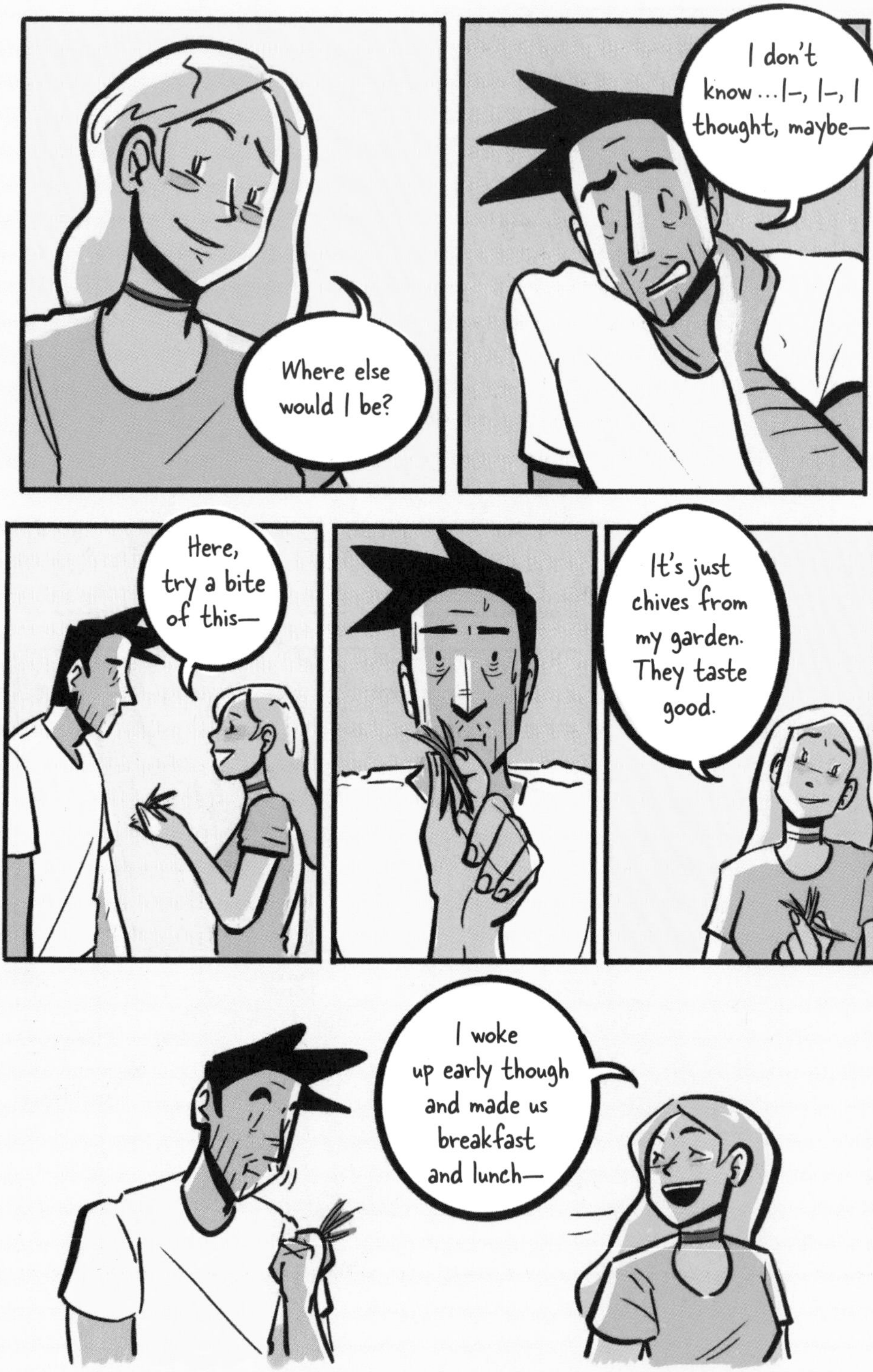
Where else would I be?
I don't know...I–, I–, I thought, maybe—
Here, try a bite of this—
It's just chives from my garden. They taste good.
I woke up early though and made us breakfast and lunch—

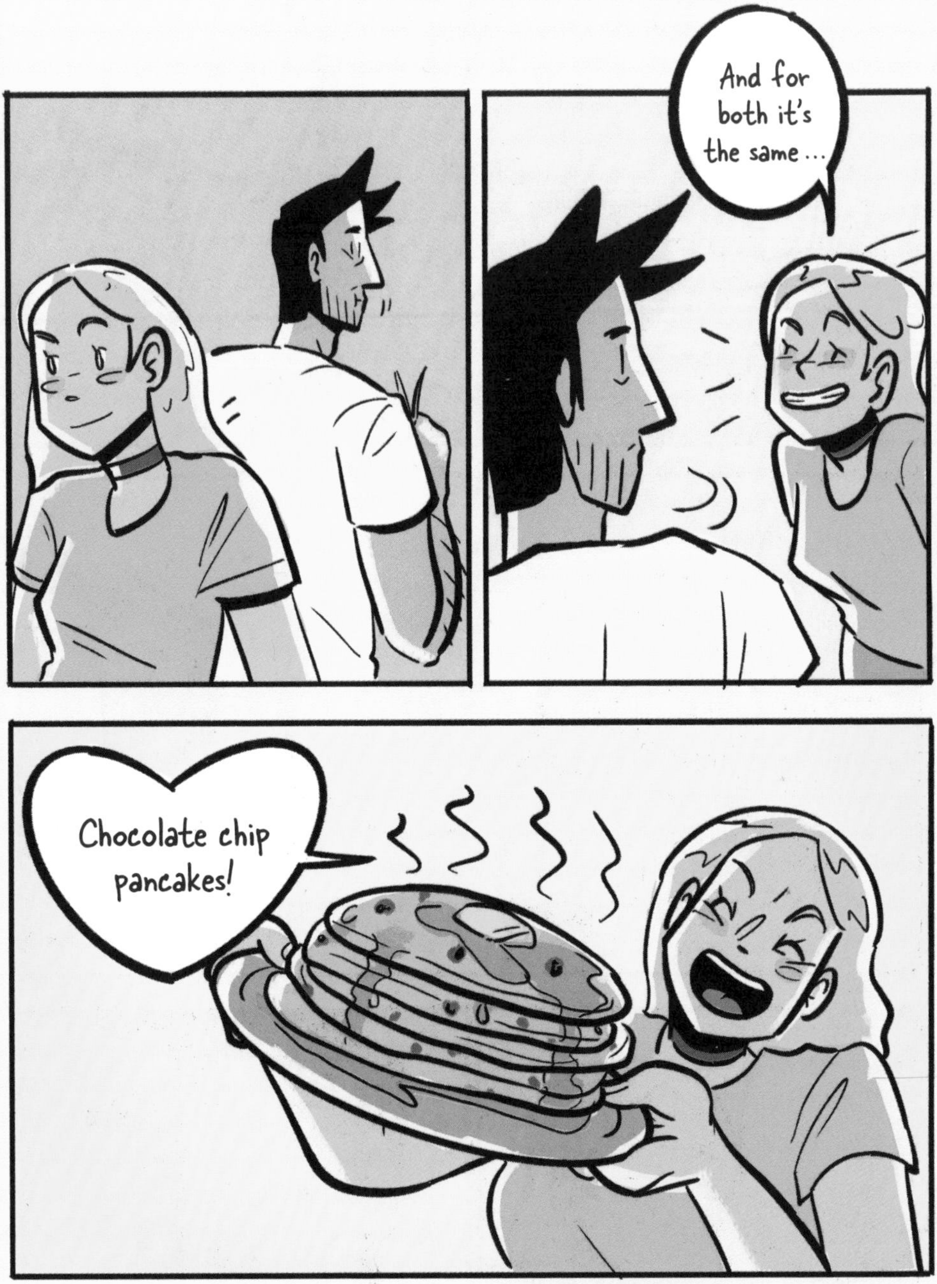
And for both it's the same...
Chocolate chip pancakes!

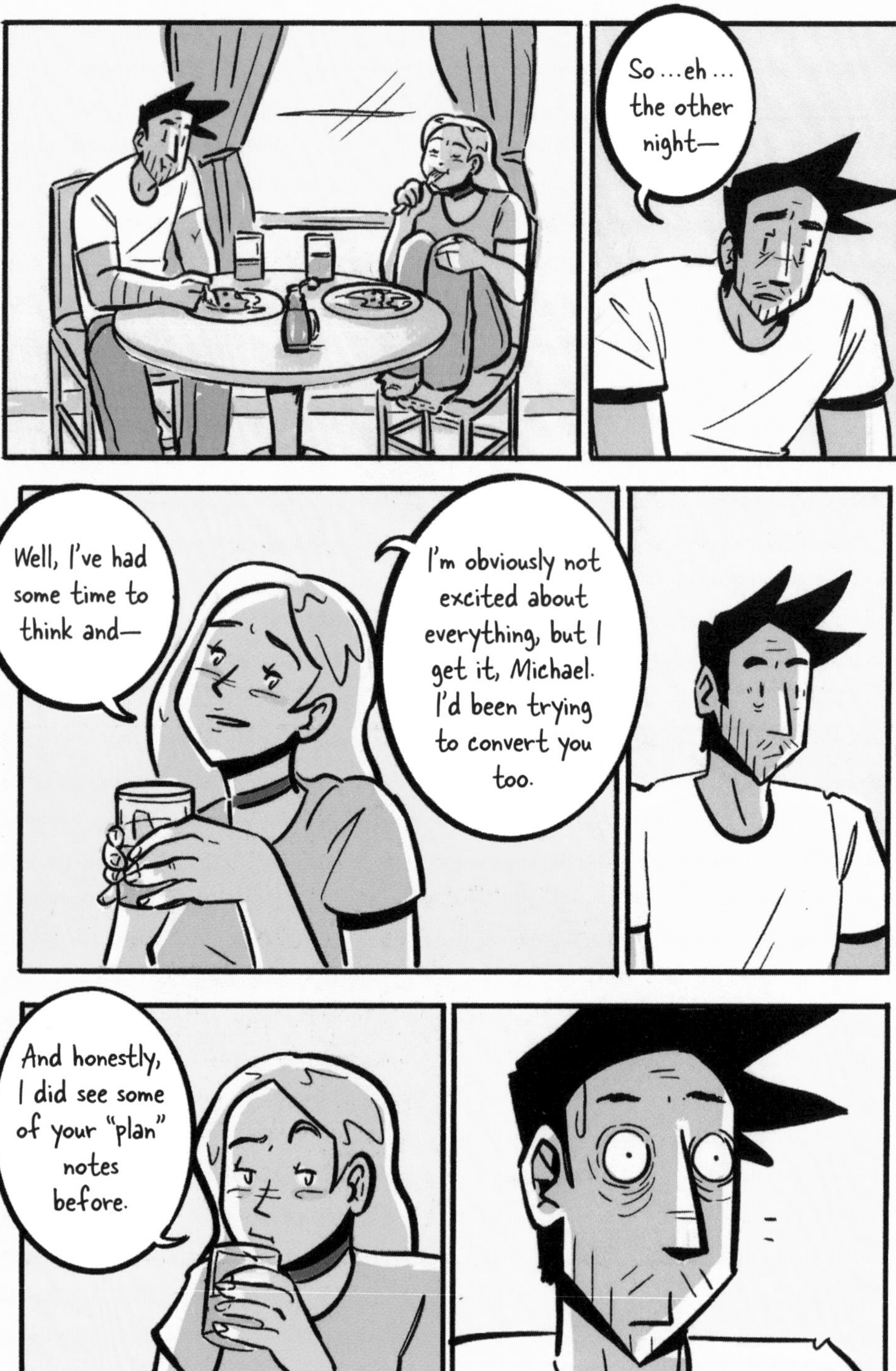

So...eh...the other night—
Well, I've had some time to think and—
I'm obviously not excited about everything, but I get it, Michael. I'd been trying to convert you too.
And honestly, I did see some of your "plan" notes before.

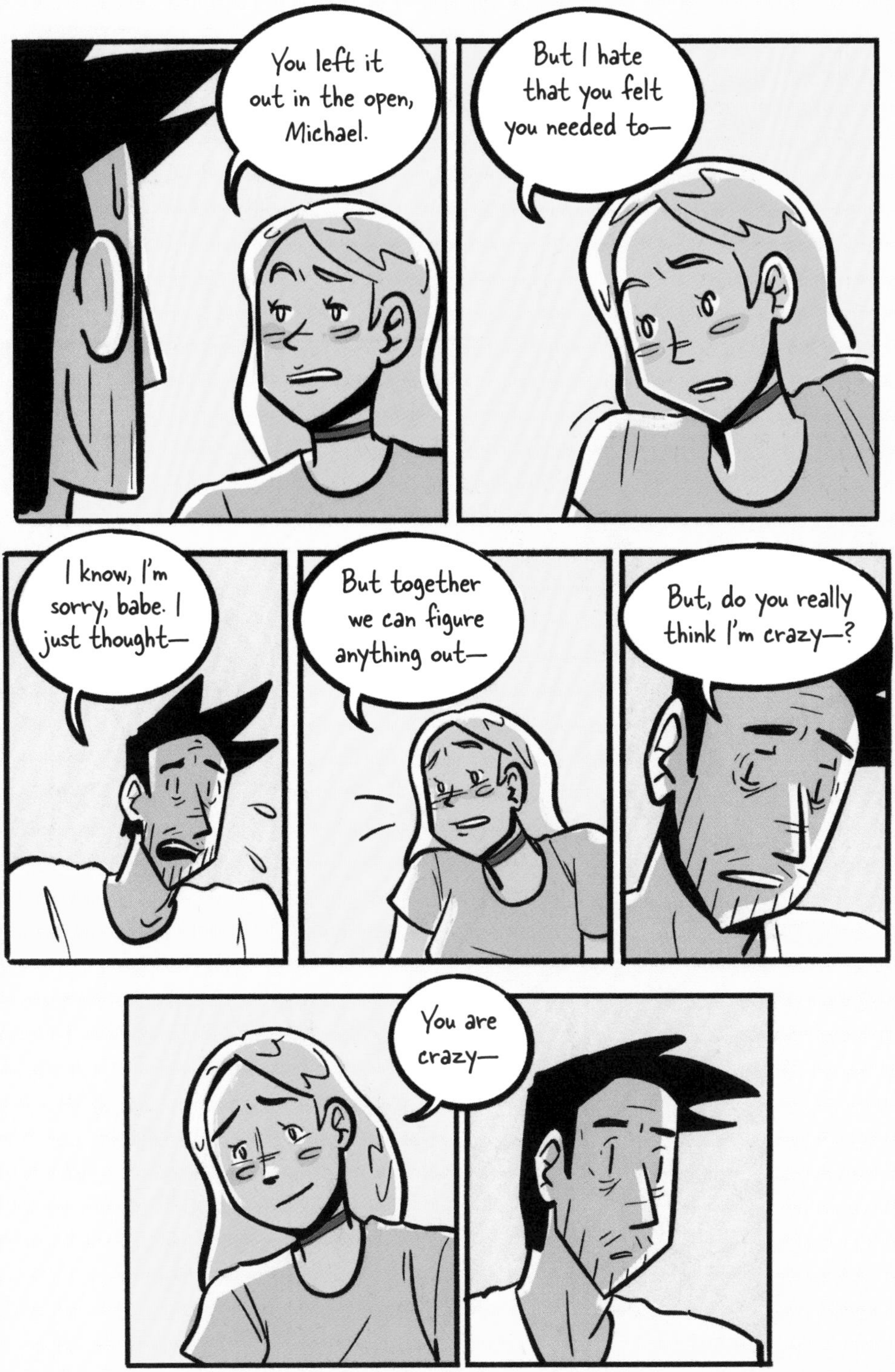
You left it out in the open, Michael.
But I hate that you felt you needed to—
I know, I'm sorry, babe. I just thought—
But together we can figure anything out—
But, do you really think I'm crazy—?
You are crazy—

—my crazy.
I've been doing some thinking too. And I think that I get it—
Oh yeah?
Yeah. You're a soldier dying for a cause—
?
Or you're a soldier living for one?
Anyway, the point is I get it.

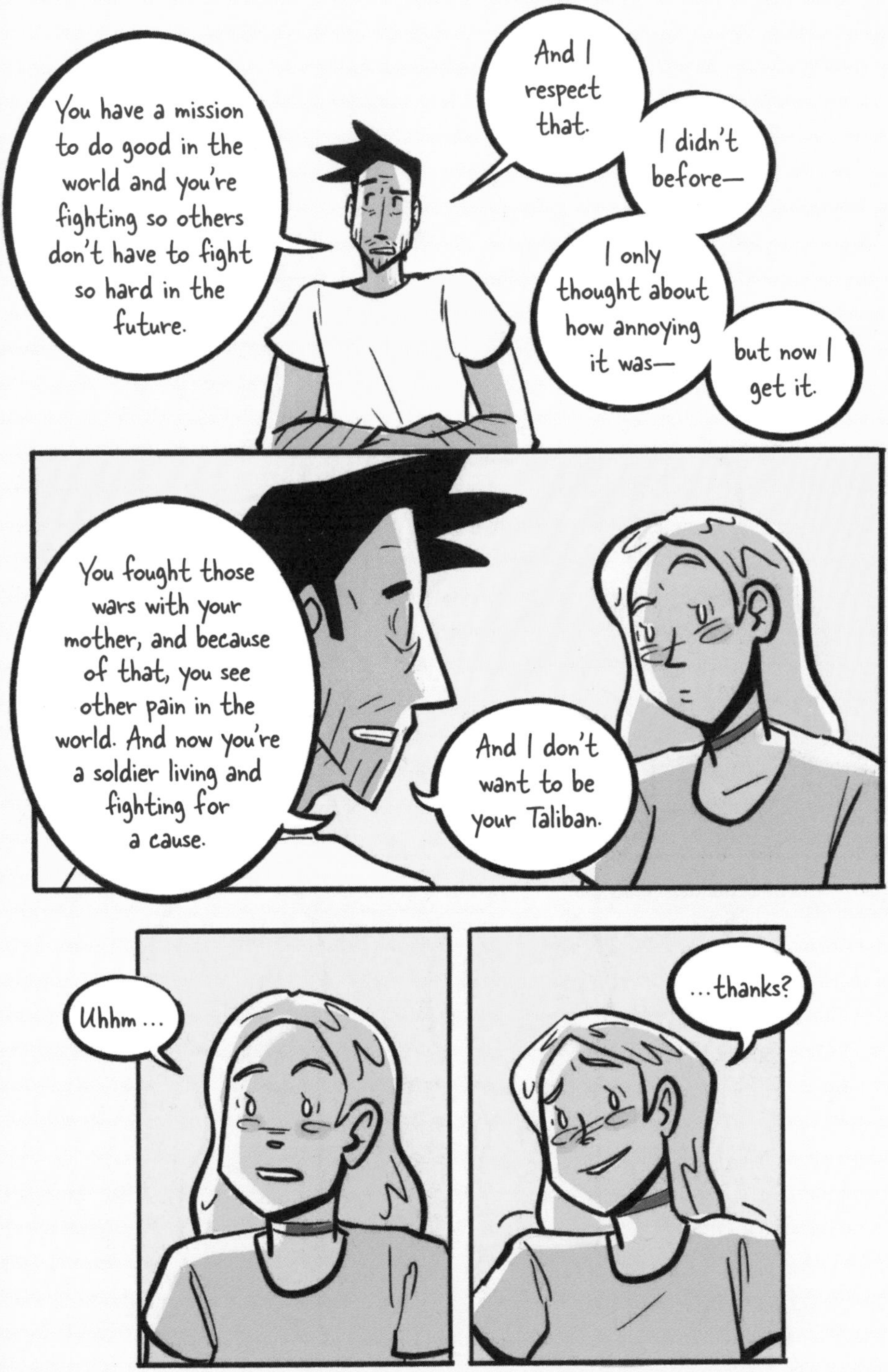
You have a mission to do good in the world and you're fighting so others don't have to fight so hard in the future.
And I respect that.
I didn't before—
I only thought about how annoying it was—
but now I get it.
You fought those wars with your mother, and because of that, you see other pain in the world. And now you're a soldier living and fighting for a cause.
And I don't want to be your Taliban.
Uhhm ...
...thanks?

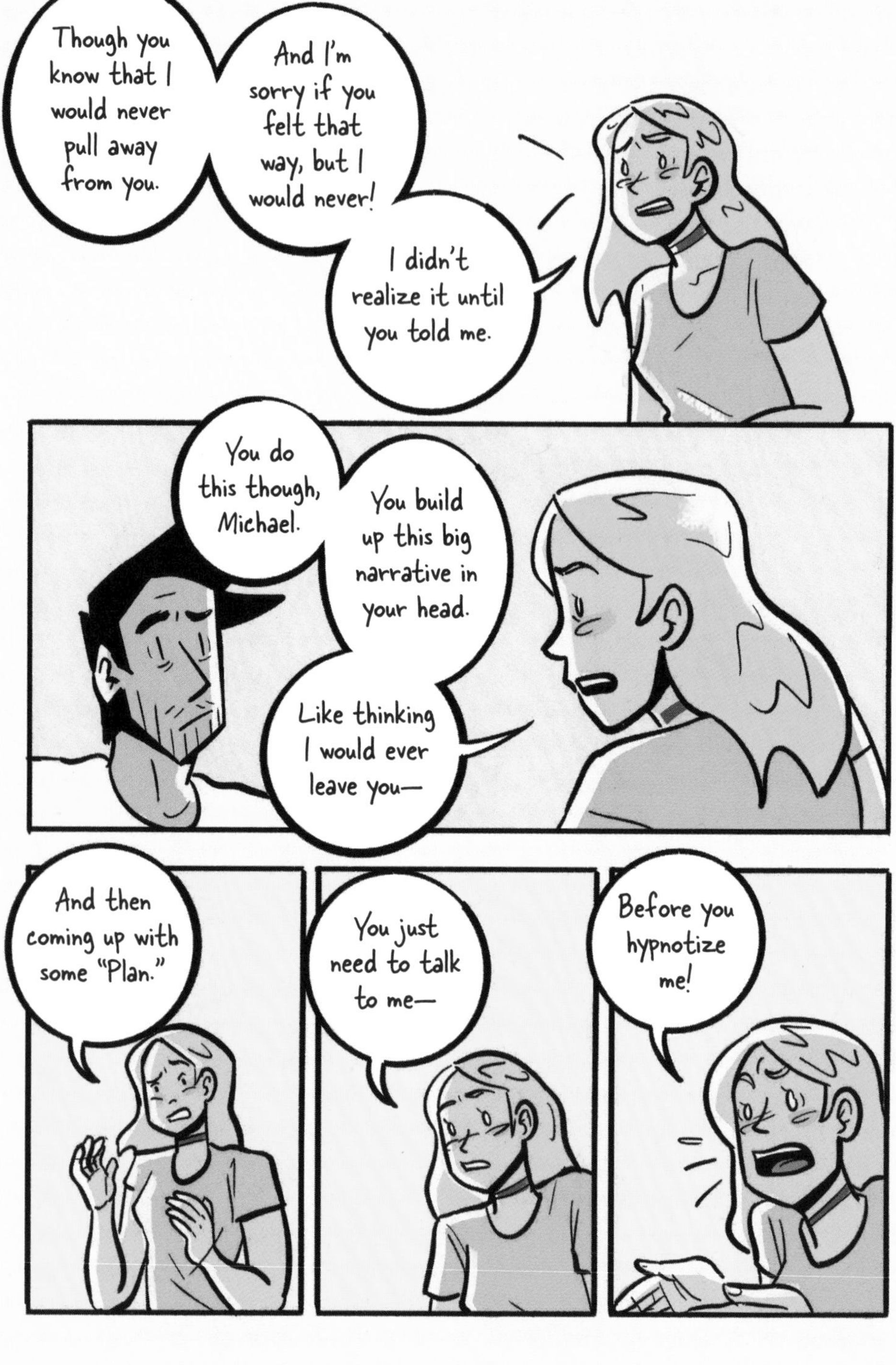
Though you know that I would never pull away from you.
And I'm sorry if you felt that way, but I would never!
I didn't realize it until you told me.
You do this though, Michael.
You build up this big narrative in your head.
Like thinking I would ever leave you—
And then coming up with some "Plan."
You just need to talk to me—
Before you hypnotize me!

But you did tell me the other day though that you were feeling physically great...
Or was that just a part of your plan?
Well, yeah, I do feel good, but—
And you did already last all these weeks as a vegetarian—

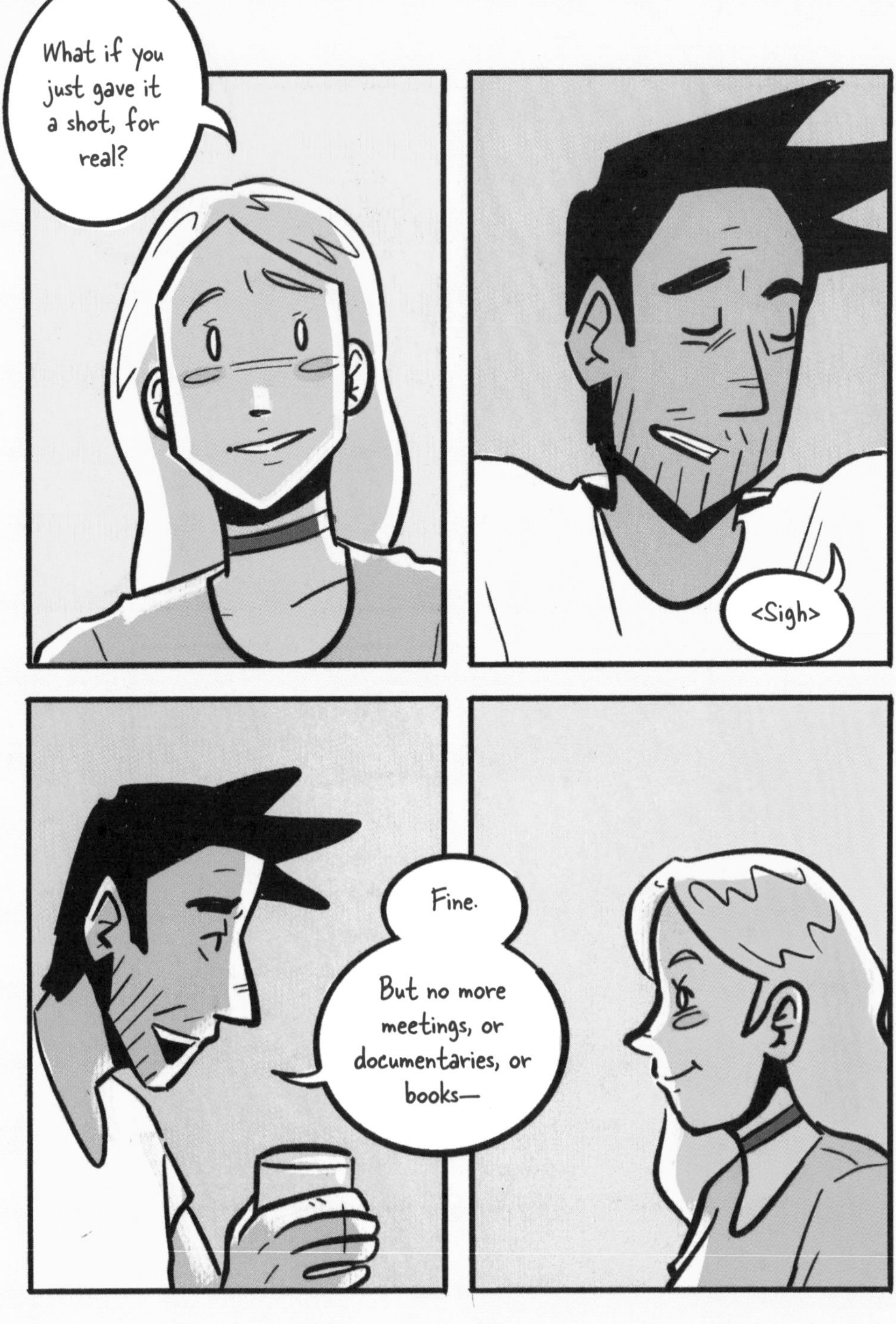
What if you just gave it a shot, for real?
<Sigh>
Fine.
But no more meetings, or documentaries, or books—

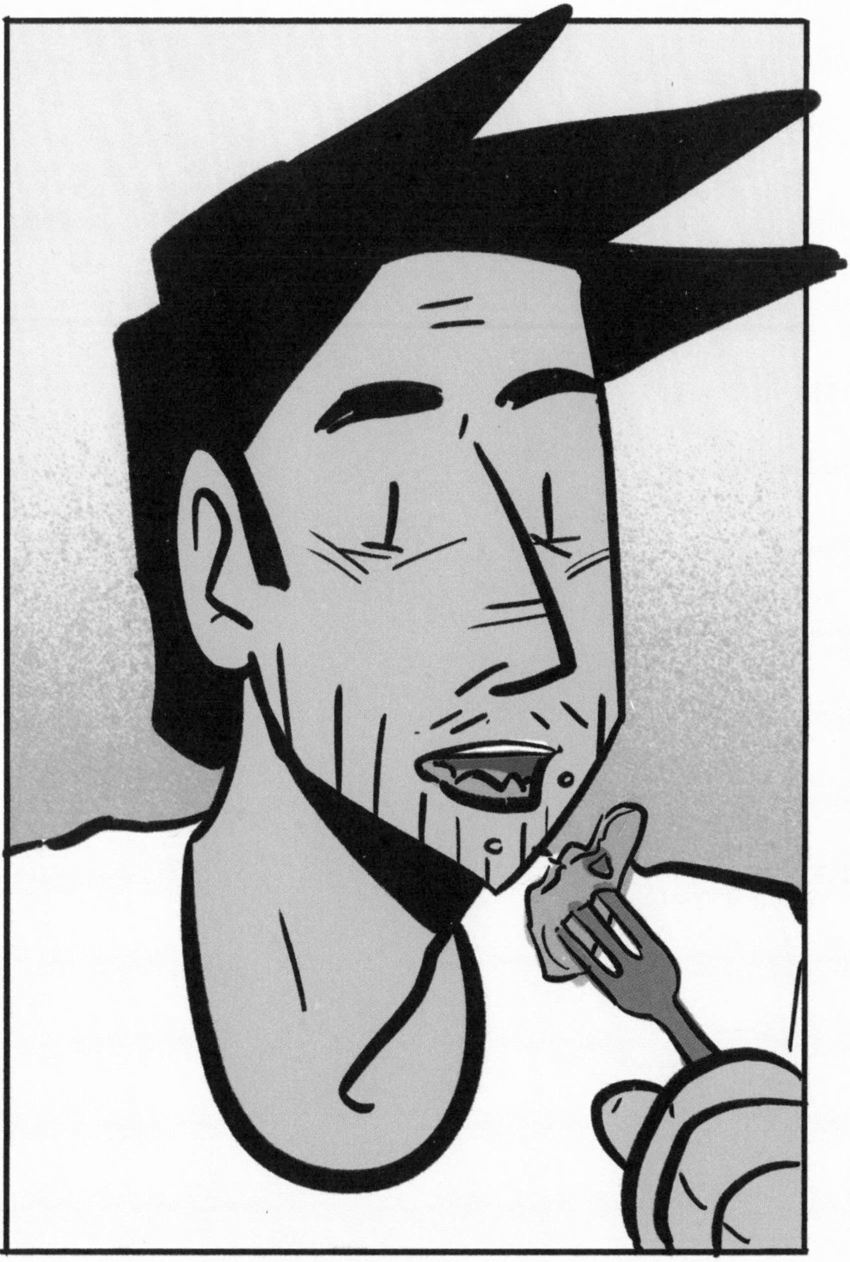

SEE . . . LOVE REALLY IS THE
ABSOLUTE WORST.

EPILOGUE

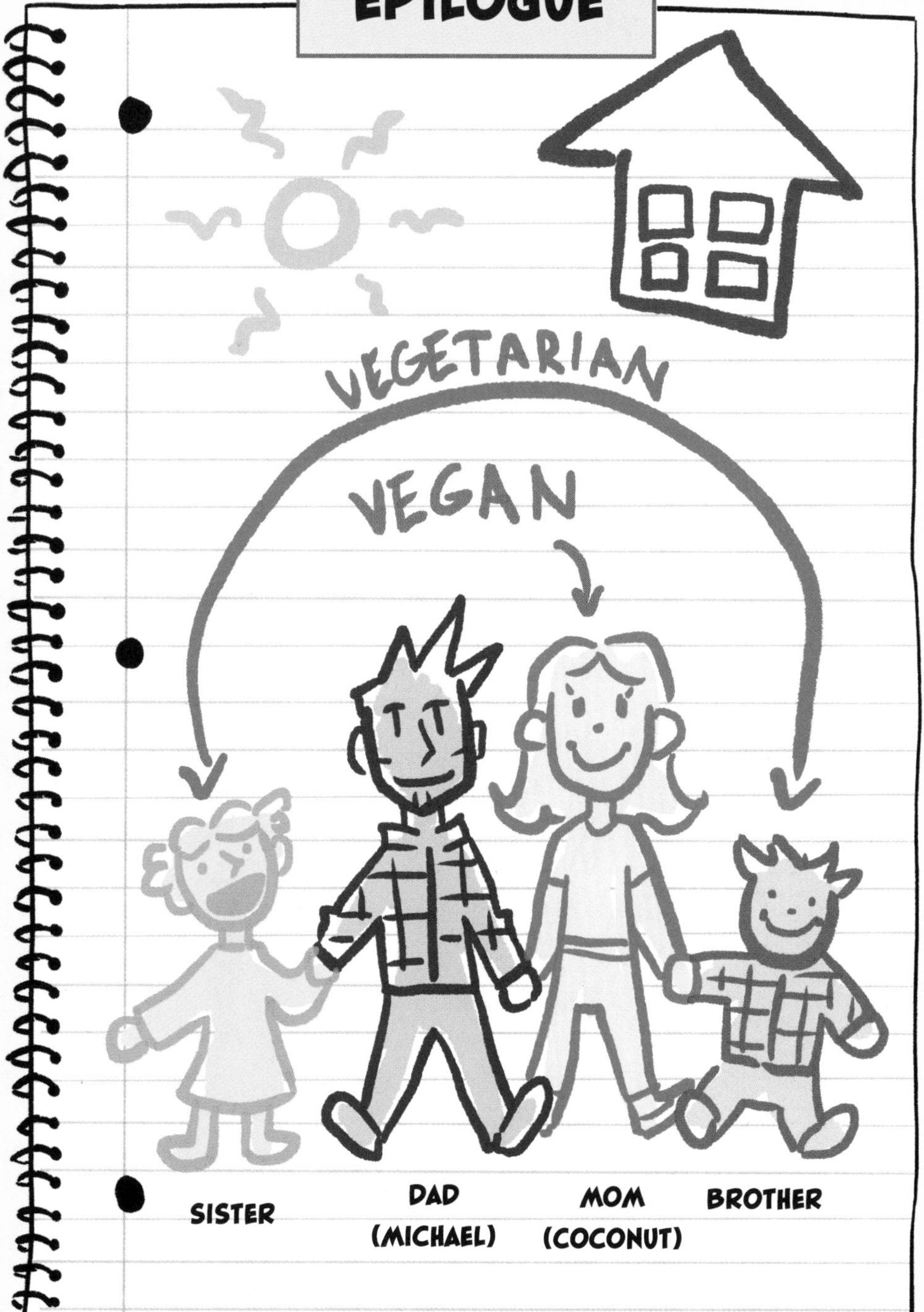

VEGETARIAN
VEGAN
SISTER
DAD
(MICHAEL)
MOM
(COCONUT)
BROTHER

Recommended Reading

Animal Liberation: The Definitive Classic of the Animal Movement
By Peter Singer

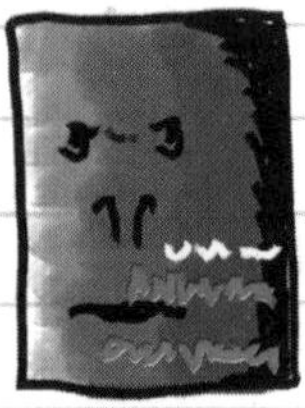

The China Study: The Most Comprehensive Study of Nutrition Ever Conducted
By T. Colin Campbell and Thomas M. Campbell II

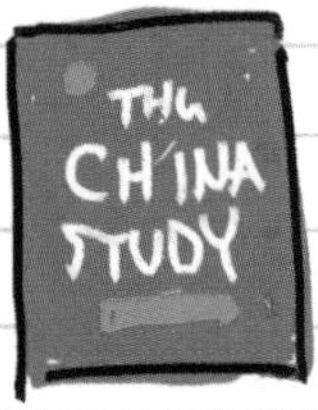
CHINA
STUDY

Eating Animals
By John Safran Foer

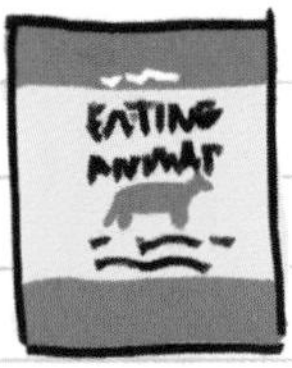

Meat Is for Pussies: A How-to Guide for Dudes Who Want to Get Fit, Kick Ass, and Take Names
By John Joseph

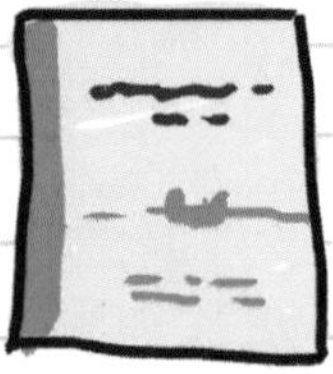

The Emotional Lives of Animals
By Marc Bekoff with foreword by Jane Goodall

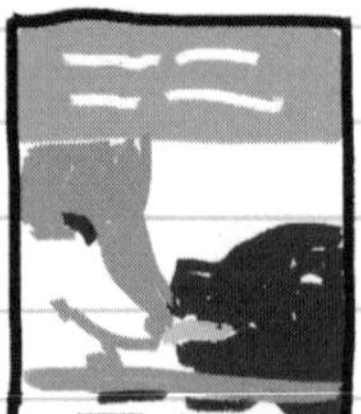

Continued

The Happy Herbivore: Over 175 Vegan Recipes
By Lindsay S. Nixon

The Joyful Vegan: How to Stay Vegan in a World That Wants You to Eat Meat, Dairy, and Eggs
By Colleen Patrick-Goudreau

Slaughterhouse: The Shocking Story of Greed, Neglect, and Inhuman Treatment Inside the U.S. Meat Industry
By Gail A. Eisnitz

Veganomicon: The Ultimate Vegan Cookbook
By Isa Chandra Moskowitz and Terry Hope Romero

MICHAEL ANTHONY

IS THE AUTHOR OF THE MEMOIRS *MASS CASUALTIES: A YOUNG MEDIC'S TRUE STORY OF DEATH, DECEPTION, AND DISHONOR IN IRAQ* AND *CIVILIANIZED: A YOUNG VETERAN'S MEMOIR*. MICHAEL HAS PREVIOUSLY WRITTEN FOR *THE WASHINGTON POST* BLOG, *BUSINESS INSIDER*, *SIGNATURE READS*, *THE FLAMING VEGAN*, *THE VEGAN VILLAGER*, AND HE HAS PREVIOUSLY PERFORMED STAND-UP COMEDY UNDER THE PSEUDONYM "THE VEGAN COMEDIAN." MICHAEL HOLDS AN MFA IN CREATIVE WRITING FROM LESLEY UNIVERSITY. A FORMER U.S. ARMY SOLDIER, HE CURRENTLY LIVES WITH HIS WIFE AND KIDS IN MASSACHUSETTS AND SPENDS HIS FREE TIME VOLUNTEERING WITH VETERANS.

CHAI SIMONE

IS AN ARTIST AND MOVIE FAN WHO GREW UP IN LAS VEGAS. SHE WENT TO THE LAS VEGAS ACADEMY OF THE ARTS, WHERE SHE DOUBLE MAJORED IN FILM AND ART AND STUDIED AT THE UNIVERSITY OF NEVADA, LAS VEGAS. CHAI CURRENTLY WORKS AS A FREELANCE ILLUSTRATOR. THIS IS HER DEBUT GRAPHIC NOVEL.